William Gunnyon

Illustrations of Scottish History

Life and Superstition from Song and Ballad

William Gunnyon

Illustrations of Scottish History
Life and Superstition from Song and Ballad

ISBN/EAN: 9783744777469

Printed in Europe, USA, Canada, Australia, Japan

Cover: Foto ©ninafisch / pixelio.de

More available books at **www.hansebooks.com**

ILLUSTRATIONS

OF

SCOTTISH HISTORY, LIFE, AND

SUPERSTITION

PRINTED BY BALLANTYNE, HANSON AND CO.
EDINBURGH AND LONDON

ILLUSTRATIONS

OF

SCOTTISH HISTORY

LIFE

AND SUPERSTITION

FROM SONG AND BALLAD

BY

WILLIAM GUNNYON

LONDON:
HAMILTON, ADAMS, & CO.
EDINBURGH: MENZIES & CO.
1877

PREFACE.

THE object of the present work is to introduce to the stores of our Song and Ballad literature those who may be ignorant of their riches, and to refresh the memories of such as may have once been familiar with them, but who have now ceased to cherish their acquaintance. These stores are not only rich but varied, and if the book proves uninteresting, the fault is due, not to the subject, but solely to defective treatment.

The usual collections of Song and Ballad have been carefully studied while preparing these chapters; but the extracts are generally, though not always, taken from Chambers's "Songs of Scotland prior to Burns," and Aytoun's tasteful recension of the texts of the Ballads. Especially valuable aid has been had from Burton's "History of Scotland." Alexander Smith's Essay on "Ballads" in the "Edinburgh Essays," and Professor Dr. J. Clark Murray's "Songs and Ballads of Scotland," have been consulted, and always with profit, though the aim of the latter work differs very materially from that of this. But the most valuable help has been had from the Songs and Ballads themselves.

WILLIAM GUNNYON.

GLASGOW, *8th August* 1877.

CONTENTS.

ERRATA.

Page 6, line 23, *for* "Turn thy sweet will to me," *read* "Turn thee, sweet Will, to me."

,, 32, ,, 3, *for* Planché's *read* Planche's.

,, 66, ,, 22, *for* Delaney *read* Deloney.

,, 82, ,, 16, *for* Altacholylachan *read* Altachoylachan.

,, 144, ,, 9, *for* shemes *read* schemes.

ILLUSTRATIONS

OF

SCOTTISH HISTORY, LIFE, AND SUPERSTITION, FROM SONG AND BALLAD.

───────

CHAPTER I.

INTRODUCTORY.

SCOTTISH Song has, for several reasons, a higher fame than any other European anthology. The exquisite pathos, the inimitable humour, the felicity, *verve*, and *pawkiness* of the lyrics themselves, together with the celebrity of at least many of the later writers, and the passion with which their names are cherished by adventurous Scots in every region of the globe, have combined to give our national songs a fame and a popularity exceptionally great. Song is indisputably the earliest form of poetic—and, indeed, of any—literature everywhere; and though the oldest Scottish specimens now existing are of comparatively moderate antiquity, we know of some that were current as early as the days of Wallace

A

and the Bruce. "The Gude Wallace," as it has
come down to us, bears in places the stamp of great
antiquity; and "When Alexander our King was
dead"—a touching lament for the wars and troubles
that followed the death of Alexander III. in 1286,
preserved in Winton's "Cronykil"—was undoubtedly
in its earliest form contemporaneous with the events
which it deplores. The form in which we have it,
as might be expected of a composition handed on by
recitation from age to age, when printing was not as
yet, and the professional antiquary not even a conception, is that of the age of the chronicler himself.
The genuineness of the fragment quoted by Fabyan
of a song represented as having been composed by
the maidens of Scotland, in which they naturally,
but somewhat maliciously, called on their sisters of
England to mourn for their lemans lost at Bannockburn, is attested by the St. Alban's "Chronicle,"
and its refrain of "heucalowe" with "rumbylowe"
is found in James the First's "Peblis to the
Play:"—

> " Hope, Calye, and Cardronow,
>   Gathered out thick-fold,
> With hey and how, rumbelow,
>   The young folks were full bold."

Fabyan has also preserved some satiric lines in
derision of the alliance formed between England and
Scotland on the marriage, in 1328, of David, son of
the Bruce, to Jane, sister of Edward. The Princess
was humorously styled Jane Makepeace, and the

verses referred to are said to have been affixed to the doors of York Cathedral by the Scottish Ambassadors. In his "History of the House of Douglas," Hume of Godscroft quotes from a song on the murder, in 1353, of the Lord of Liddesdale, while hunting in Ettrick Forest, by William, Earl of Douglas, from motives of jealousy; and it is a cogent testimony to the practice of embalming striking events in popular song, that Barbour in his " Brus " excuses himself from relating the defeat of Sir Andra Harcla by Sir John de Soulis by the blunt statement that—

> " Young women, when they will play,
> Sing it amang them ilk day."

John Mair, or Major (" De Gestis Scotorum," Paris, 1521), also assigns to the First James the composition of many songs that were popular in his day; but if his statement be correct, the songs of the royal bard have all disappeared.

The undoubted remains of ancient song are extremely scanty, but what little is extant, and the tradition of more that has been lost, prove beyond question the early prevalence of song in Scotland, and the popular delight in it. It is to be inferred further, that these songs were, for the most part, of lowly origin—the expression of overpowering passion inspired in a rustic bosom by the charms of some Hebe of the farm or fold, or the embodiment in humorous, pathetic, exultant, or wailing strains of an incident, personal or national, that had struck the fancy or the heart of some untaught bard, who—

"Sang other names, but left his own unsung."

For when we come down to the splendid galaxy of poets who illustrated the sixteenth century—Henryson, Douglas, and Dunbar—all men of culture, men of the schools—we find in their writings nothing of the nature of songs for the people. Yet with such songs they were all familiar. In Henryson's fable of "The Wolf, the Fox, and the Cadger," there occurs the line—

"The Cadgear sang, Hunt's up, up, upon hie,"

which contains the title of a song popular both in England and Scotland, being mentioned in "The Complaynt of Scotland" (1548), in Alexander Scot's poem on May (about 1560), and at the time of the Reformation converted into one of the "Gude and Godly Ballads." It is mentioned also in "Romeo and Juliet," act iii. sc. 5—

"Hunting thee hence with *Hunt's up* to the day."

In the prologue to the Twelfth Book of Gawin Douglas's translation of the Æneid, completed July 22, 1513, and first printed in 1553, we find the title of a people's song:—

"Ane sang, 'The schip salis over the salt fame,
Will bring thir merchandis and my lemane hame.'"

Dunbar (Laing's edition, vol. i., p. 98) complains—

"Your common minstrels hes no tone
But 'Now the day daws,' and 'Into Jone,'—"

a common minstrel being apparently in the eyes of the courtly poet, though himself a composer of "saugis, ballatis, and playis," a person of no account. Yet in his "Lament for the Death of the Makars" we find—

> "That scorpioun fell hes done infek
> Maister Johne Clerk and James Afflek,
> Fra ballat-making and trigidé."

The popularity of the first of the two strains mentioned by Dunbar is further attested by Douglas in these lines—

> "Thareto thir birdis singis in thair shaws,
> As menstrals plays *The joly day now dawe.*"

But we find in "Cockelbey's Sow" and in the "Complaynt of Scotland" by far the most complete list of the titles of now-forgotten songs. The author of "Cockelbey's Sow" is unknown; but from internal evidence we gather that it is posterior to Chaucer, and anterior to the middle of the fifteenth century. It was very popular about the beginning of the sixteenth century, when Dunbar and Douglas flourished. The latter refers to it thus in his "Palice of Honour," part iii. st. 48—

> "I saw Raf Coilyear with his thrawin brow,
> Craibit Johne the Reif, and auld Cowkellpi's sow."

Dr. Irving remarks that "it contains some gleanings of curious information." Among these are the illustrations it throws on the music, dances, and musical instruments in common use in the fifteenth century; "and what adds in no small degree to its interest," says Mr. Laing, "is the consideration that the names of the greater proportion of the airs, dances, and songs enumerated in it are otherwise unknown." Some of these last are :—"The sone shene in the sowth," "Cok craw thou quhill day," "Jolly lemman, daws it not day," "Be yon wodsyd," "Rusty bully with a bek, and every note in utheris nek," "Trolly lolly," &c. Dunbar refers to the poem in his "General Satire" as Cowkelbyis Gryce, and there is an allusion to it in the "Interlude of Laying a Ghaist," in the Bannatyne MS.—

> " To reid quha will this gentill geist,
> Ye herd it not at Cokilby's Feast."

The "Complaynt of Scotland," also of uncertain authorship, is a production of about a century later, having been first printed in 1548. A list of popular songs is given in pp. 100, 101, Leyden's edition (Edinburgh, Constable, 1801), and among them are some of rather tantalising promise, such as :—"The briar binds me sore," "Still under the leavis green," "Cou thou me the rashes green," "Lady, help your prisoner," "Broom, broom on hill," "Alone I weep in great distress," "Trollee, lollee, lemmen don" (this is also a title in "Cockelbey's Sow"), "The frog cam to the mill door," "Turn thy sweet will to me," "My love is lying sick, send him joy, send him joy" (evidently the model of the more modern "My luve's in Germanie, send him hame, send him hame"), &c. These lists, in the words of Mr. Cunningham, "may well excite our sympathy for the lost favourites of our forefathers. But it may serve to lessen our

regret to know that some of those songs were un-
usually licentious and indelicate." "On the whole,"
says Robert Chambers, "they give us little insight
into the general condition of song literature in those
days." However, regret is in vain ; they have passed
away from human memory, without the hope or the
possibility of recall. Yet many, we believe, have
longed more eagerly for the simple "O Bothwell
bank, thou blumest fayre," that fell on the ear of the
wanderer in Palestine as it was sung by the Scottish
mother to her child beside the dwelling of her
Moslem lord, and brought about a friendly recogni-
tion between the two compatriots of the far-off western isle, than they ever did for "the song the sirens
sang." If "The Gaberlunzie Man" and "The Jollie
Beggar," two lyrics of extraordinary merit, though
somewhat more outspoken than modern taste would
sanction, are really productions of James the Fifth,
we have mentioned the last truly national songs that
enriched our anthology for a long period. It is
singular, however, that the Bannatyne MS., made in
1568, only twenty-five years after the death of James,
contains only two pieces that have been adopted by
modern song-collectors.

A remarkable episode in the history of Scottish
song was the publication in 1597 of "Ane Compen-
dious Booke of Godly and Spiritual Songs, collectit
out of sundrie partes of the Scripture, with sundrie
of other ballates changed out of prophaine Sangis,
for avoyding of sinne and harlotrie," &c. It pro-

bably contains many of the compositions of John and Robert Wedderburn, of Dundee, the latter of whom was vicar of the town. On his return to Scotland from Paris, Calderwood informs us that " Wedderburn turned the tunes and tenour of many profane ballads into godlie songs and hymns, which were called the ' Psalmes of Dundie;' whereby he stirred up the affections of many." The intent was excellent—namely, to aid in the work of the Reformation; but the *modus operandi* was absurd and ludicrous. The songs, many of them originally indecent, preserved enough of the old leaven to suggest to the mind of the singer all that might have been conveniently forgotten. But though obviously failures as aids to piety, they serve admirably the purposes of the historical inquirer, as they preserve in their beginnings and burdens enough of the original to give us a fair conception of the songs that pleased in the sixteenth century.

> " Who is at my window, who, who ?
> Go from my window, go, go.
> Who calls there so like a stranger ?
> Go from my window, go."

Again, to the air " He's low down among the broom that's waiting for me," we find—

> " My love that mourns for me, for me,
> My love that mourns for me ;
> I am not kind, he's not in mind,
> My love that mourns for me."

Another is—

> "John, come kiss me now,
> John, come kiss me now,
> John, come kiss me by and by,
> And make no more ado."

To the tune of "Hunt's up," previously referred to, the following words were assigned—

> "With hunt's up, with hunt's up,
> It is now perfect day ;
> Jesus our King is gane in hunting,
> Wha likes to speed, they may."

Thus two modes of furthering the Reformation were adopted in connection with contemporary song and music. The one was singing obscene songs to the finest music of the Latin service, to discredit it ; the other, attempting to supplant obscene songs by substituting pious words to the same airs. From the "Merry Wives of Windsor" we learn that the Hundredth Psalm was sometimes sung to the tune of "Green Sleeves ;" and the Clown in the "Winter's Tale" exclaims, "But one Puritan amongst them, and he sings psalms to hornpipes." A satirical effusion against the vices of the Romish clergy, in language remarkable at least for its plainness, to the tune of "Hay trix, trim go trix, under the greenwood tree," occurs in the midst of these pious canticles. The following is a specimen—

> "Of Scotland well the friers of Faill,
> The limmery lang hes lastit ;
> The monks of Melros made gude kaill
> On Fryday quhen they fastit."

Then follow two lines utterly unquotable. Such efforts of the Reformers must evidently have failed of their purpose. The too sensuous groundwork remained. Meston says of a Presbyterian dame of exemplary piety—

> " She reads a letter
> In Rutherford, and seldom misses
> To light on those which mention kisses."

Numerous extracts, that appear at this day not only ludicrous but positively blasphemous—so much has taste altered—are given in that once popular book, "Scotch Presbyterian Eloquence Displayed," from the letters of Samuel Rutherford, addressed, *inter alios*, to Lord and Lady Kenmure, Lord and Lady Boyd, Lord Loudoun, Lady Culross, the Earl of Cassillis, &c., &c.

After the Restoration the songs of Scotland became so popular that they were manufactured in England, and afterwards accepted in Scotland as genuine. Many such are to be found in Durfey's "Wit and Mirth" and "Pills to Purge Melancholy." The accession of the House of Hanover called forth many humorous and some pathetic Jacobite songs. Ramsay's "Tea-Table Miscellany" introduced many of the old songs and airs into fashionable society, and some persons of quality wrote what must be confessed to be very frigid pastoral songs indeed. Others, however, as Miss Jean Elliot and Lane Anne Lindsay, wrote songs truly Scottish in language and sentiment. But, on the whole, the Scottish anthology is the outcome of the humbler ranks, and the great and undisputed monarch of the Scottish lyre, Robert Burns, gloried in the title of "the Ayrshire Ploughman." The songs to be illustrated in the following pages are confined, for the most part, to those preceding the time of Burns; but though thus limited, the field is wide and rich, for the national song is inextricably interwoven with every department of the national life and history.

CHAPTER II.

SPURIOUS BALLADS.

WHILE Scottish Song is in one sense conterminous with, and runs parallel to, Scottish history, how stands the case with the ballads? It might have been expected, *a priori*, that there would have been no such loss of compositions, consisting not, as the songs do, of crystallised sentiment, but of simple and fervid narrative, with all the artificial and conventional aids to memory which have characterised the ballad lore of every age and clime, as we know to have actually occurred with regard to lyrics once generally popular. According to the theory of Niebhur, which Mommsen has not so much controverted as exhibited in another light, Livy was enabled to construct his picturesque history of early Rome from ballads in the mouths of the common people. Macaulay in his "Lays of Ancient Rome" attempted to reproduce some of those which he conceived most likely to have been tenaciously treasured in the popular heart; and in his preface he says that "it," *i.e.*, ballad-poetry, "attained a high degree of excellence among the English and the Lowland

Scotch during the fourteenth, fifteenth, and sixteenth centuries." Further on he says—"Sir Walter Scott, who united to the fire of a great poet the minute curiosity and patient diligence of a great antiquary, was but just in time to save the precious relics of the minstrelsy of the Border."

That there are many undoubtedly ancient and historical ballads cannot be denied, but their number is much less than is generally supposed. Even Sir Walter Scott, with all his sagacity and antiquarian knowledge, is anything but a safe guide in determining the age and genuineness of many of the ballads he admitted into his collection. In the instances of "The Death of Featherstonhaugh" and "Bartram's Dirge," he was most ungenerously, not to say cruelly, imposed on by his friend and brother antiquary, R. Surtees, of Durham, whose own composition those two ballads were. Of the former, Scott was made to say—"It was taken down from the recitation of a woman eighty years of age, mother of one of the miners in Alston Moor, by the agent of the lead-mines there, who communicated it to my friend and correspondent, R. Surtees, Esq.," &c., with many more circumstances equally apocryphal. Surtees wound up with a note containing a reference to the Roman Wall, and extracts in feudal Latin from an *Inquisitio* and an *Utlagatio*, respectively *Henrici 8vi*,—baits which Scott could not resist, and to tempt him with which was as cruel as to seethe the kid in its mother's milk. The latter is introduced thus—"The follow-

ing beautiful fragment was taken down by Mr.
Surtees from the recitation of Anne Douglas, an old
woman who weeded in his garden." Evidently
Jonathan Oldbuck had not as yet dug up Aiken
Drum's Lang Ladle (A.D.L.L.) on the Kaim of Kin-
prunes, nor was there any fear of Edie Ochiltree
before his eyes. So that the dictum of Alexander
Smith in his essay on the Scottish ballads, contributed
to the "Edinburgh University Essays," and republished in "Last Leaves," that it is impossible to forge
an old ballad, must be not so much taken *cum grano*
as totally repudiated; for numerous impostors escape
detection, and not every "Phalaris" has his Bentley.
In truth, literary forgery, such, at least, as shall escape
detection for a time, and it may be for ever, unless
some peculiar audacity in the forger or some special
interest in the subject-matter attracts the notice of
experts, seems comparatively easy, and appears to
have singular charms for a certain class of minds.
In proof of this, to refer only to modern instances,
who has not heard of Macpherson's Ossian, of
Lauder's Milton, of Ireland's Shakespeare, and of
Chatterton's Rowley Poems? That Allan Cunningham should have palmed off on Cromek as antiques
productions of his own is in nowise wonderful, for
Cromek was not even a Scotchman, and "honest
Allan's" pseudo-antiques are, after all, among the
best things in the "Remains of Nithsdale and
Galloway Song." But the morality of the thing was
questionable; though the enormity of the offence is

much modified, according to the spectacles through which it is looked at. In "The Book-Hunter," John Hill Burton characterises Cunningham's offences as so many harmless peccadilloes, so many " rises " taken out of a Cockney, who, with however excellent intentions, was intermeddling with a subject of which he was totally ignorant. Not so did they appear to William Motherwell, for in speaking of the "Remains" in the introduction to his " Minstrelsy Ancient and Modern," he thus relieves his mind :—" There never was, and never can be, a more barefaced attempt to gull ignorance than what this work exhibits. It professes to give as ancient ballads and songs things which must have been written under the nose of the editor. More pretension, downright impudence, and *literary falsehood* seldom or ever came into conjunction." And again, when speaking of Cunningham's practice of " improving " ancient song, he breaks forth—" It is an unholy and abhorrent lust which thus ransacks the tomb, and rifles the calm beauty of the mute and unresisting dead "—a procedure which a little further on is stigmatised as " the *heinousness* of his offending."

The ballads alluded to never had any extraordinary popularity, were not looked upon as national heirlooms, or as in any way especially illustrative of history and manners. But there were others which had come to be regarded with peculiar pride and affection, and were pointed to as proofs that Scotland had a traditionary ballad lore not only rivalling, but in many respects transcending, that of any other nationality. Among these were "Hardyknute," "Sir Patrick Spens," "Gilderoy," "Gil Morrice," "Edward, Edward," &c. In the middle of the eighteenth century British poetry had fallen into a most lethargic state. There were versifiers in plenty after the manner of Pope, with all the defects of the school of which he was the acknowledged head, but with none of his sense, point, or vigour. The language of nature and of common life, and consequently of truth and passion, was no longer familiar to the Muse of Britain. Pope, in his "Song by a Person of Quality," an evident burlesque, gives, as it were prophetically, an exquisite exemplar of the sort of rubbish which a century later should pass among his imitators for poetry—

> "Flutt'ring spread thy purple pinions,
> Gentle Cupid, o'er my heart ;
> I a slave in thy dominions—
> Nature must give way to Art."

And the melancholy fact was now *so*. Now, among the first and most effective agencies in disrupting this artificial school of rhymsters was the publication, in 1765, of Percy's "Reliques of Ancient English Poetry." Southey says—"Two works which appeared in the interval between Churchill and Cowper promoted beyond any others this growth of a better taste than had prevailed for the hundred years preceding. These were Warton's 'History of English Poetry' and Percy's 'Reliques,' the publication of which must form an epoch in the continuation of that history." The national taste was speedily revolutionised; once more truth and nature inspired the voice of song; once more the sunshine and the rain, the breeze of heaven and the early dew, gladdened, stirred, and refreshed the flowers of poesy; once more

> " The common air, the earth, the skies,
> To men were opening Paradise."

Among the gems of Percy's collection, the ballads which we have enumerated, and others having a certain family resemblance to them, were not the least brilliant; to them the book owed much of its popularity and influence; to their publication was due in no small measure the revival of British poetry by breathing into it a purer and fresher spirit. Of these, "Hardyknute" was early discovered to be a forgery; but in 1859 the lovers of ballad literature were startled from their propriety by the publication of "The Romantic Scottish Ballads: their Epoch and Authorship," by Robert Chambers, in which an attempt was made to prove "that the high-class romantic ballads of Scotland are not ancient compositions—are not older than the early part of the eighteenth century—and are mainly, if not wholly, the production of one mind;" and that there was "a great *likelihood* that the whole were the composition of the authoress of 'Hardyknute'—namely, Elizabeth, Lady Wardlaw of Pitreavie."

Here there was no lack of boldness of assertion:

B

not by an obscure, but by an eminent person; not
by a rash man, but by one known for eminent fair-
ness and sobriety of judgment; not by a dilettante
dabbler in the field, but by one who had cultivated
it successfully for years, and who had, indeed, in
1829, published the most admirable and tasteful
collection of Scottish ballad poetry that had up till
that time appeared. Among the ballads included
in this sweeping charge were—"Sir Patrick Spens,"
"Gil Morrice," "Edward, Edward," "The Jew's
Daughter," "Gilderoy," "Young Waters," "Edom
o' Gordon," "The Bonny Earl of Murray," "Johnie
of Bradislee," "Mary Hamilton," "The Gay Gos-
Hawk," "Fause Foodrage," "The Lass o' Loch Ryan,"
"Clerk Saunders," "The Douglas Tragedy," "Willie
and May," "Margaret," "Young Huntin," "Fair
Annie," "Burd Ellen," "Sweet William's Ghost,"
"Tamlane," "Sweet Willie and Fair Annie," "Lady
Maisry," "The Clerk's Twa Sons o' Owsenford,"
"and a Scotch 'Heir of Linne,' besides others which
must rest unnamed." Of the first-mentioned
seven or eight of these, Mr. Chambers adds—"Indeed, it might not be very unreasonable to say that
they have done more to create a popularity for
Percy's 'Reliques' than all the other contents of the
book." If Mr. Chambers's finding be correct, it
might be asked, Why should a person of such exquisite
gifts—by far the most accomplished poet of the
time—studiously conceal her light under a bushel?
Who can account for an idiosyncrasy? It is proved

that Lady Wardlaw *did* conceal her authorship of
"Hardyknute;" that while she was alive her friends
gave divers disingenuous and improbable accounts of
its origin, or rather of its discovery; and that her
authorship was not disclosed till forty years after
her death. It is also pertinent to observe that, with
the exception of Burns, the greatest of all Scottish
song-writers is Carolina, Baroness Nairn; and that
while "Caller Herrin'," "The Laird o' Cockpen,"
"The Land o' the Leal," and many others no less
excellent, were "familiar in men's mouths as household words," the authoress was never suspected, and
at her death at the age of seventy-nine only one
person was possessed of her secret.

Mr. Chambers opens his case thus—

"In 1719 there appeared in a folio sheet at Edinburgh a
heroic poem styled 'Hardyknute,' written in affectedly old
spelling, as if it had been a contemporary description of events
connected with the invasion of Scotland by Haco, King of
Norway, in 1263. A corrected copy was soon after presented
in the 'Evergreen' of Allan Ramsay, a collection professedly
of poems written before 1600, but into which we know the
editor admitted a piece written by himself. 'Hardyknute'
was afterwards reprinted in Percy's 'Reliques,' still as an
ancient composition; yet it was soon after declared to be the
production of a Lady Wardlaw of Pitreavie, who died so lately
as 1727. Although, to modern taste, a stiff and poor composition, there is a nationality of feeling about it, and a touch of
chivalric spirit, that has maintained for it a certain degree of
popularity. Sir Walter Scott tells us that it was the first
poem he ever learn by heart, and he believed it would be the
last he should forget."

His mode of eliciting what he proposes to be proof

of his conclusion already quoted is this—The authorship of "Hardyknute" being undisputed, from a comparison of favourite modes of expression, and of the
entire treatment of each subject, his finding is that
"Sir Patrick Spens" comes from the same hand, only,
however, after having acquired a little more cunning.
David Laing, the man in Scotland whose opinion on
a subject of this kind is of the most value, had intimated a similar suspicion as early as 1839. The
revised and improved edition of "Gil Morrice," from
certain resemblances in diction and treatment to the
two abovenamed, is attributed to the same author;
and so on with the list already enumerated. There is
always a danger of a man's riding his hobby to death,
and of his becoming unconsciously the victim of a per-
verted ingenuity. Nor do we think that Mr. Chambers
has altogether escaped either of these dangers. Still
he insists, not without reason, on the absence of
any ancient manuscripts, or of any proof that these
ballads were known or recited before the eighteenth
century; on their elegance and freedom from coarse-
ness in the midst of ballad simplicity; and of a
common confused and obscure reference to known
events in Scottish history. It might be possible
that his theory as to the common authorship of
"Hardyknute" and "Sir Patrick Spens" should be
correct, and the rest of it not so. We shall state
Mr. Chambers's arguments somewhat *in extenso,* and
lay over against them the arguments that may be
advanced on the other side, as these are given with

much knowledge and ability in a pamphlet published at Aberdeen in 1859, entitled, "The Romantic Scottish Ballads and the Lady Wardlaw Heresy," by Norval Clyne. These arguments have been reproduced by Mr. Clyne in a note to his "Ballads from Scottish History," Edinburgh, 1863. That the ballads named should be of use for our purpose, it is necessary that we should have an intelligent idea of their epoch and genuineness. Still, as this is a case of probabilities, we are not entitled to call for more evidence than the case admits of.

Percy's folio MS. was long unjustly regarded as a myth; but we will not acquit Hogg, any more than Surtees, of having taken an occasional "rise" out of Scott. The MSS. cited by Scott under the name of Mrs. Brown of Falkland, and vouched for by Professor Thomas Gordon, King's College, Aberdeen, as having been written down by his grandson as his aunt (Mrs. Brown) sang them, were as opportune as they were valuable. But in a case of this kind it is possible, as Hamlet says, to inquire too curiously.

In "Dejection: an Ode," Coleridge, no mean judge of poetic excellence, refers to

"The grand old ballad of 'Sir Patrick Spens.'"

Mr. Chambers likewise admits its excellence, but denies that it is old, and removes it from the category of the Historical ballads into that of the Romantic, asserting that it has no established historic basis,

though he had held a contrary opinion in 1829. In
1843 he broached his theory of the Wardlaw authorship in "Chambers's Edinburgh Journal;" though it
may be questioned if this was an independent judgment, and not rather an elaboration of the opinion
of Mr. David Laing, as expressed in his Notes to
"Johnson's Scots Musical Museum" in 1839. Mr.
Laing's words are—"Notwithstanding the great
antiquity that has been claimed for 'Sir Patrick
Spens,' one of the finest ballads in our language, very
little evidence would be required to persuade me that
we were not also indebted for it to Lady Wardlaw."
Further on in the same volume he says—"That the
ballad was intended to embody some remote event in
Scottish history is quite evident; and it would have
been difficult to fix on a more poetic incident than it
presents, although not strictly adhering to historical
facts. Had the ballad really possessed any claims to
such high antiquity as would fix its composition
near to the epoch of Margaret the 'Maiden of
Norway,' on whom her grandfather, Alexander the
Third, had devolved the crown of Scotland before
the close of the thirteenth century, it is hardly con-
ceivable that it should never have been heard of till
it was sent to Bishop Percy, in 1765, by some of his
correspondents in Scotland, along with other traditionary ballads of still more questionable antiquity.
Since his time it has been printed in a hundred
different shapes, generally with some additional
verses or improvements, 'fortunately recovered,' &c.,

but most of which improvements are palpable interpolations."

That the ballad has undergone revision by a skilful hand is not denied; but the question whether it be a genuine or only a spurious antique will be much simplified if it can be proved to have a reference to an undoubted event in the national history. This Mr. Clyne considers highly probable; and he attempts to reconcile the ballad with the fact by a careful collation of four different texts—(1.) Percy's, containing eleven stanzas; (2.) Scott's, twenty-one, omitting five supplied by Mr. Hamilton, as they appear redundant; (3.) Jamieson's, eighteen; and (4.) Buchan's, twenty-nine. The common opinion was that the ballad referred to an expedition sent in 1290 to bring home the Maid of Norway, daughter of Eric, King of that country, and of Margaret, daughter of Alexander III., as heiress of the Scottish throne, after the death of her grandfather. But "this view," says Professor Aytoun, " may be dismissed as quite irreconcilable with the main facts of the ballad." That such an embassy was sent is matter of history, the commissioners being Sir David Wemyss of Wemyss, and Sir Michael Scott of Balwearie, the famous wizard. Scott hazarded a conjecture that the expedition of Sir Patrick Spens was previous to this embassy, and if this conjecture coincides with fact, it is maintained that all difficulties are removed. Motherwell first showed that it did, and that the expedition in question was the one that in 1281 con-

veyed Margaret, Alexander's daughter, to Norway on
the occasion of her marriage to King Eric.　To reconcile the received text of the ballad with the fact, a
slight verbal emendation is necessary.　Instead of

> " To Noroway, to Noroway,
> 　　To Noroway o'er the faem ;
> 　The King's daughter *of* Noroway,
> 　　It's thou maun tak' her hame,"

it is proposed to read, and Aytoun does read—

> " The King's daughter *to* Noroway," &c. ;

On which Mr. Chambers remarks—" I apprehend
such liberties with an old ballad are wholly unwarrantable."　Perhaps so ; but, unfortunately for
his position, in his collection of 1829 he had accepted
Mr. Motherwell's theory, which justifies the emendation.　We give his note, in which the historical
incidents claimed by Motherwell as the basis of the
ballad are fully and fairly stated :—" We owe it to
Mr. Motherwell that the occasion of the ballad is now
known to have been the expedition which conveyed
Margaret, daughter of King Alexander III., to
Norway, in 1281, when she was espoused to Eric,
King of that country."　Fordun, in his History of
Scotland, relates the incident thus :—" A little before
this (namely, in the year 1281), Margaret, daughter of
Alexander III., was married to the King of Norway,
who, leaving Scotland on the last day of July, was
conveyed thither in noble style, in company with
many knights and nobles.　In returning home, after

the celebration of her nuptials, the Abbot of Balmuri-
noch, Bernard of Monte-Alto, *and many other persons,
were drowned"*—*et alii plures sunt submersi.*

Again, if the ballad be "so rounded and complete,
so free, moreover, from all vulgar terms," that it is
almost certainly printed in the condition in which it
was left by the author, what about the numerous
variations and additions in the versions above referred
to?—what about "our Scots nobles" and the "Scots
lords"? No explanation of the necessity of their
presence in the ship is given. Scott's version helps
to make the narrative more intelligible, but by no
means complete—"'Tis *we* must fetch her hame."
The companions of the voyage required to be of rank,
and consequently the "Scots lords" were properly
selected as her attendants. Then, on what other
hypothesis can the following lines be explained—

> " Ye Scottish men spend a' our king's gowd,
> And a' *our queenis fee*" ?

The contract of marriage between the Princess
Margaret and King Eric, dated 25th July, 1281, will
be found in Rymer's " Fœdera." In terms of it
Margaret was to receive a dowry of 14,000 merks, a
fourth part of which was to be taken with her to
Norway, and it is evidently in reference to this that
" our queenis fee " is introduced. Buchan's version,
which cannot be charged with literary roundness
and completeness and freedom from all vulgar terms,
having been indubitably moulded in the mouths of
the common people into conformity with current

phraseology and modes of thought, as happens
necessarily with all literature preserved by tradition,
makes everything plain, illustrating what is obscure
in the other versions, and the ballad is now complete :—

> " But I maun sail the seas the morn,
>   And likewise sae maun you,
>   To Noroway wi' *our King's daughter,*
>   *A chosen queen* she's now."

Its preservation by a class of reciters quite different
from the Lady Wardlaw type is further manifest from
what follows :—

> " They hadna stayed into that place
>   A month but and a day,
>   Till he caused the flip in mugs gae roun',
>   And wine in cans sae gay.
>
> " Then out it speaks an auld skipper,
>   An inbearing dog was he—
>   Ye've stayed ower lang in Noroway,
>   Spending your King's monie."

And this is confirmed by Buchan's account of how he
procured his version :—" It was taken down from the
recitation of ' a wight of Homer's craft,' who, as a
wandering minstrel, blind from his infancy, has been
travelling in the North as a mendicant for these last
fifty years.   He learned it in his youth from a very
old person, and the words are exactly as recited, free
from those emendations which have ruined so many
of our best Scottish ballads."   Now, accepting only
the half of this as true, it throws insuperable difficulties in the way of Mr. Chambers's hypothesis.

Buchan's " Ancient Ballads and Songs of the North
of Scotland " were published in 1828. His blind
minstrel had been reciting " Sir Patrick Spens " for
fifty years, which brings us back to 1778, and *he had
learned it from a very old person.* Disregarding this
latter statement, though it might be insisted on as
being valuable *pro tanto*, between 1778 and 1765, the
date of the publication of Percy's " Reliques," is a
period of thirteen years, and we submit that it is not
only incredible but impossible that a ballad of eleven
stanzas, that indicates but does not tell a complete
story, and polished like a rare gem, should in the
course of thirteen years have spread from the select
region of Percy's " Reliques " into the rounds of a
" blind crowder " in the North, expanded into twenty-
nine stanzas, telling a connected and intelligible
story, tallying exactly with an interesting and important historical incident, and bearing unmistakable
evidence in conception and language of its popular
origin. Further, it is inconceivable that a ballad in
this form should have been skilfully forged in a
popular shape, and harmonised with facts stretching
so far back in the national history—facts, too, which
for a time escaped the notice of persons the most
likely to have known and remembered them. Yet
it does so tally ; for the marriage is correctly recorded
in the " Scotochronicon," with the additional circumstance of the disaster attending it; and in the
" Scottish Chronicle " of Raphael Hollinshed, partly
founded on Fordun's work, it is recorded that " a

number of the Scottish nobilitie, which had attended
the Lady Margaret into Norway, were lost by shipwreck." That Sir Patrick Spens is not mentioned by
the chronicler among the number of those lost is no
matter of surprise or suspicion. He was not one of
the leaders charged with the guardianship of the
future queen; he was simply the "good skipper"
selected by Alexander for his nautical skill, and
more interesting to the ballad-maker than any mere
abbot or noble, whose position of eminence might
have been but the accident of an accident. As a
further proof of this, Percy mentions that in some
modern copies the name of Sir Andrew Wood of
Largo—the Scottish Nelson, so to speak—is, though
an anachronism, substituted for that of Sir Patrick
Spens.

As we wish to put Mr. Chambers's argument as
strongly as possible, it is right to mention that Percy
had remarked in a note—"An ingenious friend
thinks the author of 'Hardyknute' has borrowed
several expressions and sentiments from the foregoing
and other old Scottish songs in this collection." On
this Mr. Laing observes—"It was this resemblance,
with the localities Dunfermline and Aberdour, in the
neighbourhood of Sir Henry Wardlaw's seat, that led
me to throw out the conjecture whether this much-
admired ballad might not have been written by Lady
Wardlaw herself, to whom the ballad of 'Hardyknute' is now universally attributed." Mr. Chambers
also lays stress on the localities mentioned, as being

in the immediate neighbourhood of the mansions
where Lady Wardlaw spent her maiden and her
matron days, adding that a poet is most disposed to
write about those localities with which he is familiar,
and that some are first inspired by the historical
associations connected with their native scenes. But
Dunfermline was a favourite residence of the Scottish
kings, and the writer who opens a ballad thus—

> " The King sits in Dunfermline towne,
>   Drinking the blude-red wine,"

is unfairly construed as belonging in all likelihood
to the locality. Equally unwarrantable is a similar
inference from—

> " Half ower, half ower to Aberdour,
>   It's fifty fathom deep ; "

for Aberdour was a neighbouring and convenient
seaport. Hence we reject the suggestion that the
Aberdeenshire Aberdour is meant, as well as the
various reading of Scott—

> " O, forty miles off Aberdeen ; "

the assonance, or resemblance of sound, in three
words of the line being in favour of the form we have
given. And Aytoun remarks very justly, that " ' Half
ower to Aberdour ' signifies nothing more than that
the vessel went down half-way between Norway and
the port of embarkation."

It must be confessed that the want of ancient
manuscripts of this and other ballads of the group

challenged by Mr. Chambers as modern fabrications
is unfortunate, if not suspicious.   But such a want
would tell with equal force against the antiquity of
the great mass of ballads collected by Scott and
others, many of which, though unvouched for by
manuscript authority, are from internal evidence
undoubted antiques—at least in form and substance
—though having necessarily, in the course of transmission by oral tradition, undergone such a succession
of changes as would keep them alive.   But Mr.
Chambers is least happy in his verbal criticism,
introduced to prove from the ballad itself that it
cannot be genuine.   For example, Sir Patrick tells
his friends before starting on his voyage—" Our ship
must sail the faem."   On this Mr. Chambers remarks
—" No old poet would use *foam* as an equivalent for
the *sea;* but it was just such a phrase as a poet of
the era of Pope would love to use in that sense."
Now, not to quote from the group of the twenty-five
suspected ballads, which is, however, too chivalrous
a concession, nor from others in Jamieson's collection,
and in the " Minstrelsy of the Border"—which have
not been branded with suspicion—we will adduce a
single instance, but that a decisive one, to discredit
the critic's assertion that *foam* would not be used by
any old poet as an equivalent for the *sea.*   In Gavin
Douglas's translation of the " Æneid," completed on
July 22, 1513—surely a date sufficiently remote
from the era of Pope—we read in the prologue to the
Twelfth Book—

> " Ane sang, ' The schip salis over the salt fame,
> Will bring thir merchandis and my lemane hame,'"

the title of a song popular in 1513, and probably
composed much earlier. It has been said, however,
that the elliptical form "sail the fame," for "sail
over the fame," indicates a comparatively modern
authorship. But such an ellipsis has been common
in all eras of our literature. In one of the "Tales of
the Three Priests of Peblis," assigned to the early
part of the sixteenth century, occur these lines—

> "Then bocht he wool, and wyselie couth it wey ;
> And efter that sone saylit he the sey."

Equally infelicitous is another piece of verbal
criticism. In some remarks on the "Lass o' Lochryan" he says—"It chances that there is here, as
in 'Sir Patrick,' one word peculiarly detective—
namely, 'strand,' as meaning the shore." Now, the
word does not occur in Percy's version, nor in Jamieson's, nor in Buchan's, though it does in Scott's, and
that probably by an inadvertence. In his own collection of Scottish ballads, Mr. Chambers had remarked
that in some modern copies of the ballad the word
strand had been injudiciously substituted for *sand*,
which shows that in the present instance he is inclined to push his theory too hard. The mention of
hats, fans, cork-heeled shoon, and *feather-beds* proves
perhaps that liberties have been taken with the
ballad in the course of transmission, even that
stanzas may have been interpolated, but not that

the whole is a modern fabrication. Sticklers for the genuineness of the ballad in its present form refer to Planché's "History of British Costume" for the antiquity of the first three articles, and while admitting that the era of the introduction of *feather-beds* into Scotland is unknown, they show that their use on the Continent was of earlier date than the reign of Alexander III. In the attempt to saddle the other ballads of the group on Lady Wardlaw, the same minute, and sometimes equally unhappy, criticism is had recourse to. The recurrence of a number of stock phrases in the compositions under review is also insisted on as proving identity of authorship, as they are to be found hardly at all in any of the rustic or homely ballads. These are such as—"Johnie tarries lang," "He set his bent bow to his breast and lightly lap the wa'," "Kissed baith cheek and chin," "Wan water," "Bonny boy," "Hose and shoon," "Blood-red wine," "Upon the nurse's knee," &c., &c. Besides, there is a tone of *breeding* pervading these ballads not to be found in the productions of rustic genius; there are luxurious descriptions of masculine beauty, arrayed in elegant attire, the mercery being of the eighteenth and of no earlier century; there is the pathos of deep female affections, and the sacrifice and suffering which these so often involve. Wherefore, says Mr. Chambers, these ballads are the composition of Lady Wardlaw, the acknowledged authoress of "Hardyknute," which is a very palpable *non sequitur.*

I have thus shown, in reference to one ballad, that the theory of Mr. Chambers rests on no solid basis. The charges against the others will be considered as they occur in the course of our illustrations. Regarding ballads avowedly imitations, it is unnecessary to speak.

CHAPTER III.

PART I.

§ I. CHEVY CHASE.

WE have already seen that we have no very ancient historical songs, and that such of our historical ballads as refer to incidents of a remote period are not, at least in their present form, themselves of great antiquity. This, however, is not matter of surprise, for they could not have been transmitted orally from one generation to another without continual transformations, by which they were insensibly assimilated to the current speech of the successive narrators. "A story may thus be preserved," says Dr. Irving, "when most of the original words have been changed." Assuming that "Sir Patrick Spens" has an historical basis in the incidents attending the conveying of the Princess Margaret to Norway in 1281, and in the disaster that befell the Embassy while returning to Scotland, the next memorable incident illustrated by ballad lore is the Battle of Otterburn, fought between the Douglas and the Percy on the 19th of August 1388. It was simply a raid for plunder, as is avowed in the most candid and business-like manner in the Scottish version—

> "The doughty Earl of Douglas rade
>   Into England to fetch a prey."

The more popular and famous ballad of the "Chevy Chase," though, by a pardonable poetic licence, assigning as the cause of quarrel a defiant hunting by a great noble in the forest of his hereditary foe, and materially inverting other important circumstances, undoubtedly commemorates the same event, "Chevy Chase" being but a corruption of the French *chevauchée,* a predatory raid on horseback, and only connected with the Cheviot Hills by an intelligible association resulting from similarity of sound and local propriety. That the incidents commemorated in both sets of ballads are identical is further proved by the following stanza from the version attributed to a Richard Sheale, supposed by Hearne to be the same with a person of that name who was alive in 1588, but who is considered by Percy to have lived at an earlier date—

> "This was the hontynge of the Cheviat,
>   That tear began this spurn,
> Old men that knowen the ground well enoughe
>   Call it the Battell of Otterburn."

But the date may be accepted as correct. It is only forty years later than that of "The Complaynt of Scotland," in which the ballad is referred to as "The Huntis of Chevet," and in which two lines are quoted, though not precisely as they are given by

Sheale, the variation resulting probably from their being quoted from memory—

> "The Perssee and the Mongumrye mette
> That day, that day, that gentil day."

An interest altogether apart from the historical accuracy of the narrative gathers round "Chevy Chase" from the three following circumstances:— (1.) From Froissart having given in his Chronicle an extremely vivid and picturesque account of the battle, derived from persons who had been engaged in either army, and which we shall consider more particularly when we attempt to disentangle the actual incidents from the conflicting statements of the minstrels, who have severally ascribed the honour of the victory to the nationality with which they themselves were connected. (2.) To the glowing testimony of Sir Philip Sydney, in his "Defence of Poetry," to the inspiring character of the strains of the rude, uncultured singer:—"I never heard the old song of Percie and Douglas that I found not my heart moved more than with a trumpet: and yet it is sung but by some blinde crowder, with no rougher voice than rude style; which, beeing so evill apparelled in the dust and cobweb of that uncivill age, what would it work trimmed in the gorgeous eloquence of Pindare!"   And (3.) from Addison's well-known laudatory criticism in Nos. 70 and 74, May 21 and 25, 1711, of the "Spectator." For this he was taken to task by Dr. Johnson—

undoubtedly a great man, but a poor critic—in these terms:—"By a serious display of the beauties of 'Chevy Chase' he exposed himself to the ridicule of Wagstaff, who bestowed a like pompous character on 'Tom Thumb;' and to the contempt of Dennis, who, considering the fundamental position of his criticism, that 'Chevy Chase' pleases, and ought to please, because it is natural, observes that 'there is a way of deviating from nature by bombast or tumour, which soars above nature, and enlarges images beyond their real bulk; by affectation, which forsakes nature in quest of something unsuitable; and by imbecility, which degrades nature by faintness and diminution, by obscuring images and weakening effects.' In 'Chevy Chase' there is not much of either bombast or affectation; but there is chill and lifeless imbecility. The story cannot possibly be told in a manner that shall make less impression in the mind."

Now, Johnson is the poorest critic in our literature of any man of real eminence. An excellent critic by square and rule, he would have been admirable as a college tutor, whose style of criticism may not unaptly be called word-mongering without insight. But in the higher region of imagination and passion, where above all things sympathy is a *sine quâ non*, he could not tread. Witness his utterly blind and false, perverse and tasteless, strictures on Milton's "Lycidas." Had he not been a really great man these would have inevitably crushed

him to the level of Dennis and Oldmixon. As was
to be expected in one so obstinate and dogmatic,
his estimate of "Chevy Chase" was never in the
least degree modified; for in a journal kept by Mr.
Windham, in which he preserved minutes of conver-
sations held with Johnson at Ashbourn in August,
1784, we find the following dictum of the Doctor's:
—"'Chevy Chase' pleased the vulgar, but did not
satisfy the learned; it did not fill a mind capable
of thinking strongly." It must be remembered,
however, that the ballad criticised by Addison was
the more modern and inferior version, composed,
probably, soon after the death of Elizabeth, and
which falls very far short of the dignity of the
ancient copy. The stanza, for instance, in which the
catastrophe of the gallant Witherington is related is
absolutely ludicrous—

> "For Witherington needs must I wayle,
>   As one in doleful dumpes;
> For when his legs were smitten off,
>   He fought upon his stumpes;"

which is thus burlesqued by Butler, in "Hudibras,"
part i., canto iii., ll. 95, 96—

> "As Widdrington, in doleful dumps,
>   Is said to fight upon his stumps;"

"For which reason," says Addison, "I dare not so
much as quote it." The corresponding stanza in the
old version labours under no such disadvantage, and
is indeed full of simple pathos—

> " For Witherington my heart is woe,
> That ever he slain should be ;
> For when his legs were hewn in two,
> He knelt and fought on his knee."

" Dumpes," with its undignified rhyme ' " stumpes,"
is particularly unfortunate.   Yet it was not originally
suggestive of the same comic idea as it is now ; for
in a sonnet ascribed to Richard Edwards in the
" Paradise of Daintie Devises," and referred to by
Shakespeare in his " Romeo and Juliet," it occurs
without any ludicrous application, and is allowed to
pass without censure by Shakespeare in the passage
alluded to, though the expression, "Musicke with her
silver sound," which occurs in the following line, is
playfully ridiculed —

> " Where griping griefs the heart would wound,
> And doleful dumps the mind oppress," &c.

In fact, "dumpes," is the exact equivalent of
" vapours," hypochondriacal affections that were
supposed to be caused by vapours from the humours
of the body, and is just the Dutch "domp" and
English " damp."

Addison was evidently amazed at his own boldness
in attempting to do justice to what must have
appeared to the bulk of his contemporaries only a rude
ballad, and his attempt was quite at variance with
his usual habit of thought.   But he sheltered himself
under the authority of Sir Philip Sydney, already
quoted, and of Ben Jonson, who used to say that he
would rather have been the author of the old song

in question than of all his works. But he could not
entirely divest himself of the prevailing exclusive
classical taste, and he instanced parallelisms of language and conception in Virgil and Horace. "I
shall only beg pardon," he wrote, "for such a pro-
fusion of Latin quotations, which I should not have
made use of but that I feared my own judgment
would have looked too singular on such a subject,
had not I supported it by the practice and authority
of Virgil." In fact, his critique is one of the earliest
instances in what was called "polite literature" of
an English author having any conception that his
own country had a splendid past, as deserving of
being referred to, and as apt for illustration, as the
history of Greece or of Rome. By the time of Gray
there was a general improvement in taste in this
respect, and it was growing; for in the original draft
of the "Elegy," instead of the names of Hampden,
Milton, and Cromwell, which occur in one of the most
striking stanzas of the poem as published, there were
set down those of Cato, Tully, and Cæsar. Addison's
criticism was naturally pitched on a defiant key, but
it scarcely deserves the epithet of "extravagant"
applied to it by so competent and so cool a critic as
Robert Bell.

Professor Morley claims the latter part of the
fifteenth century as the date of the composition of
the "ballads of 'Robin Hood,' 'Chevy Chase,' and
other such pieces, which usually survive in later
versions." The battle of Otterburn was fought on

the 19th of August 1388, when the King of Scotland
was Robert II., and the King of England was
Richard II. In the ballad of "Chevy Chase," however, "Jamy the Skottishe King" is mentioned,
while the "fourth Harry" is represented as having
been at the same time King of England. The
"Battle of Otterburn" is evidently the earlier of the
two ballads, as actual incidents are transferred from
it to the other, almost *in ipsissimis verbis.* We have
here, therefore, some data, however slight, for enabling
us to fix the era of their authorship. There was no
Scottish King of the name of James till 1424, and
Henry the Fourth of England died in 1413. This
trifling discrepancy may be disregarded, the important circumstance to note being that the name James
was familiar to the singer as that of a King of Scotland. Percy, who assigns the poem to a date not
lower than the reign of Henry VI., remarks that
during that long reign no fewer than three Jameses
had mounted the Scottish throne; a circumstance
which, coupled with "the long detention of one of
them in England, would render the name familiar to
the English, and dispose a poet in those rude times to
give it to any Scottish King he happened to mention."
This points to the latter part of the fifteenth century,
and thus agrees with the assumption of Professor
Morley.

The ballad of "Chevy Chase," as given in the
"Reliques," is an English production, and is coloured
by a pardonable national partiality. The Scottish

version, the "Battle of Otterburn," as given by Scott in the "Border Minstrelsy," is evidently the same as that mentioned by Hume of Godscroft, and therefore has documentary evidence for an antiquity almost as high as the ballad of Richard Sheale. Hume, however, notes an important difference in the popular ballads of the two countries. "The English 'Hunting of Cheviot,'" he says, "seemeth indeed poetical, and a mere fiction, perhaps, to stir up virtue; yet a fiction whereof there is no mention, either in the Scottish or English chronicle." In fact, it is rather based on the ordinary chronic warfare on the Borders between the chiefs of the great houses, though an actual and well-known incident is introduced. Hume proceeds— "Neither are the songs that are made of them both one, for the Scots song made of Otterbourne telleth the time, about Lammas, and also the occasion, to take preys out of England; also the dividing armies betwixt the Earls of Fife and Douglas, and their several journeys, almost as in the authentic history." The superiority of the English version, as a poem, over the Scottish must be admitted; but we shall show by-and-by that the latter abounds in those touches of nature which make the whole world kin.

With regard to the supposed incident on which the English ballad is founded—namely, that the Percy had made a vow to God to hunt three days in the mountains of Cheviot, "in the manger of doughty Douglas,"—it may be remarked that we learn from the "Memoirs of Carey, Earl of Monmouth," of a custom

the Borderers had when they were at peace of arrang-
ing for a hunting within each other's marches; and
that if they took this liberty without leave asked and
obtained, the Warden of the district violated proceeded to punish the invaders. Regarding the actual
incidents, however, as relating to the historical battle
of Otterburn, let us see how the minstrels of the
two countries represent the respective forces engaged,
and the issue of the fray. The English minstrel
says—

> " Of fifteen hundred archers of England,
>   Went away but fifty and three ;
> Of twenty hundred spearmen of Scotland,
>   But even five and fifty."

Which last line is in the modern version with less
generosity rendered—

> " Scarcely fifty-five did flye."

The leaders on both sides are slain—Douglas by an
English arrow, and Percy by the spear of Sir Hugh
Montgomery. In the Scottish version the respective
numbers are not given. Douglas, who had hurried to
the battle with so much haste that he forgot to don
his helmet, was brought to the ground by a mortal
stroke on the brow from the sword of Percy, while
the Percy himself was captured by Sir Hugh
Montgomery. With the money obtained for his
ransom Montgomery built the castle of Polnoon, in
Renfrewshire, not in Ayrshire, as erroneously stated
both by Scott and Aytoun. There is a spice of
poetry and romance about the Douglas, which accords

well with one so unselfishly chivalrous. When he is
informed by his page of the approach of the English
he exclaims—

> " I ha'e dreamed a dreary dream
>   Ayont the Isle of Skye—
> I saw a deid man win a fight,
>   And I think that man was I."

When he feels his wound to be mortal, he bids his
little footpage run speedilie—

> "And fetch my ac dear sister's son,
>   Sir Hugh Montgomerie.
>
> "' My nephew guid,' the Douglas said,
>   ' What recks the death of ane ?
> Last night I dreamed a dreary dream,
>   And I ken the day's thy ain !
>
> "' My wound is deep ; I fain would sleep !
>   Take thou the vanguard of the three,
> And bury me by the bracken bush
>   That grows on yonder lily lea.
>
> "' O bury me by the bracken bush,
>   Beneath the bloomin' brier ;
> Let never living mortal ken
>   That a kindly Scot lies here !'
>
> " He lifted up that noble lord,
>   With the saut tear in his e'e ;
> And he hid him by the bracken bush,
>   That his merry men might not see."

There is something exquisitely touching in this formidable warrior, when stricken down in the heady
fight under the clear moon,

> " While spears in flinders flew,"

wishing for sleep with the earnestness of a little child, and desiring to be laid in his resting-place by his "ae dear sister's son." He was not, however, buried at the bracken bush, but in Melrose Abbey, where his tomb may yet be seen.

The real circumstances, as far as they can be gathered from the narrative of Froissart and from other sources, were these. To inflict a blow on England, 50,000 Scottish troops assembled on the Border, in conformity with the decision of a conference held at Aberdeen. The bulk of the army was to advance by the west on Carlisle, and the Earl of Douglas, to distract the enemy's attention, was to make a flying raid across the eastern border. His force, according to Froissart, was composed of 300 mounted men-at-arms and 2000 spearmen, who were soon at the gates of Durham. On their return, the Scots remained three days before Newcastle, where Sir Henry Percy, the famous Hotspur, had collected a considerable force. In a skirmish under the walls Douglas secured the Percy's pennon, which he swore he would display on his castle of Dalkeith. This the Percy vowed he should never do, and Douglas told him to come at night and take it from before his tent. The matter became thus one of chivalry, and the Scots, strongly entrenching themselves, awaited the attack of the English. These, led by Hotspur, advanced on Otterburn, their numbers being 8000 footmen and 800 mounted men-at-arms, or more than three to one. They attacked the foe, who were in some measure taken by surprise; but the Scots having previously arranged a very skilful mode of defence, when the attack was made swept round their camp, and took their assailants in flank. The English strength lay in their archers, but the battle was a hand-to-hand one, and there was no room for archery. The superior weight of the English at first bore the Scots back. Douglas, perceiving this, made a rush on the foe with his battle-axe, and after performing prodigies of valour, was stricken down and trampled under foot of horse and men. There is a tradition, however, that he was not slain by the enemy, but by a groom of his chamber, whom he had roughly chastised the day before for some remissness in his duty. This man, meditating revenge, is said to have left a part of Douglas's armour behind unbuckled, and in the heat of the fight, watching his opportunity, to have stabbed him where his harness was loose. But this story may be dismissed as fabulous. Froissart reckoned the English taken or left dead in the field at 1040, 840 taken or killed in the pursuit, and upwards of 1000 wounded. Of the Scots, 100 were slain and 200 made prisoners.

"That there was a memorable slaughter in this affair," says Mr. Burton, "a slaughter far beyond the usual proportion to the numbers engaged, cannot be doubted; nor was there ever bloodshed more useless for the practical ends of war. It all came of the capture of the Percy's pennon. The Scots might have got clear off with all their booty; the English

forgot all the precautions of war when they made a
midnight rush on a fortified camp without knowledge
of the ground or the arrangements of their enemies.
It was for these specialties that Froissart admired it
so." The English for a long time smarted under the
issue of this battle, and their minstrels did what
they could to slur over the defeat. It was a battle,
however, in which, while there was defeat, there
was no loss of honour. The descendants of those
who were engaged in it look back upon it with a
sort of pious pride, and cherish with devotion every
memento of it. When the Douglas fell, one of his
dying charges was, "Defend my standard." It was
borne by his natural son, Archibald Douglas, ancestor of the family of Cavers, who was charged to
defend it to the last drop of his blood. It is still
preserved by his descendants as a glorious heirloom.
The pennon of the Percy, the *causa teterrima belli*—
carried to Scotland by Lord John Montgomery—
Hugh, his son, was slain in the action—is still preserved with pride at Eglinton Castle; and when a
Duke of Northumberland asked it to be returned,
the then Montgomery laughingly answered, after the
manner of the Douglas, "There is as good lea-land
at Eglinton as there was at Otterburn; come and
take it." The least pleasing reminiscence in connection with any descendant of the combatants is thus
narrated by William, Earl of Shelburne, First Mar-
quess of Lansdowne, in his Life by Lord Edmond
Fitzmaurice (London, 1873). It is to be premised

that Lord Shelburne had been introduced at Holyrood to the last Duke of Douglas, John Home, author of "Douglas," being present. "When anything was said about his family, he nodded to Mr. John Home to narrate what regarded it. I told him I had seen a house he was building in the Highlands. He said he heard that the Earl of Northumberland was building a house in the North of England, the kitchen of which was as large as his whole house, on which the Duchess of Douglas observed, that if the Douglasses were to meet the Percies once more in the field, then would the question be whose kitchen was the largest! Upon this the Duke nodded to Mr. Home to state some of the great battles in which the Douglas family had distinguished themselves." Shelburne could not speak well of our countrymen, for of Lord Mansfield he wrote that, "like the generality of Scotch, he had no regard to truth whatever." What a superb English "snob"! At the same time what he said about the Duke of Douglas was perhaps too true.

§ 2. THE RED HARLAW.

In the list of songs and ballads already mentioned as occurring in the "Complaynt of Scotland," "The Battel of Hayrlau" immediately precedes "The Huntis of Chevet," which we have identified with the "Battle of Otterburn," thus reversing the order of time, though perhaps preserving that of popularity. Otterburn was fought on 19th August 1388, and

Harlaw on 24th July 1411. The greater nearness
in time of the one, which is really trifling, could give
it little precedence over the other in the matter of
popularity, though circumstances might, and very probably did, do this. The victory at Otterburn did not
relieve the country from any fate it greatly dreaded,
or to which it was unused. Experience had frequently
been had of an English foe, and, in the case of
Edward I., of the worst he could or would do. He
had often been met in fair fight, and been found not
invincible; indeed, on one most memorable occasion
—namely, at Bannockburn, when his power had
culminated and seemed irresistible—he had been
ignominiously routed. What is familiar has comparatively few terrors for us; it is the unknown that
appals. *Omne ignotum pro terrifico.* Had Percy
been victorious at Otterburn, he might have fetched
a prey, and the south-eastern districts suffered tem-
porary inconvenience; but to the great bulk of the
nation the affair would never have been more than as
a tale when it is told, bringing with it neither loss of
goods nor loss of honour. Besides, the Percy, Hotspur though he was, was a gentle foeman, who fought
on rules dictated by the code of chivalry; and soon
after the foray was over, the Marchmen might have
met in not unfriendly conference at tryst or hunting-
match. But the Islesmen of Donald and their
Highland allies were regarded in quite another light.
Different in race, speech, institutions, dress, and mode
of warfare, they inspired their Lowland compatriots

D

with a terror strange and deep in proportion as the
objects of it were alien and unknown. This may help
to explain the assertion of Mr. Burton, that "the
defeat of Donald of the Isles was felt as a more
memorable deliverance even than that of Bannockburn." The genesis of the war, of which Harlaw was
fortunately the only battle, may be thus explained :—

The Lord of the Isles was at this period, and had
been for a long time before, regarded by the Irish or
Dalriad Scots, who peopled the Western Highlands
and Islands, as their natural leader and protector
against the subjects of the King of Scotland, who
were steadily encroaching on their territory. In fact,
his power and pride were so great that he claimed to
be an independent sovereign, and had even proceeded, after the feudal fashion, to have feudatories
under him, despite the widely divergent code of law,
or rather of custom, between Celt and Teuton. In
the War of Independence he was of sufficient power
and importance to be courted by England as an ally,
and in 1389 he was a party to the treaty of peace
between France and England as an ally of the latter.
As late as three years before Harlaw he was recognised by Henry IV. as having a diplomatic standing.
The time had therefore come for a decisive struggle
for supremacy between the Teutonic and Celtic constituents of the population ; and the Celts, from their
preference to subsist by robbery rather than by industry, gave ample handle to their adversaries to

attempt to subject them, if not to absolute power-
lessness, at least to law-abiding habits. At this time
the Earldom of Ross, to which appertained large
possessions north of the Moray Firth, fell to an
heiress, who took the veil, and Donald, the then
Lord of the Isles, claimed it as the husband of her
aunt. But it was wanted by the Regent Albany for
his second son, the Earl of Buchan. The Earl of
Mar, illegitimate son of Alexander Stewart, the Wolf
of Badenoch, who had once held the disputed Earldom
in right of his wife—himself a nephew of Albany,
and now a great feudal lord in virtue of a forcible
but condoned marriage with the Countess of Mar—
was naturally an interested observer of the proceedings of what may be called the foreign claimant. He
had, besides, to rehabilitate himself in the eyes of the
Government; for he himself had been a leader of
Highland caterans, and, sweeping down from the
braes of Angus in 1392, had gained the battle of
Gasklune, driving the Lowlanders of Angus and
Mearns like chaff before the wind, as he rushed on
them with his savage and impetuous mountaineers.
And just as a lady of dubious virtue, who has retained or contrived to gain a footing in society, is the
most rigid censor of an erring sister, so Mar, the
ci-devant marauder, was now to show himself the stern
represser of those by whose aid he had formerly
profited.

Donald, who imagined that he was to be deprived
of his rights, prepared to assert them by the strong

hand. It was the policy of the Government to resist him to the utmost, for his success would have made him master of half the kingdom. With a Douglas in the south and a Lord of the Isles in the west and north, the Scottish King would have been a sovereign only on sufferance. Donald would, besides, have enriched his followers with whatever lands they coveted, and the clansmen would have eaten up, like locusts, all the labours of the fields. The interests, therefore, as well as the fears, of all classes united them against him; and when, with ten thousand followers at his back—Islesmen, Macintoshes, Mackenzies, and Macleans—he came down through the mountains of the north to Benachie, and thence to the moor of Harlaw, in the Garioch, he was met, ten miles north-west of Aberdeen, by a small but well-equipped force of nobles and gentlemen with their retainers and tenants, and a force of burghers from the towns, all led by the Earl of Mar. The combat was bloody, but in one respect decisive. The Highlanders rushed on their seemingly insignificant foe, time after time, like a torrent, with the most reckless prodigality of life. But in vain; and they had to withdraw to their mountains. Both parties suffered severely, and though there was not much of a victory to boast of, the Low Country, and indeed the monarchy, were saved. On the side of Donald, the chiefs of Macintosh and Maclean were slain, with about 1000 men. Mar lost nearly 500, among whom were many men of rank, including the Lords Saltoun

and Ogilvy, Scrymgeour, Constable of Dundee, Irvine
of Drum, and Sir Robert Davidson, Provost of Aberdeen. The loss of their Provost is said by Francis
Douglas, in his "Description of the East Coast" (1782),
to have affected the citizens so much that they
adopted a resolution that for the future no Provost
should go beyond the immediate territory of the
town in his official capacity—a statement adopted
by Sir Walter Scott. But Mr. Joseph Robertson, in
the "Book of Bon-Accord," remarks, that "no trace
of this regulation is to be found in the city record,
and it may be therefore fairly set aside as apocryphal." But it was absolutely necessary to meet
Donald before he and his caterans should fall on the
comparatively wealthy city of Aberdeen, to which he
was on his direct march when he was stopped at
Harlaw.

> "To hinder this proud enterprise,
>   The stout and mighty Earl of Mar,
> With all his men in arms did rise,
>   Even frae Curgarf to Craigievar ;
>   And down the side of Don right far,
> Angus and Mearns did all convene,
>   To fight, ere Donald came sae near
> The royal brugh of Aberdeen."

The battle "appears," says Mr. Laing, "to have
made a deep impression on the national mind. It
fixed itself on the music and the poetry of Scotland ;
a march, called 'The Battle of Harlaw,' continued to
be a popular air down to the time of Drummond of
Hawthornden, and a spirited ballad on the same event
is still repeated in our own age."

The ballad referred to by Mr. Laing is the well-known—

"Frae Dunidier, as I cam' through," &c.

He speaks of an edition printed in the year 1688 as being "in the curious library of old Robert Mylne." But no printed copy is known to exist of older date than that to be found in Ramsay's "Evergreen" (1724), and by many it is suspected that Ramsay, though he may have had a genuine antique to work upon, took, as was his wont, many liberties with it. Pinkerton thought—but, unfortunately for his authority, he was much given to think whatever suited his theory—that it might have been written soon after the event. Ritson, a most competent critic, and of inflexible honesty, said that, so far as either internal or external evidence went, it might be as old as the fifteenth century. Lord Hailes, Mr. Sibbald, and Professor Aytoun concur in the opinion that it has been at least retouched by a more modern hand, and that it is probably as recent as the days of Queen Mary or James the Sixth. In the second stanza occur these lines—

"But sin' the days of auld King Harry
Sic slaughter was not heard nor seen."

"This slaughter," says Mr. Sibbald, "most probably alludes to some bloody engagement between the English and the Scots. If so, under what 'auld King Harry' did this happen? No battle answers such a description excepting that of Flodden in

1513; and I venture to say that the author meant
no other, notwithstanding the absurd anachronism
with which he is chargeable." Aytoun supposes
that the ballad is by the same author as that of the
"Raid of the Reidswire," and the most cursory
comparison of the two more than confirms his happy
conjecture. "The Raid of the Reidswire" is contained in the Bannatyne manuscript (1568), which
would give an authorship not more modern than
the early part of the reign of James VI. Assuming
it, then, to have an origin at least as remote as this
date, we may premise that the ballad, though
pedantic, prosy, and long-winded, is historically
valuable, as being faithful in details, and giving a
minute and circumstantial narrative of the origin
and incidents of the battle—

> "Great Donald of the Isles did claim
>   Unto the lands of Ross some right ;
> And to the Governor he came
>   Them for to have, gif that he might ;
>   Wha saw his interest was but slight,
> And therefore answered wi' disdain.
>   He hasted home baith day and night,
> And sent nae bodword [notice] back again.
>
> "But Donald, right impatient
>   Of that answer Duke Robert gave,
> He vowed to God omnipotent
>   All the haill lands of Ross to have,
>   Or else be graithit in his grave."

His purpose was to make himself master of Scotland
to the Forth, and he issued a proclamation that his
adherents should assemble at Inverness. Mar met

him, as we have seen, at Harlaw, and fortunately checked his career, the numbers being stated, probably with poetic license, as ten to one.

As an instance of the pedantry referred to above, the following stanza will suffice. It may be not uninteresting to note the sententiousness of the conclusion—

> "This is (quoth he) the right report
>   Of all that I did hear and knaw ;
> Though my discourse be something short,
> Take this to be a right sooth saw.
> Contrarie God and the King's law,
> There was spilled meikle Christian blude,
> Into the battle of Harlaw ;
> This is the sum, sae I conclude."

The last of the following lines, which conclude the list of the leaders slain on the side of Mar, has a peculiarly modern—one would say, were it not for the anachronism, a peculiarly Byronic-ring—

> "The Knight of Panmure, as was seen,
> A mortal man in armour bright ;
> Sir Thomas Murray stout and keen,
> *Left to the world their last good-night.*"

This coincidence is no doubt suggested to one by the peculiarly lumbering line which immediately precedes Childe Harold's farewell to his native land—

> "Thus to the elements he poured his last ' Good-Night.' "

The Childe's " Good-Night " was suggested by Lord Maxwell's " Good-Night," first published in " The Minstrelsy of the Border." According to Alexander

Smith, it surpasses Childe Harold's in tenderness and pathos. He might have added that it surpasses it also in concentration and intensity, as much as the real surpasses the imaginary, and actual calamity dominates a self-conscious sentimentalism. Another line of the "Pilgrimage" may have had a similar genesis—

"And chiefless castles, *breathing stern farewells.*"

The date of the engagement is given with a very singular periphrasis, the 24th of July 1411, being thus expressed—

"In July, on St. James his even,
   That four-and-twenty dismal day,
Twelve hundred, ten score, and eleven
   Of years sin' Christ, the sooth to say."

This is evidently of much earlier construction than the time of Ramsay.

The ballad we have been reviewing *may* be the one referred to in the "Complaynt of Scotland," for the opinion of Ritson as to its possible antiquity is entitled to the greatest weight. But Professor Aytoun published another version, for which he was indebted to Lady John Scott, and which he designates the "traditionary version." It is still popular in Aberdeenshire, where it was taken down as sung. It is an ancient ballad of a high class, and has much greater swing and directness than that published in the "Evergreen." Aytoun thinks it by no means improbable that this is the original. It gives the

number of the Highlandmen at 50,000 — a very
natural exaggeration. The ferocity of the combat is
thus graphically described —

> " The Hielandmen wi' their lang swords,
>   They laid on us fu' sair ;
> And they drave back our merry men
>   Three acres breadth and mair."

The corresponding passage in the other ballad is by
no means of equal picturesqueness and strength, and
has still the same fatal taint of pedantry—

> " There was nae mows [jesting] there them amang,
>   Naething was heard but heavy knocks ;
> That Echo made a dulefu' sang
>   Thereto resounding frae the rocks."

With reference to the duration of the struggle, it says
truthfully but prosaically, " The bluidy battle lasted
lang."   How much more poetically striking the other,
though it shoots with a very long bow indeed !

> " On Mononday at morning,
>   The battle it began ;
> On Saturday at gloamin',
>   Ye'd scarce ken'd who had wan.

> " Of fifty thousand Hielandmen
>   Scarce fifty there went hame ;
> And out of a' the Lowlandmen
>   But fifty marched wi' Græme.

> " And sic a weary buryin'
>   I'm sure ye never saw,
> As was the Sunday after that,
>   On the muirs aneath Harlaw.

> " Gin anybody speer at ye
>   For them we took awa',

> Ye may tell them plain, and very plain,
> They're sleeping at Harlaw!"

This last line is quite in the spirit of the best Greek epigram.

It is amusing to remark in the common set of the verses how the Teutonic hatred of the Celt breaks out—

> "These lazy loons might well be spared,
> Chasit like deers into their dens,
> And gat their wages for reward."

This battle and its legendary accompaniments powerfully affected the imagination of Scott. Every reader of " The Antiquary "—and the name must be legion—will remember that powerful chapter in which Oldbuck, with his nephew Captain M'Intyre, and Edie Ochiltree, is represented as visiting the cottage of Saunders Mucklebackit, the fisherman, to glean information, if he could, from Elspeth Mucklebackit, Saunders's mother, about the lost child of Lord Glenallan :—" As Oldbuck lifted the latch of the hut, he heard the tremulous voice of the old woman chanting forth to her grandchildren snatches of old ballad poetry. Suddenly her strain changed from the romantic to the historical—

> ' Now haud your tongue, baith wife and carle,
> And listen, great and sma',
> And I will sing of Glenallan's Earl
> That fought on the Red Harlaw.

> ' The coronach's cried on Bennachie,
> And down the Don and a',
> And Hieland and Lawland may mournfu' be
> For the sair field of Harlaw.'

'It's an historical ballad,' said Oldbuck, eagerly, 'a genuine and undoubted fragment of minstrelsy! Percy would admire its simplicity—Ritson could not impugn its authenticity.' The old crone continued—

> ' They saddled a hundred milk-white steeds,
>   They hae bridled a hundred black,
> With a chafron of steel on each horse's head,
>   And a good knight upon his back.'

'Chafron!' exclaimed the Antiquary, 'equivalent, perhaps, to " cheveron;" the word's worth a dollar;' and down it went in his red book."

This is the true spirit of a black-letter ballad-collector. Without enthusiasm, and a slight touch of what Horace sportively calls an amiable insanity, it is impossible to be a successful explorer in this out-of-the-way, but by no means barren, field. Elspeth Mucklebackit's " croon," under the title of " Glenallan's Earl," is in the later editions of the " Minstrelsy of the Border." It concludes thus in the words of Roland Cheyne, Glenallan's " squire so gay "—

> " My horse shall ride through ranks sae rude,
>   As through the moorland fern ;
> Then ne'er let the gentle Norman blude
>   Grow cauld for Highland kerne."

This contrast it was that embittered the contest— the contrast of Norman knight as against Highland kerne. It is even now difficult for men to realise the declaration of Paul that " God hath made of one blood all nations of men for to dwell on all the face of the earth." But however bitter the strife may be between nationalities, that between races is infinitely more so. During the lull of an armistice, the French and the German, the English and the Scottish knight could interchange the civilities and courtesies of the lists and the banqueting-hall, as during the Peninsular war the British and French outposts could exchange canteens till the trumpet sounded once more to arms. But between the soldier of the Black Watch and the soldier of King Koffee Calcalli no such civilities could exist under any circumstances. And somewhat similar was the feeling then of the Norman or Teuton to those whom the French used to call the savages of Scotland. Happily no such feeling exists now, and the people of this island are all the better that to the Saxon solidity have been superadded the Celtic grace and self-respect.

Mr. Clyne has directed my attention to some investigations of his own respecting this "brim battel of the Harlaw." Among those slain on the side of Mar was, according to the ballad—

> " Gude Sir Robert Davidson,
> Who Provost was of Aberdeen."

Mr. Clyne shows that the Provost's knighthood is purely imaginary; for in the account of the battle given by the contemporary author Walter Bower, the continuator of Fordun's "Scotichronicon," as well as in the local records, Davidson's name always occurs in the form of that of a simple burgess. He kept a " Taberna," or wine dealer's booth, where wine was not only sold but consumed on the premises. He was Provost, or " Alderman," the title then given to the chief magistrate, for the first time in 1402, and seems to have been a public-spirited, sagacious, hearty man, equally ready to dispense a cup of good wine, or to buckle on his armour and head the burgesses against a common foe. Mr. Clyne is not disposed to dispute Aytoun's assigning the authorship of the ballad to a date not more modern than the early part of the reign of James VI. In fact, he shows it to be almost certain that the writer had Boece's " Historiæ Scotorum " (1526) before him, particular sentences and phrases in the ballad approaching to a translation of Boece's Latin. Boece was proverbially fallacious, and the author of the ballad has reproduced his errors, and, among others, that of making *Robertus Davidstoun, Aberdoniæ præfectus*, a knight, or *eques auratus*.

§ 3. DARK FLODDEN.

The battle of Flodden—called in the English despatches the battle of Brankstone Moor—was fought on the 9th of September 1513, between the Scots, led by James IV. in person, and the English, commanded by the Earl of Surrey. The English had about 5000 slain, and the Scots probably twice that number. But these figures, eloquent as they are, do not in any adequate degree represent the dis-

parity of loss; for the English lost very few persons
of distinction, while the Scots, from the one extremity
of the kingdom to the other, were deprived of their
natural leaders. Among their dead were the King,
two bishops, two mitred abbots, twelve earls, thirteen
lords of Parliament, the provost and magistrates of
Edinburgh, and the head or some member of almost
every distinguished family in the kingdom. Some
of the Border towns—as Selkirk, Hawick, and Jedburgh—had nearly the whole of their adult male
population cut off, and in the ballad of the " Flowers
of the Forest" we still hear an echo of the wail that
arose from widow and orphan, and maiden bereft of
her lover, in that region so happily described by
Wordsworth as now characterised by—

> " The grace of forest charms decayed,
>   And pastoral melancholy."

Of the Scottish ballads commemorating this melancholy catastrophe, a broken stanza or two are all
that remain, but the ancient air is preserved in the
Skene Manuscript, with the title of " The Flowres
of the Forreste." The following lines alone are preserved—

> " I've heard them lilting at the ewes' milking,
>   The Flowers of the Forest are a' wede away."

And this other imperfect line, with the refrain—

> "I ride single on my saddle,
>   For the Flowers of the Forest are a' wede away,"

picked up by Scott, who observes that it " presents

a simple and affecting image to the mind." The
two first quoted are respectively the first and the
fourth lines of the first verse of the exquisite stanzas
to the air already named, written by Miss Jean Elliot
of Minto. "The manner of the ancient minstrels is
so happily imitated," says Scott, "that it required
the most positive evidence to convince the editor
that the song was of modern date." Miss Elliot was
born in 1727, and her ballad was published anony-
mously, probably about 1755. By many it was considered old, but its recent composition was detected
by Burns, who wrote:—"This fine ballad is even a
more palpable imitation than Hardyknute. The
manners are indeed old, but the *language* is of yesterday. Its author must very soon be discovered."
The origin of the ballad is thus described by Mr.
Laing in his Notes on Stenhouse, in the 4th vol. of
"Johnson's Museum:"—Miss Elliot's father, Gilbert
Elliot of Minto, Lord Justice-Clerk of Scotland, con-
versing with her one day about the Battle of Flodden,
offered a bet that she would not compose a ballad
on that subject. It thus came to pass that she took
up the fragments of the old lost ballad, and restored
them, as it were, to life in her well-known song,
which is thus in some measure the legitimate offspring of the muse of the older minstrel. The same
cannot be said of two other ballads composed to the
same air, both of great merit, and both written by
females. That commencing with—

    " I've seen the smiling of fortune beguiling,"

written by Miss Alison Rutherford of Fernylee,
Selkirkshire, married in 1731 to Patrick Cockburn,
Advocate, does not refer to Flodden, but, as expressed
by Mr. Chambers, "to a crisis of a monetary nature,
when seven good lairds of the Forest were reduced
to insolvency, in consequence of imprudent specu-
lations," though this, if correct, was unknown to
Scott, who says that "the verses were written without peculiar relation to any event, unless it were the
depopulation of Ettrick Forest." The following is
said to have been its genesis :—A gentleman one day
overhearing a shepherd playing a peculiarly plaintive
air, made him repeat it several times till he had
mastered it, when he noted it down. The air was
"The Flowers of the Forest." He requested Miss
Rutherford to supply appropriate verses, which she
did in the song just referred to. The third ballad to
the same air was written by Miss Anne Home, sister
of Sir Edward Home, and married in 1771 to the
celebrated anatomist, John Hunter. It begins—

"Adieu, ye streams that smoothly glide."

After she was a widow she published a volume of
poems at London in 1806. Mr. Laings says he
cannot ascertain where the different sets of these
beautiful lyrics were first published. He says,
further, that it is doubtful which of them should
claim priority of composition. Miss Rutherford's set
was printed in "The Lark," p. 37, Edinburgh, 1765.
Miss Elliot's set appeared in the same volume, and

Mr. Laing asserts of it that "there is not perhaps in the whole range of our lyrical poetry a finer adaptation of old words handed down by tradition." In Herd's Collection (1776) both sets are incorporated as part of a long narrative ballad of inferior merit.

But if the Scottish poets are silent regarding this disastrous battle, Pitscottie's prose narrative is minute, garrulous, and picturesque. The English bards, also—and this should occasion us no surprise—have not failed to commemorate so great a triumph to their national arms. Some of them treat of the matter with something like a crow of triumph that is in exceedingly bad taste; but others speak of the calamity to the King of Scots and his army with the respect that gallant men owe to each other. In Ritson's "Ancient Songs" there is a copy of verses on the subject. His introductory note is as follows:—
"The following ballad may be as ancient as anything we have on the subject. It is given from 'The most pleasant and delectable history of John Winchcomb, otherwise called Jack of Newberry,' written by Thomas Delaney, who thus speaks of it: 'In disgrace of the Scots, and in remembrance of the famous achieved victory, the commons of England made this song, which to this day is not forgotten of many.'" The ballad has little poetical merit. As an instance of its spirit and taste the following extract will suffice—

"Then bespake good Queen Margaret,
  The tears fell from her eye!

'Leave off these wars, most noble King,
    Keep your fidelity.

" ' The water runs swift and wondrous deep,
    From bottom unto the brim ;
My brother Henry hath men good enough,
    England is hard to win.'

" ' Away,' quoth he, ' with this silly fool !
    In prison fast let her lie ;
For she is come of the English blood,
    And for these words she shall die.'

" With that bespake Lord Thomas Howard,
    The Queen's chamberlain that day,
' If that you put Queen Margaret to death,
    Scotland shall rue it alway.'

"Then in a rage King Jamie did say,
    ' Away with this foolish mome ;
He shall be hanged, and the other burned,
    So soon as I come home.' "

In this ballad the title of the battle is " Brani-
stonegreen." The fullest collection of pieces on the
subject is to be found in a volume entitled "The
Battle of Flodden Field," a poem of the sixteenth
century, edited by Henry Weber, Edinburgh, 1808.
It contains the various readings of the different
copies, a historical narrative, a glossary, and an
appendix containing ancient poems and historical
matter relating to the same event. The editor says—
"The author's object was to procure his fellow-
countrymen of the North of England, particularly
those attached, like him, to the noble House of
Stanley, an accurate and minute account of a victory
in which they had gained so much renown." Though
the only ancient manuscript is of no latter date than

1636, there can be little doubt that the poem was produced during the preceding century, probably as early as the middle of it.   It is in nine fits, and in it the battle is named Brampton.   The following is a specimen of it—

> " But when the English archers shot,
>   On each part did so pierce and gall,
>   That, ere they came to handy strokes,
>   A number great on ground did fall.
>
> " The King himself was wounded sore,
>   An arrow fierce in's forehead light,
>   That hardly he could fight any more,
>   The blood so blemished his sight.
>
> " Yet like a warrior stout he stayed,
>   And freely did exhort that tide,
>   His men to be nothing dismayed,
>   But battle boldly there to bide.
>
> " But what availed his valour great,
>   Or bold device ?   All was but vain ;
>   His captains keen fell at his feet,
>   And standard-bearer down was slain."

The following stanza deserves to be quoted, as it records an interesting fact not generally known—

> " The Archbishop of St. Andrews brave,
>   King James his son in base begot,
>   That doleful day did death receive,
>   With many a lusty lord-like Scot."

This son, who must have been a very young archbishop, was of the highest promise.   Had he survived, it is surmised that the Scottish Reformation might have been differently coloured, and this might probably have been not disadvantageous.   The Dean of Westminster, in an address at St. Andrews on the occasion of his inauguration as Lord Rector of the University, passed a high eulogium on him, and referred gracefully to the fight at Flodden, in which an ancestor of his own had taken so prominent a part. The skull of the youthful archbishop used to be shown in the museum of the United College at St. Andrews. It was of dazzling whiteness, and had an ugly gash in it, inflicted doubtless by an English billman.

In the "Mirour of Magistrates" (London, 1587), there is a poem entitled "The Lament of King James IV., slayne at Brampton." It is of little value. He blames the King of France for the disaster to himself and his people. The refrain is a Latin verse—

"Miserere mei Deus et salua me."

There is in the "Flower of Fame" another lament of King James of Scotland, who was slain at *Scotfield*. It is by Ulpian Fulwell. The following is from the first-mentioned lament, and is not without a certain pathos—

" Farewell, my Queen, sweete, lovely Margaret ;
   Farewell, my Prince, with whom I used to play ;
I wot not where we shall together meet ;
   Farewell, my Lords and Commons, eke for aye.
Adieu ! ye shall no ransom for me pay ;
   Yet I beseech you, of your charity,
To the High Lord merciful that you pray—
   Miserere mei Deus et salua me."

When we mention "The Laird of Muirhead,"

who with 200 of his name from Torwood and the Clyde laid down their lives at Flodden, we have mentioned nearly all the old poetic literature bearing on the subject.

There is, however, one notable exception, that is, "The Souters o' Selkirk." Eighty of the gallant Souters appeared on the fatal field, and the most of them never returned from it. It may be held a settled point that the ballad refers not to a contest at football between the Souters and the men of Hume, as has been contended, but to the different behaviour of themselves and the followers of Lord Hume at Flodden—at least to the tradition on the subject; for Hume had nothing to gain but everything to lose by the success of the English. Sir Walter Scott, himself a "Souter," has made this matter sufficiently plain. The second of the lines we quote is unintelligible on any other supposition—

> "And up wi' the lads of the Forest,
>   That ne'er to the Southron would yield;
> But deil scoup o' Hume and his menzie,
>   That stude sae abeigh on the field."

Pinkerton remarks that "the Scottish nation were so very unwilling to yield any advantage on the English part, that they seem actually to have set up pretensions to the victory." It is to this that the scurrilous Skelton, Henry VIII.'s poet-laureate, refers in the subjoined lines—

> "Against the proud Scotte's clattering,
>   That never will leave their trattlying,

Wan they the field and lost theyr king ?
They may well say fie, on that winning !
Lo these fond sottes and trattlying Scottes,
How they are blinde in their own minde,
And will not know theyr overthrow.
At Branxton moore they are so stowre,
So frantike mad, and say they had,
And wan the field with speare and shielde ;
This is as true as black as blue."

The details of the contest are so well known that
we have purposely refrained from mentioning them.
Scott's "Marmion" is, or ought to be, familiar to
every one ; and in that poem, and in the notes to it,
the events that preceded and accompanied the fight
are detailed with singular vividness and power.
Indeed, the description of the fight is the most powerful battle-scene in modern literature. To find its
equal we must resort to Homer, and in no translation
of the old Greek that we know of is anything equal
to Scott to be found. In "Good Words" (July 1875),
Principal Shairp discourses on the Homeric element
in Scott, and some of his remarks are so apposite that
in this connection there is no apology needed for
quoting them :—" It is in ' Marmion ' that whatever
was epic in Scott found fullest vent. He had chosen
a national and truly heroic action as the centre or
climax of the whole poem—the battle of Flodden.
Flodden had been the most grievous blow that Scotland ever received. It had penetrated the national
heart with an overpowering sorrow, so pervading and
so deep, that no other event, even Culloden, ever
equalled it. And it had lived on in remembrance

down to Scott's boyhood as a source of the most pathetic refrains that ever blended with the people's songs."

If it be asked how this great calamity overtook the nation, it will suffice to say that it was due to the character and personal popularity of the monarch. It has been remarked, that instead of being led by a general, the Scots had at their head a knight-errant bent on distinguishing himself by his personal prowess. Had the English been attacked before the whole of their army had crossed the Till, there might have been a victory equal to that gained by Wallace at Stirling. The only redeeming feature where there was so much blundering was the devotion with which the nobles sacrificed themselves for their monarch when they discovered how fatally he had erred. This explains Sir David Lindsay's remark in his "Complaint of the Papingo"—

> " I never read in tragedy nor story,
>   At ane tournay so mony nobillis slane
>   For the defence and luve of their soveraine."

It was a letter from the young and beautiful queen of Louis XII. of France that precipitated James's rupture with his brother-in-law, Henry VIII. She believed, says Pitscottie, "that he wold raise ane army and come three foot on English ground for her sake; and to that effect she sent him ane ring off her finger, worth fifteen thousand French crowns." This was attacking James on his weak side. He was so notorious for his gallantry, that in the attempt made to dissuade him from war with England, the figure dressed up to represent St. John, that appeared to him in the Church of Linlithgow, cautioned him against frequenting the society of women and using their counsel. Even when on English ground with his army, which had gradually melted away from 100,000 men that had assembled on the Borough Moor, to 35,000, instead of striking a decisive blow against the enemy's country, he trifled away his time in an intercourse of gallantry with Lady Heron of Ford, who succeeded in diverting him from the purpose of the expedition till the arrival of an English army. His own soldiers sang ribald ballads in derision of his conduct, but his heroic action in the field, and his great popularity with all ranks of his subjects, made his error to be in a great measure condoned.

§ 4. MINOR COMBATS: CORRICHIE, BALRINNES, AND DRYFFE SANDS.

The Scotch are a martial, not a military people, having no delight in "the pomp and circumstance of glorious war" as such. We scarcely remember an instance in the national history in which anything like military splendour was exhibited except that gathering on the Borough Moor, which met the eye of Marmion as he drew nigh the capital, and which preceded the sad defeat of Flodden. The motto of the people is "Defence, not offence;" and though

the doughty Earl of Douglas, and many a less conspicuous personage, may have at times ridden into
England to fetch a prey, they had no intention of
annexing territory and abiding there. As soon as
they had secured their beeves and driven them off,
their purpose was accomplished. And it was defen-
sive in this sense, that it was a spoiling of the Ama-
lekites, because by every beeve thus abstracted, the
common enemy was so much the weaker. As war
so conducted had little sentiment connected with it,
we should not expect the idea of it to have informed
much of song or poetry. And the case is so. It is
not till we come to a later period—indeed, to that
of the two men of whom Scotland has most reason
to be proud in recent times, Burns and Scott—that
we find the martial spirit expressed with power and
splendour. Burns's—

" Farewell, thou fair day, thou green earth, and ye skies," &c.,

has been much admired. There is undoubtedly great
force of expression in it, and striking images of tenderness, terror, and patriotism are combined. But it
has always seemed to us too melodramatic, to savour
too much of the fiddlers and the footlights. This,
however, may be pardoned for its uncommon power,
and spirit, and from the fact that it is actually presented as part of a drama. Much better, in our
opinion is—

" Scots wha ha'e wi' Wallace bled ;"

but better, perhaps, than either is—

"Does haughty Gaul invasion threat?"

It contains, indeed, what seem needless vulgarisms to the more refined—or shall we say to the more squeamish?—taste of the present day. But it is to be remembered that it was written at a period of extraordinary excitement, and had a reference to engrossing current events. Moreover, the poet had for a season been relegated to the cold shade of unpopularity with the influential for suspected disloyalty, and he may have deemed it necessary to express himself on the occasion with unusual energy. It is worth while noticing, in the present connection, that in the expression *red-wat-shod*, occurring in another poem, Burns has borrowed, probably unconsciously, from the ballad of "Otterbourne"—

"The Gordons gude in English *blude*
They *wat* their hose and *shoon*."

Scott, again, is full of the martial spirit. If ever there was a born soldier he was one. His battle-piece in "Marmion" has been already commented on. But everywhere throughout his works, poetic and prose, this spirit breaks out. The combat between Fitz-James and Roderick Dhu in the "Lady of the Lake" is one of the first lengthened poetic pieces that arrest the attention of high-spirited boys. And in his novels, *passim*, are combats either on a large or a small scale, a battle or a duel, which are described as only the born soldier could do. In "The Monastery" occurs perhaps the best and most inspiriting march ever written—

"March ! march ! Ettrick and Teviotdale."

When the Blue Bonnets should come over the Border, if they were animated individually by the spirit of their laureate, the boast—

> " England shall many a day
> Tell of the bloody fray,"

would not prove a mere *brutum fulmen*. This march is modelled on what is known as " General Leslie's March to Long Marston Moor," beginning—

> " March ! march ! why the deil dinna ye march ? "

in which the Presbyterian spirit breaks out so fiercely against " Popish relics," " hoods," " the sark of God," and " the kistfu' of whistles," and asserts very characteristically that—

> " There's nane in the right but we
> Of the auld Scottish nation."

And Thomas Campbell has proved himself a very Tyrtæus in his martial lyrics—" The Battle of Hohenlinden," " The Battle of the Baltic," and " Ye Mariners of England "—the last two of which have become national and highly-treasured inheritances ; while " Rule Britannia " is the joint production of Thomson and Mallet, or the production of one or other of them —both our countrymen.

It is natural, therefore, to expect that our countrymen should have conducted themselves nobly in war. And they have :—nobly on many a bloody field. But we think it may be confessed that the Lowland portion of them have no great natural aptitude or taste for being soldiers, and that they require to be highly disciplined, and wisely handled, before they mount into the highest rank. Led by a Bruce, whose military capacity was pre-eminent, and his action uncontrolled, they could perform wonders. Led even by a Wallace, whose action was cramped and thwarted by men incapable and often treacherous, they failed even against a foe not superior in numbers and appliances. On many occasions their defeats by the English were absolutely humiliating. Of this the most conspicuous example was the affair at Solway Moss. But when highly disciplined and wisely led, they never found their victors on anything like equal terms. The Scottish Guard of the French Kings were the foremost individual soldiers in Europe; and the Scottish battalions that fought with the great Gustavus, and were led by Munros, Leslies, Lumsdens, and many an unnoted Dalgetty, all duly registered, no doubt, in "The Scot Abroad," found no superiors in Continental armies. If we mistake not, it was a regiment of Frasers that covered the British retreat at Fontenoy. Had they not been subjected to proper discipline, the same men would either not have charged at all, deeming themselves injured on some punctilio of clan honour, or having charged and vanquished, would have dispersed in quest of plunder, and been themselves vanquished in turn by troops under better control. Scott's description of the warriors of his country in "The

Vision of Don Roderick" is truthful and spirited; and it shows how much public sentiment had altered in little more than half a century from Prestonpans and Culloden, that the typical Scottish soldier is the once-dreaded Highlander with waving tartans and screaming pibroch, and only he.

These remarks on the Scottish soldier at his worst and best are not inappropriate here, as we have touched on the most important of the battles dealt with in our old ballad lore. We shall now notice three minor combats commemorated in ballad, and singularly illustrative each of its place and era—the battle of Corrichie, fought 28th October 1562; the battle of Balrinnes, fought 4th October 1594; and the battle of Dryffe Sands, fought 7th December 1593. As a bloody crime resulted from this, we shall refer further to the celebrated ballad of Lord Maxwell's "Good Night," connected with that crime.

The circumstances that led to the battle of Corrichie and the result of it may be thus briefly summarised:—"The Cock of the North," the Earl of Huntly, was so powerful in the North that he kept princely state in Strathbogie Castle, and his fourth son, Sir John Gordon, is said to have even lifted his eyes to the Queen (Mary). Huntly, being the head of the Catholic party, was obnoxious to Murray, the Queen's brother, and head of the Congregation; and, besides, he held in occupancy the estates of the Earldom of Murray. It was, therefore, both the policy and the interest of Murray to crush him, and accordingly he persuaded Mary to accompany him northwards with a sufficient force. Huntly, who dreaded this visit, though nominally only a royal progress, kept out of the way till the Queen and her brother returned to Aberdeen after some rough work at Inverness Castle. However he now thought his best policy was to fight, which he did at Corrichie, sixteen miles west of Aberdeen. He was defeated, and was found among the slain after the battle—smothered, says Buchanan, by his armour, being a portly man. Three days after, Sir John, the Queen's reputed lover, was beheaded at Aberdeen, the Queen herself being a spectator. How Mary could act thus may seem inexplicable. In spite of her high spirit the crafty Murray may have persuaded her that it was politic. But her conduct can scarcely be determined by a reference to ordinary Scottish motives. She had learned the deepest dissimulation in the court of her mother-in-law, Catherine de Medici. As, however, according to the ballad, Sir John

> " Had broken his ward in Aberdeen,
>   Thro' dreid o' the fause Murray,"

his execution may have been technically right; but none the less was Mary's conduct not only unqueenly but unwomanly.

Whatever merit the ballad has, it has that of historic fidelity. It says of Murray's adherents—

> " Murray gar'd raise the tardy Merns men,
>   An' Angus, and mony ane mair ;

Erle Morton, and the Byres Lord Lindsay,
    And campit at the Hill o' Fair."

The battle, having begun, was going against the
royal forces—

" Then fause Murray feignit to flee them,
    An' they pursued at his back ;
When the half o' the Gordons deserted,
    An' turned wi' Murray in a crack.
Wi' heather in their bonnets they turnit,
    The traitor Haddo at their head,
An' slay'd their brothers and their fathers,
    An' spoilit, and left them deid."

These circumstances are nearly identical with those
mentioned in Maitland's history. Maitland informs
us that Murray's foot giving way, he would certainly
have been defeated had it not been for the gallantry
of the cavalry under Morton and Lindsay. We have
mentioned that the Earl, being corpulent, was supposed to have been smothered in his armour. The
ballad-monger—who, by the way, is said to have
been John Forbes, schoolmaster at Maryculter, Dee-
side—admits the Earl's corpulency, but makes his
death more befitting a warrior, probably for poetical
effect—

" Then Murray cried to tak' the auld Gordon,
    An' mony ane ran wi' speid ;
But Stuart o' Inchbraik had him sticket,
    An' out gush'd the fat lurdane's bleid."

The author of the " Innocence of Mary " affirms that
Huntly was killed by Murray's express orders. On
one thing only does the soft-hearted schoolmaster

differ from history. He exonerates the Queen. The wish is evidently father to the thought, and he seeks to harmonise fact with propriety—

> " But now the day maist waefu' cam',
>   That day the Queen did greet her fill,
> For Huntly's gallant stalwart son
>   Was headed on the headin' hill."

His heart is in the right place, and he concludes with the most pious wishes—

> " I wis' our Queen had better friends ;
>   I wis' our countrie better peace ;
> I wis' our lords wadna discord ;
>   I wis' our wars at hame may cease ! "

The battle of Balrinnes was also fought by an Earl of Huntly, grandson of the preceding, and who had less than three years before signalised himself by killing "the bonny Earl of Murray," son-in-law of the Regent Murray, for the evils he had brought upon the house of Gordon. The present Earl, equally powerful with his grandfather, and, like him, the head of the Catholic party, was suspected, on the evidence of what are known in the history of the period as "the Spanish blanks," of having conspired with Errol, Angus, and Gordon of Auchendoun, Huntly's nephew, to introduce Spanish troops into the country to restore the Popish faith. Huntly's rival in power was Argyle, who was commissioned to attack the northern potentate—a process which suited well the unenterprising character of James, saving him at once trouble and expense. This

F

Argyle, young and eager, readily undertook, and, in the capacity of King's lieutenant, soon brought ten thousand men to the sources of Spey, and marching down the haughs along the river fell in with Huntly and Errol on the Livet, with a force of not more than two thousand men.   Mr. Burton notes that this small force came mainly from the district whence Mar had procured the handful of troops that defeated Donald of the Isles at Harlaw in 1411, that the battlefields were within thirty miles of each other, and that the results were similar.   Gordon and Huntly had six field-pieces, an arm long dreaded by the Highlanders.   Argyle's men, after repeated attempts to break through the compact line of their enemy, were completely routed.   The battle has three names—Altacholylachan, Glenlivet, and Balrinnes.

The ballad, like many others narrating battles, is given in the first person by an individual who, having to proceed—

"Frae Dunnoter to Aberdeen,"

had risen too soon ; but—

"On Towie Mount I met a man
    Well graithed in his gear ;
Quoth I, ' What news !' then he began
    To tell a fit of weir,
Saying, ' The ministers I fear,
    A bloody browst have brewn,'" &c. ;

which gives at once an idea of the structure of the ballad, and that the battle was regarded as a religious one. The ballad in its complete state may be

found in Dalzell's "Scottish Poems of the Sixteenth
Century." It is extraordinarily prolix, consisting of
forty-one double stanzas, or three hundred and
twenty-eight lines. When Huntly and Errol joined
their forces, there were two days of fine hearty
soldierly " high jinks "—

> " Then players played and sangsters sang
> To glad the merry host," &c.

> " They for two days would not remove,
> But blithely drank the wine ;
> Some to his lass, some to his love,
> Some to his lady fine.
> And he that thought not for to blyne [stop]
> His mistress' token tak's ;
> They kisst it first, and set it syne
> Upon their helms and jacks."

When the armies came in presence Huntly's men
were for rushing to battle—

> " ' Gae to, assay the game !' said some ;
> But Captain Ker said, ' Nay !
> First let the guns before us gae,
> That they may break the order.' "

This Captain Ker was the real perpetrator of the
atrocities mentioned in "Edom o' Gordon." There
is generous mention of the gallantry of the enemy,
even after they had fled—

> " They cried out, O, and some, Alace,
> But never for mercy sought ;
> Therefore the Gordons gave nae grace,
> *Because they craved it not.*"

The Maclean maintained his ground long after Argyle

had fled. Being forced, however, reluctantly to follow his leader, it was suggested that he might easily be overtaken—

> " But noble Errol had remorse,
>   And said, ' It is not best ;
> For the Argyle has got the worst,
>   Let him gang with the rest.
> Therefore, gude fellows let him be ;
>   He'll dee before he yield ;
> For he with his small company,
>   Rade langest in the field.' "

This is truly chivalrous. Not so much can be said of anything that occurred at the battle of Dryffe Sands, which happened the year before, between the rival houses of the Johnstones of Annandale and the Maxwells of Nithsdale. This skirmish, which belongs properly to the Border warfare, may be treated here both as a much more considerable skirmish than usual between the Border clans, and as exhibiting a ferocity—a want of chivalry—entirely at variance with that of Errol noticed above.

After feuds and reconciliations the Johnstones and Maxwells were at peace, when the peace was broken in consequence of a raid, or cattle-lifting, of the Johnstones on the lands of the Lairds of Crichton, Sanquhar, and Drumlanrig, who induced Lord Maxwell secretly to accept from them bonds of manrent, he, in turn, binding himself to maintain their quarrel. This being discovered by the Johnstones, war was immediately entered into, and Maxwell, though armed with the royal authority and followed by 2000 men, was defeated at Dryffe Sands, near Lockerby. Maxwell himself, unhorsed and prostrate, stretched forth his hand for quarter, which was at once severed from his body, and himself slain. Many of his followers were killed, and many cruelly wounded, especially by slashes in the face, such wounds being thence termed a " Lockerby lick." The hand is said to have been struck of by Willie Johnstone of the Kirkhill, his chief having before the battle promised a five-merk land to the man who should that day cut off Lord Maxwell's head or hand.

The origin of this petty war was a raid, as we have seen. Johnstone of Wamphray, called " The Galliard," was a noted freebooter. In " The Lads of Wamphray " it is said—

> " For the Galliard and the gay Galliard's men,
> They ne'er saw a horse but they made it their ain."

The Galliard having gone to Nithsdale " to steal Sim Crichton's winsome dun," made a strange mistake for such a man ; for

> " Instead of the dun, the blind he has ta'en.
> ' Now, Simmy, Simmy of the Side,
> Come out and see a Johnstone ride !
> Here's the bonniest horse in a' Nithside,
> And a gentle Johnstone aboon his hide." [1]

But he had calculated without his host. His blind horse was no match for those that at once pursued, and the Galliard being taken, was instantly hanged. His nephew Willie, who—it is not explained how— witnessed the execution, vowed revenge, which he

executed by that driving of a prey that brought about
the battle, defeating with slaughter those who pursued to rescue their property. There was great risk
in this kind of life, but great excitement, and actual
fun. After boasting that

> " For every finger of the Galliard's hand
>   I vow this day I've killed a man,"

Willie finished by this generous invitation—

> " Drive on, my lads, it will be late ;
>   We'll hae a pint at Wamphray gate."

Lord Maxwell, son of him whose hand was so
cruelly struck off at Dryffe Sands, vowed vengeance,
and in spite of the entreaties of the King—even
breaking out of Edinburgh Castle, where he was confined—he executed his purpose by treacherously
shooting Sir James Johnstone at Auchnamhill with
two poisoned bullets in the back. He escaped to
France ; but having ventured to return to Scotland,
was captured, tried, and executed. His famous
" Good Night," which suggested that in " Childe
Harold," and is much superior, must have been
composed some time between 1608 and 1613.

> " Adieu, madame, my mother dear,
>   But and my sisters three !
> Adieu, fair Robert of Orchardstane !
>   My heart is wae for thee.
> Adieu, the lily and the rose,
>   The primrose, fair to see !
> Adieu, my ladye, and only joy !
>   For I may not stay with thee."

The spirit of unappeasable revenge, occasionally mingled with something like feminine tenderness, breathes throughout the ballad. His lady, sister to the Marquis of Hamilton, and whose death has been attributed—it is to be hoped without foundation—to his harsh treatment, entreats him to go with her to her brother, who will succour him with "the Hamiltons and Douglas baith." But he has a mind of his own—

> " Thanks for thy kindness, fair my dame,
>   But I may not stay with thee."

> " Then he tuik aff a gay gold ring,
>   Thereat hang signets three ;
> ' Hae, tak' thee that, mine ain dear thing,
>   And still hae mind o' me :
> But if thou take another lord,
>   Ere I come ower the sea—
> His life is but a three days' lease,
>   Though I may not stay with thee.' "

The " Good Night " is a poem of a very high order.

§ 5. HISTORICAL-TRAGICAL.

In the " Bride of Lammermoor," old Alice says to the Lord-Keeper, Sir William Ashton, " Remember the fate of Sir George Lockhart." Sir William repudiated the parallel, but she continued,—" Therefore, I may well say, beware of pressing a desperate man with the hand of authority. There is blood of Chiesley in the veins of Ravenswood, and one drop of it were enough to fire him in the circumstances in which he is placed. I say beware of him."

The circumstance alluded to by old Alice is familiar to readers of Scottish history. Sir George Lockhart of Carnwath, Lord President of the Court of Session, having in his capacity of arbiter in a suit for aliment raised against John Chiesley of Dalry by his wife, from whom he had been separated, decided against him, Chiesley followed him from church on Sunday, 31st March 1689, and shot him down in the Lawnmarket, close to his own door, in presence of numerous spectators. He made no attempt to escape: on the contrary, he boasted of his deed. "This incident," says Scott, "was long remembered as a dreadful instance of what the law-books call the *perfervidum ingenium Scotorum.*" In other words, the Scots were credited with having something dangerous in their blood that might impel them to the greatest and most unexpected atrocities.

A still more appalling instance of this phase of national character was that exhibited by John Mure of Auchindrane, in Ayrshire, on whose strange atrocities Scott based his Ayrshire tragedy, by far the finest of his dramatic efforts. "Yet I doubt," says Mr. Lockhart, "whether the prose narrative of the preface be not, on the whole, more dramatic than the versified scenes." Scott says of Mure that he was "bold, ambitious, treacherous to the last degree, and utterly unconscientious—a Richard the Third in private life, inacessible alike to pity and remorse." Such crimes as those of Mure, horrible as they may

be, are redeemed from the category of mere vulgar
atrocities, inasmuch as they are motived not by the
love of gold or of sensual indulgence, but by ambition
and love of vengeance. In the case of Mure, given
the first crime, the rest of the series are the necessary
corollaries; and having taken the devil's erles, he
could not be let off without doing the devil's work.
About such a criminal there could be nothing weak
—no nervous tremors; no compunctious visitings.
Having formed a carefully-deliberated plan, from
which impulse was eliminated, he would work it out
remorselessly to the end, however bitter for himself
and others. Every obstacle had to be removed from
his path at however great a price.

Ballad lore furnishes at least two instances of
this same strange and almost inconceivable *perfervidum ingenium,* in its most cold-blooded and fero-
cious aspect. We refer to "Edom o' Gordon" and
"The Burning of Frendraught." In the battles
of Corrichie and of Balrinnes the Gordons were
principal actors, and in both of the two ballads
mentioned they are conspicuous, either doing or
suffering. "Edom o' Gordon" was Adam Gordon of
Auchendoun, brother and deputy of the Marquis of
Huntly. After having gained several successes over
the clan Forbes, the neighbours and feudal enemies
of the Gordons, the chronicler of the history of King
James VI. remarks of him, that "what glory and
renown he obtained by these two victories were all
casten down by the infamy of his next attempt; for

immediately after his last conflict he directed his soldiers to the Castle of Towie, desiring the house to be rendered to him in the Queen's name, whilk was obstinately refused by the lady, and she burst forth with certain injurious words. And the soldiers being impatient, by command of their leader, Captain Ker, fire was put to the house, wherein she and the number of twenty-seven persons were cruelly burned to the death." This happened in 1571.

One or two points may here be noted. In the ballad Edom o' Gordon is charged as the perpetrator, while the chronicle saddles the guilt on Captain Ker. Ker was the real culprit, but as he was acting under the commission of Gordon, and was never even called in question for his inhuman conduct, Gordon with true poetic justice is himself branded as the criminal. In some versions of the ballad, the "Castle of Towie," called in Archbishop Spottiswoode's "History of the Church of Scotland" Tavoy, appears as the "House o' the Rodes," which is in Berwickshire. Such changes of name, says Aytoun, "deserve note, as they indicate the district in which the poems were taken down, though they afford no evidence as to the part of the country in which they originated." The ballad is not a Border one, but belongs to the North Countrie. It deserves to be mentioned that in Percy's folio MS. it is entitled *Captain Adam Carre*, and is in the English idiom.

Edom o' Gordon is represented as saying to his

men in the cold, windy weather of the Martinmas time
that they must repair to a shelter, the most convenient
being the Castle of Towie. The lady, standing on the
battlements, and seeing the host of mounted men
spurring towards the castle, thought that it was her
husband returning with his retinue. She accordingly
withdrew to attire herself suitably, and to welcome
her lord with a comfortable repast—

> "She had nae suner buskit hersel',
>   Nor putten on her goun,
> Till Edom o' Gordon and his men
>   Were round about the toun.
>
> "They had nae suner supper set,
>   Nor suner said the grace,
> Till Edom o' Gordon and his men
>   Were light about the place."

The lady ran to the tower to see if she could pacify
him with fair words, but the ruffian replied to her
with the most insulting proposals. Her womanly
pride was offended, and she gave utterance to injurious
language, Gordon's reply to which was—

> "'Gie owre your house, ye ladie fair,
>   Gie owre your house to me,
> Or I shall burn yoursel' therein,
>   But and your babies three.'"

On this she discharged two bullets at him, which
missed his heart but grazed his knee—

> "'Set fire to the house!' quo' the false Gordon,
>   All wude wi' dule and ire ;
> 'False ladie! ye shall rue that shot,
>   As ye burn in the fire.'"

She beholds among the savages below "Jock," her man, who had pulled out the "grund-wa-stane," and let in the fire to her, and upbraids him with his perfidy.

> " O then bespake her youngest son,
>   Sat on the nourice' knee ;
>   Says, ' Mother, dear, gie owre this house,
>   For the reek it smothers me.'
>
> " ' I wad gie a' my gowd, my bairn,
>   Sae wad I a' my fee,
>   For ae blast o' the westlin' wind
>   To blaw the reek frae thee ! ' "

The following verses are unsurpassed in popular poetry—

> " O then bespake her daughter dear—
>   She was baith jimp and sma'—
>   ' O row me in a pair o' sheets,
>   And tow me owre the wa' ! '
>
> " They row'd her in a pair o' sheets,
>   And tow'd her owre the wa' ;
>   But on the point o' Gordon's spear
>   She gat a deadly fa'.
>
> " O bonnie, bonnie was her mouth,
>   And cherry were her cheeks ;
>   And clear, clear was her yellow hair,
>   Whereon the red blude dreeps.
>
> " Then wi' his spear he turned her owre,
>   O gin her face was wan !
>   He said, ' You are the first that e'er
>   I wish'd alive again.'
>
> " He turned her owre and owre again,
>   O gin her skin was white !
>   ' I might hae spared that bonnie face,
>   To hae been some man's delight.

> " ' Busk and boun, my merrie men a',
>   For ill dooms I do guess ;
>   I canna look on that bonnie face,
>   As it lies on the grass ! ' "

Two snatches of criticism are subjoined—the one
from Burton's "History of Scotland," the other from
Alexander Smith's essay on "Scottish Ballads," his
earliest published composition in prose. " The scene
supposed to have passed within that burning house
—a scene in which the heroic mother is tortured
between the duty of feudal hatred and the appeals of
her smothering children—is one of the finest among
the touching and beautiful pictures in the popular
ballads of the Scots people." "The writer of ' Edom
o' Gordon ' had no theories of art. He uttered only
what he saw and felt ; but what words could add to
that picture of the burning tower, the unutterable
sigh of the mother for ' ane blast o' the western wind,'
and the mute reproach of the face on the grass, more
terrible to the marauder than the gleam of hostile
spears ? "

The ballad was first printed at Glasgow by Robert
and Andrew Foulis, 1755, 8vo (twelve pages). Percy
improved and enlarged it with several fine stanzas
from a fragment in his folio MS. Even Mr. Chambers
admits that it is old, though modernised and improved, of course, by Lady Wardlaw. He says, " All
that can be surmised here is that the revision was the
work of the same pen with the pieces here cited."

And it must be confessed that there is great

similarity of workmanship between portions of this
ballad and others of "Young Waters," the "Bonny
Earl of Murray," "Sir Patrick Spens," &c., of what
he designates the Wardlaw group.

But a deed even still more diabolical than that of
Captain Ker is commemorated in "The Burning of
Frendraught," which occurred as late as 1630—provided the interpretation put upon it by the Gordons
be correct, and it was universally accepted at the
time. The last ballad represented the Gordons at
feud with the Forbeses; the one under review represents them at feud with the Crichtons. Charles I.
had rather been encouraging the Crichtons, that they
might have sufficient power and influence in some
measure to balance the local feudal power of the
overgrown house of Huntly. In a skirmish between
the Crichtons and some of the Gordons, January 1,
1630, Gordon of Rothiemay was killed. The Marquis
of Huntly succeeded in getting the matter com-
pounded, the Crichtons agreeing to pay to the widow
and children of the slain Rothiemay an assythment,
or compensation, of 50,000 merks. On Thursday,
October 7th, all parties to the arrangement were
present in Huntly's Castle of Strathbogie, but Frendraught had in the meantime got himself into fresh
difficulties by severely wounding the son of Leslie of
Pitcaple, who had vowed revenge. In fact, it was
known that Pitcaple was lying in wait with an
armed band to attack Frendraught on his way home.
Huntly, therefore, thought it advisable to send a

strong convoy with Frendraught, commanded by his
son and heir, Viscount Aboyne. The son of the
slain Rothiemay also accompanied the party. On
reaching the stronghold of the Crichtons, the Gordon
leaders were strongly pressed, especially by the lady
of the house, to spend the night, and partake of
hospitality in turn. They consented, and spent a
jovial evening. The square tower of Frendraught
was assigned to them for sleeping-quarters, and it
was remarked that none others slept in it. It consisted of three wooden-floored chambers, one above
the other. The lowest of the three, in which Aboyne
with two servants slept, was over a chamber
vaulted with stone, in which there was a round hole
for communicating with the floor above by means of
a ladder. Immediately over Aboyne's chamber slept
Rothiemay with some servants beside him, and three
others occupied the topmost chamber. At midnight
of October 8th according to Spalding, October 18th
according to the ballad, the conflagration of the
tower was visible for miles around, and its occupants
were soon all reduced to ashes. And herein this
crime exceeded the other in atrocity—it was premeditated, and it was a direct violation of the laws of
hospitality, generally held sacred in the most unci-
vilised communities. To a man of the evidently
irascible and passionate temperament of Frendraught,
with his brain never clear at the best as to moral
distinctions, probably at the time inflamed with wine,
and smarting under the humiliation and loss of hav-

ing to pay a ransom-money so large, the temptation presented by circumstances was overpowering. The son of the judge who had mulcted him, the heir of his great feudal enemy, and the man who was to profit by the penalty to be exacted, were both under his roof. The Gordons asserted that the whole affair had been planned, and that the vaulted chamber had been filled with combustibles. The fastenings of the doors and windows were carefully secured, and Lady Frendraught is said to have mocked the wretches from the outside as they tore in vain at the window bars. Aytoun says there is no reason to suppose that Frendraught and his lady originated the fire. Be that as it may, Ichabod was thereafter written on their door-posts; they became a common prey; even the famous Gilderoy brought his band to plunder from the distant Loch Katrine, and at the Revolution the family disappears.

"This ballad," says Aytoun, "was supposed, both by Ritson and Finlay, to have been lost, and they gave instead of it an acknowledged modern composition called 'Frennet Ha.'" It was, however, still current in the North, and versions differing very little from each other have been given by Mr. Motherwell and the editor of the "North Countrie Garland." Even Mr. Chambers admits it to be a genuine unsophisticated production, a contemporaneous metrical chronicle of the event it describes.

The events are detailed in the ballad somewhat as we have given them above—

> "They had not long cast off their clothes,
>   And were but new asleep,
> When the weary smoke began to rise,
>   Likewise the scorching heat.
>
> " 'O waken, waken, Rothiemay,
>   O waken, brother dear ;
> And turn ye to our Saviour—
>   There is strong treason here !' "

Having risen and dressed, they found the doors
and windows fast, and "the roof-tree burning down."

> "When he stood at the wire-window,
>   Most doleful to be seen,
> He did espy her, Lady Frendraught,
>   Who stood upon the green.
>
> "Cried, ' Mercy, mercy ! Lady Frendraught !
>   Will ye not sink with sin ?
> For first your husband killed my father,
>   And now you burn his son !'
>
> "O then out spoke her, Lady Frendraught,
>   And loudly did she cry,
> ' It were great pity for good Lord John,
>   But none for Rothiemay,
> But the keys are casten in the deep draw-well—
>   Ye cannot get away !' "

She was a genuine she-wolf. If a woman becomes
untrue to the kindlier instincts, her heart waxes
harder than the nether millstone. The tender
mercies of the wicked are said to be cruel, but
never more cruel than when the wicked one is a
female.

> "While he stood in this dreadful plight,
>   Most piteous to be seen ;
> Then called out his servant Gordon,
>   As he had frantic been,

G

> " ' O loup, O loup, my dear master,
>   O loup down frae the tower ;
>   I'll catch you in my armis two ;
>   But Rothiemay may smoor ! ' "

This last line is conjectural. It is to be hoped that the reading is erroneous. On the other hand, the sentiment is quite in keeping with the feeling of the time and of the subject of it. The faithful servant and retainer was indifferent to everything but the safety of his master. The response, however, is noble—

> " ' The fish shall never swim the flood,
>   Nor corn grow through the clay,
>   If the fiercest fire that ever was kindled
>   Twine me and Rothiemay.

> " ' But I cannot loup, I cannot come,
>   I cannot win to thee ;
>   My head's fast in the wire-window,
>   My feet burning frae me !

> " ' My eyes are southering in my head,
>   My flesh roasting also ;
>   My bowels are boiling with my blood ;
>   Is na that a woeful woe ?

> " ' Take here the rings from my fingers,
>   That are so long and small ;
>   And give them to my lady fair,
>   Where she sits in her hall.

> " ' So I cannot loup, I cannot come,
>   I cannot loup to thee ;
>   *My earthly part is all consumed,*
>   *My spirit but speaks to thee ! ' "*

This is all too dreadful. We are made to sup our fill of horrors. We know of nothing in the whole range of poetry more weird and powerful than these verses of an obscure ballad by an unknown poet. Neither Dante nor Shakespeare has transcended the conception of them. In parts the ballad-writer is as prosaic as a bulletin, but here he rises into the sublimest region of poetry, exhibiting an imaginative power of almost unique vividness and splendour. To the enthusiast about ballads such a passage as this is a reward at once and an excuse for his toils, and his apparently trivial pursuit then acquires in his eyes an importance and a dignity that differentiate it favourably from the most eager pursuit of the ruck of contemporary facts by the most complacent quidnunc of the day.

The Marquis of Huntly, instead of avenging himself by reprisals, appealed to the law, and John Meldrum, at one time a servant of Frendraught's, and who afterwards married a sister of Pitcaple, was tried at Edinburgh, and condemned, on merely presumptive evidence, to be hanged and quartered. Viscountess Aboyne, Sophia Hay, the "bonnie Sophia" of the ballad, did what she could to bring the perpetrators of the crime to justice. Spalding says that, like the turtle-dove, she all her after-life disdained the company of man. Arthur Johnston wrote her Plaint for the death of her husband— "Querela Sophiæ Hayæ de morte mariti," published in "Delitiæ Poetarum Scotorum," Amst., 1637, tom. i., pp. 585, &c.

PART II.

THE BATTLES OF THE COVENANT.

The battles of the Covenant may be ranked in two classes—first, those fought when the Covenant was powerful, and the leaders of its armies the foremost nobility of the kingdom, in the time of Charles I.; and, second, those fought in the reign of Charles II., when the Covenant was discredited by the nobility, and its supporters were mainly the rural populace of the Western shires.   So far as ballad literature bears on these, to the first class belong " Lesley's March " and " The Battle of Philiphaugh ; " and to the second the battles of " Rullion Green," of " Loudon Hill," and of " Bothwell Bridge."   We have already referred to " Lesley's March," first published by Allan Ramsay, and " played," says Scott, " in the van of this Presbyterian crusade "—that is, when the Scots sent a well-disciplined army of upwards of twenty thousand men, under Alexander Lesley, Earl of Leven, to the assistance of the Parliament of England.   Reference to the destination of this force is thus made in the " March "—

> " Front about, ye musketeers all,
>   Till ye come to the English border.
>   Stand till't, and fight like men,
>   True gospel to maintain ;
>   The Parliament's blythe to see us a' coming."

Lesley's army bore a distinguished part in the battle of Long Marston Moor, fought 3d July 1644; and,

in the words of Mr. Laing, " the victory was equally
due to Cromwell's iron brigade of disciplined Independents and to three regiments of Lesley's horse."
These were led by General David Lesley, a man of
greater military talent even than his chief. He
commanded that portion of the Scottish army that
was despatched from England to check the advance
of Montrose after his victory at Kilsyth, 15th August
1645. Lesley entered Scotland by the way of
Berwick, and completely surprised the army of
Montrose at Philiphaugh, near Selkirk, 13th September 1645. Lesley's force consisted of five or six
thousand men, chiefly cavalry. Under cover of a
thick mist, he attacked Montrose's infantry, between
whom and his cavalry ran the Ettrick, and gained a
complete victory, Montrose himself escaping with
difficulty. Scott says—" Upon Philiphaugh Montrose lost in one defeat the fruit of six splendid
victories; nor was he again able effectually to make
head in Scotland against the Covenanted cause."
The ballad, preserved by recitation in Selkirkshire,
has little merit as a poem, but is valuable as an
accurate record of facts.

> " Sir David frae the Border cam',
>   Wi' heart an' hand cam' he ;
> Wi' him three thousand bonny Scotts,
>   To bear him company.

> " Wi' him three thousand valiant men,
>   A noble sight to see !
> A cloud o' mist them weel concealed,
>   As close as e'er might be.

> " When they cam' to the Shaw Burn,
>   Said he, ' Sae weel we frame,
> I think it is convenient
>   That we should sing a psalm.' "

The singing of a psalm was a favourite prelude to battle with the " saints," as they were called, whether Independents or Covenanters. We may, therefore, credit some malignant Cavalier with the various reading, " That we should take a dram." " The glory of the victory," says Aytoun, " was sullied by an indiscriminate massacre of prisoners." The common soldiers were shot in cold blood in the courtyard of Newark Castle, and their bodies hastily interred at a place called, from the circumstance, " Slain-men's Lee." This is said to have been done by the command of Lesley, and with the approval of the ministers, some of whom were spectators of the butchery. But this evidence is given by Wishart, chaplain to Montrose, in his " Memoirs " of that hero, and must be taken with proper deductions. Eight of the most distinguished Cavaliers were, at the instigation of the clergy, condemned by the Parliament to be executed—a sentence carried out in the case of seven of them, Lord Ogilvy, the eighth, having escaped from prison in his sister's clothes. But for the neighbourhood of Hairhead Wood, in which the fugitives found shelter and concealment, the prisoners, and consequently the executions, would have been much more numerous. This wood is referred to in the first verse of the ballad—

> " On Philiphaugh a fray began,
>   At Hairhead Wood it ended ;
> The Scotts out o'er the Græmes they ran,
>   Sae merrily they bended."

The severity exercised on these prisoners may in some measure explain the terrible retaliation of the next reign. There can be no doubt that the preachers were satisfied of the righteousness of their counsel, and in all probability would have expected similar treatment had they been on the losing side.

But the chief interest of the battles of the Covenant centres in the three engagements referred to above as occurring in the reign of Charles II., both from the religious enthusiasm of the persecuted people and the marked individuality of several of the leaders on both sides, such as Dalziel of Binns, Graham of Claverhouse, Hackston of Rathillet, and Balfour of Burley. The struggles of that time have an extremely racy and valuable literature of their own, including Wodrow's " History of the Sufferings of the Church of Scotland, from the Restoration to the Revolution ; " the " Biographia Scoticana," better known as the " Scots Worthies," of honest John Howie of Lochgoin ; " The Cloud of Witnesses," " The Hind let Loose," " Faithful contendings Displayed," " Peden's Prophecies," " The Life and Death of Three Famous Worthies," by Peter Walker, at the Bristo Port of Edinburgh, pedlar, a notable person in the eyes of douce David Deans of St. Leonard's, &c., &c. Two of the battles of the Cove-

nant—those of Drumclog and of Bothwell Bridge—
have been described with his usual power and
picturesqueness by Scott in "Old Mortality." They
are also chronicled in the "Memoirs of Captain John
Creichton, collected from his own materials, by Dean
Swift." Creichton was as pronounced a fanatic, in
his own way, as any field-preacher among the Covenanters, and had the lurking-places of what he conceived to be sacrilegious rebels revealed to him in
dreams, after, it may be supposed, a night's hard
drinking. Swift compares Creichton's Memoirs to
those of Philip de Comines, as being "told in a
manner equally natural, and with equal appearance
of truth." Scott, no friend to the Covenanters,
reproves Swift for his hardness of heart and deadness
of feeling. "That a soldier of fortune like Creichton,
bred up, as it were, to the pursuit of the unfortunate
fanatics who were the objects of persecution in the
reigns of Charles II. and James II., should have felt
no more sympathy for them than the hunter for the
game which he destroys, we can conceive perfectly
natural; nor is it to be wondered at that a man of
letters, overlooking the cruelty of this booted apostle
of Prelacy in the wild interest of his narrations,
should have listened and registered the exploits
which he detailed. But what we must consider as
shocking, and even disgusting, is the obvious relish
with which these acts are handed down to us in
Swift's own narrative."

The three ballads relating to the three battles

alluded to were first published in "The Minstrelsy
of the Border." "The Battle of Pentland Hills,"
otherwise known as "The Battle of Rullion Green,"
was taken down by Mr. Livingston of Airds from the
recitation of an old woman residing on his estate.
The insurrection which it commemorates had its
beginning at Dalry, in Galloway, on Tuesday,
November 13, 1666. Four "hill-folk," who had
come down to the village to get some refreshment,
rescued an old man from some soldiers who were
about to torture or maltreat him. They knew they
had committed themselves, and, resolving to proceed
to extremities, they surprised and disarmed twelve
soldiers at a neighbouring post. Their number having increased to fifty horsemen and a considerable
party of footmen, they marched to Dumfries, and
seized the notorious Sir James Turner, then levying
fines from the Nonconformists, disarmed his soldiers,
and possessed themselves of a considerable sum of
money which he had collected as cess. An unsup-
ported tradition represents this money as having
been carried off by "one Andrew Gray, an Edinburgh merchant, who immediately deserted them."
Their numbers rapidly increasing, they resolved to
march on Edinburgh, in the expectation that their
friends in that quarter would join them. At Lanark
their numbers reached 3000; but by the time they
reached Rullion Green, cold, want of provisions, the
marked antipathy of the peasantry of Lothian, and
the arming of the city of Edinburgh against them,

had reduced their numbers to about 900. Their
leader, Colonel Wallace, an experienced soldier, drew
up his men on the ridge of a hill to await the attack
of General Thomas Dalziel, who, having gone as far
as Lanark to intercept them, returned on his footsteps, and found them thus posted.   Two attacks by
detachments on the position of the Covenanters
having failed, Dalziel charged with his whole force,
and succeeded in breaking and dispersing them.
Comparatively few were killed in the attack and
rout, which Scott accounts for by the cavalry of
Dalziel being chiefly gentlemen, who pitied their
oppressed and misguided countrymen.   It would be
pleasing to believe this, and it may be in some
measure true; but darkness had come on before the
ranks of the hill-people were broken, and to this is
chiefly to be attributed the comparative bloodlessness
of the engagement.   The remnant of the army of the
Whigs suffered more from the peasantry in the
vicinity of the field of battle than from the troopers
of Dalziel, ruthless as that General was justly held
to be.   The battle was fought 28th November 1666.
It was here that the Covenanters first discovered that
Dalziel had sold himself to the devil, for they imagined that they saw the leaden bullets rebounding,
harmless, from his buff coat.   The ballad is evidently
a Royalist production, and if by " the gallant
Grahams from the West" of the initial stanza he
meant the troopers of Graham of Claverhouse, it
must have been written some considerable time after

the event it chronicles, as Claverhouse was then an
officer in the Dutch service, and did not hold an
independent command in Scotland till nearly twelve
years later. The Royalist bard represents the Whigs
as gaining accessions to their numbers principally
from "souters and taylors," and makes merry over
their robbing the pedlars of their packs. He states
their number at Mauchline Muir to have been ten
thousand—a gross exaggeration.

> " General Dalyell, as I hear tell,
>   Was our Lieutenant-General."

He is represented as addressing the Whigs in the
following moderate terms :—

> " ' Lay down your arms, in the King's name,
>   And ye shall all gae safely hame ; '
> But they a' cried out wi' ae consent,
> ' We'll fight for a broken covenant.'

> " ' O well,' says he, ' since it is so,
>   A wilfu' man never wanted woe ; '
> He then gave a sign unto his lads,
> And they drew up in their brigades.

> " The trumpets blew, and the colours flew,
>   And every man to his armour drew ;
> The Whigs were never so much aghast
> As to see their saddles toom sae fast.

> " The cleverest men stood in the van ;
>   The Whigs they took their heels and ran ;
> But such a raking was never seen
> As the raking o' the Rullion Green."

These last two lines make the blood run cold.

Dalziel of Binns was a singular character, as sincere
a fanatic in his loyalty and religion as those whom

he oppressed were in their attachment to the Covenant, and this made him all the more ruthless in his treatment of them.   He had been taken prisoner at Worcester, and committed to the Tower, whence escaping, he proceeded to Muscovy, and entered the service of the Czar.   This service increased his natural ferocity, and we learn from Fountainhall's "Decisions," that he struck a man under examination at the Council-table on the teeth with his sword-hilt for calling him "a Muscovy beast who roasted men." After the Restoration he was made Commander-in-Chief of the Forces in Scotland, a situation he held till his death, with the exception of a fortnight, during which he was superseded by the Duke of Monmouth some days before the battle of Bothwell Bridge.   In token of his loyalty he never shaved after the execution of Charles I., and his beard, white and bushy, reached almost down to his middle.   Creichton gives a graphic description of his appearance in London, with a crowd of boys after him, whom he always thanked for their attendance, and informed them when he would next appear.   When he accompanied Charles II. in the Park, "the King could hardly pass for the crowd; upon which his Majesty bid the devil take Dalziel for bringing such a rabble of boys together to have their guts squeezed out, while they gaped at his long beard and antique habit; requesting him at the same time (as Dalziel used to express it) to shave and dress like other Christians, to keep the poor bairns out of danger."

In the trials that followed this battle the boot and thumbkins were freely used as instruments of torture, to the disgrace of the criminal jurisprudence of the country. The courts were so oppressed with work that a separate justiciary was appointed in the West. Business was facilitated by the illegal procuring of convictions in absence, and the convenient " bonds of lawburrows " were resorted to to maintain peace in the West, so that Dalziel and other functionaries were soon by process of law gifted with forfeitures and fines.

The battle of Drumclog, or of Loudon Hill, was the solitary gleam of success that gilded the cause of the Covenanters at this crisis in their affairs. It was fought on Sunday, 1st June 1679, shortly after the assassination of Archbishop Sharp on Magus Muir, and sprang in some measure from that tragical event. Sharp was detested by the Presbyterians as a Judas who had betrayed their cause ; and their hatred was intensified by their dread of his ruthless nature, and their horror of him as one who had made a compact with Satan. Accordingly, when Balfour and his confederates despatched him in the presence of his daughter, shortly after he had enjoyed his last pipe with the parson of Ceres, in the belief that he was bullet-proof by favour of his master they haggled him with their broadswords—the confession is their own —three-quarters of an hour before life was extinct. Balfour and Hackston having escaped to the West, joined themselves to a party of eighty horsemen commanded by Robert Hamilton, brother of the

Laird of Preston, who at Rutherglen, on the 29th of May, extinguished the bonfires blazing in honour of " the happy Restoration." They proceeded thence to Loudon Hill, where a great conventicle was to be held. While the services were proceeding, information was given by the watchers that Graham of Claverhouse, with the Guards, was at hand, and the worshippers proceeded to form in order of battle, the ground being chosen with singular skill. The result is well known. Graham and his Guards were defeated, thirty-six of his force being killed, and amongst them his nephew, Cornet Graham, while only three of the Covenanters fell. Claverhouse himself escaped with difficulty. In his despatch to the Earl of Linlithgow he says—" With a pitchfork they made such an opening in my rone horse's belly that his guts hung out half an elle, and yet he carried me af an myl." Creichton says the rebels were eight or nine thousand strong—a ridiculous exaggeration to palliate an unlooked-for and humiliating defeat. Claverhouse further said that when he came upon them " they wer not preaching, and had got away all there women and shildring." This justifies Scott's description of Graham's spelling as that of a chamber-maid. This presence of women and children is referred to by Guild in his " Bellum Bothuellianum," which contains an account of the skirmish at Drum-clog—

" Turba ferox, matres, pueri, innuptæque puellæ."

The mishap to Claverhouse's horse is thus noticed—

> " Vix dux ipse fugâ salvus, namque exta trahebat
> Vulnere tardatus sonipes generosus hiante."

The ballad commemorating the battle is the com-
position of one of the Covenanting party, and is
singularly free from the least suspicion of poetry.
After wishing for prosperity to the Gospel lads of the
West Country, and invoking malisons on wicked
Claver'se, he proceeds to describe the engagement—

> " But up spak cruel Claver'se then,
>   Wi' hastie wit an' wicked skill ;
> ' Gae fire on yonder Westlan' men :
>   I think it is my Sovereign's will.'
>
> " But up bespake his cornet then,
>   ' It's be wi' nae consent o' me !
> I ken I'll ne'er come back again,
>   And mony mae as weel as me.
>
> " ' There is not ane of a' yon men,
>   But wha is worthy other three ;
> There is na ane amang them a'
>   That in his cause will stop to die.
>
> " ' An' as for Burly, him I knaw ;
>   He's a man of honour, birth, an' fame ;
> Gi'e him a sword into his hand,
>   He'll fight thysel an' other ten.' "

The rest of the ballad is equally prosaic and feature-
less.

But the ballad on the battle of Bothwell Bridge,
also a Covenanting production, is a strain of a higher
mood, and informed with both pathos and poetry—

> " ' O billie, billie, bonny billie,
>   Will ye go to the wood wi' me ?
> We'll ca' our horse hame masterless,
>   An' gar them trow slain men are we.'

" ' O no, O no ! ' says Earlstoun,
  ' For that's the thing that maunna be ;
For I am sworn to Bothwell Hill,
  Where I maun either gae or die ! ' "

Earlstoun, who has a premonition of his death, thus
takes leave of his family—

" Now, fareweel, father, and fareweel, mother,
  An' fare ye weel, my sisters three ;
An' fare ye weel, my Earlstoun,
  For thee again I'll never see ! "

Full justice is done to the humane character of the
vacillating and undecided Monmouth, who commanded the Royal troops on this occasion, and whose
lenience provoked the ire of the more pronounced
and firmer-charactered Royalists. Dalziel arrived in
the camp the day after the battle, armed with a commission to supersede Monmouth as commander-in-
chief. Creichton says that Dalziel upbraided the
Duke publicly with his lenity, and heartily wished
his own commission had come a day sooner, when, as
he expressed himself, " these rogues should never more
have troubled the King or country ! " Monmouth,
adds Creichton, though publicly rebuked before the
whole army, sneaked among them at the town of
Bothwell till the following Saturday, when he set out
by Stirling to Fife on a visit to the Duke of Rothes.
Claverhouse was especially hot in pursuit of the
rebels, as he called them, to avenge the death of his
nephew, Cornet Graham, and in retaliation of his
defeat at Drumclog. In the ballad Monmouth is
represented as upbraiding him for his cruelty—

" Then wicked Claver'se turned about,
     I wot an angry man was he ;
 And he has lifted up his hat,
     And cried, ' God bless his Majesty ! '

" Then he's awa' to London town,
     Ay e'en as fast as he can dree ;
 Fause witnesses he has wi' him ta'en,
     An' ta'en Monmouth's head frae his bodie "—

a gross historical perversion. Graham at Killiecrankie, as Viscount Dundee, achieved a victory and
met a fate that raised him from the category of a
heartless oppressor of a singularly intelligent, high-
souled, and devout peasantry, into that of a hero.
Yet his memory will ever, in the minds of his Presbyterian countrymen, be associated with blood and
violence. Scott, with whom he was a favourite,
though unable to deny the charge of seeming effemi-
nacy in his hero, accords to him the possession of
" such a countenance as limners love to paint and
ladies love to look upon." Burton, in comparing the
two Grahams, Montrose and Dundee, says :—" We
have good portraits of both heroes, preserving faces
that haunt the memory." Of Dundee, who is represented as not having enough of the common intel-
lectual culture of the day to save him from ridicule
as a blockhead, he says, " Remove from his likeness
anything identifying the soldier, and we have in flesh
and lineaments a woman's face of brilliant complexion
and finely-cut features. But there is in it nothing of
feminine gentleness or compassion—it might stand
for the ideal of any of the classical heroines who have

H

been immortalised for their hatred and cruelties." A fanatic of this complexion could not but prove a scourge of scorpions to the adherents of the Covenant.

The Cavaliers give their version of the current of events from Rullion Green to Bothwell Bridge in " Whurry, Whigs, awa' " with such inimitable candour that the reading of it suggests some curious psychological questions. It is evident that from their point of view Cavalier and Covenanter belonged to two different genera, and that the Covenanter was made to be hunted down as much as a fox or a badger, or any other denizen of firth or forest. There is a cool ferocity about the subjoined extract that could have been engendered only by political and religious animosity—

> " The restless Whigs, with their intrigues,
>   Themselves they did convene, man,
>   At Pentland Hills and Bothwell Brigs,
>   To fight against the King, man ;
>   Till brave Dalyell came forth himsel'
>   With loyal troops in raws, man,
>   To try a match with powther and ball :
>   The saints turn'd windlestraws, man.

> " The brave Dalyell stood i' the field,
>   And fought for King and Crown, man ;
>   Made rebel Whigs perforce to yield,
>   And dang the traitors doun, man.
>   Then some ran here, and some ran there,
>   And some in field did fa', man,
>   And some to hang he didna spare,
>   Condemned by their ain law, man.

> " Yet that would not the carles please,
>   Did you not hear the news, man,

How, at Drumclog, behind the bog,
   They gae the deil his dues, man?
With blessed word and rusty sword
   They wrought a wondrous feat, man;
For, ten to ane, they wan the day,
   And wow but they were great, man!

" But, wae's my heart! it was nae sport,
   Though they were set on ill, man,
'To see them fa' like silly sheep
   That day on Bothwell Hill, man.
The Royal Duke his men forsook,
   And oe'r the field did ride, man,
And cried aloud to spare their blude,
   Whatever might betide, man.

" But Colonel Graham, of noble fame,
   Had sworn to have his will, man,
No man to spare in armour there,
   While man and horse could kill, man.
O then the Whigs from Bothwell Brigs
   Were led like dogs to die, man;
In Heaven's might they couldna fight,
   But raised a horrid cry, man."

PART III.

§ 1. JACOBITE SONGS AND BALLADS.

THE term Jacobite means an adherent of Jacobus, or
James, that is, of James II. of England and VII. of
Scotland, after his abdication of the British throne
by his flight to France in 1688, and is consequently
the direct opposite of a Williamite, or adherent of
William, Prince of Orange, James's son-in-law and
successful rival. It, however, was extended to the
adherents of James's unfortunate son, the Chevalier

de St. George, better known as the Old Pretender, and to those of *his* son, Prince Charles Edward, the Young Chevalier, and in the two latter instances is opposed to Hanoverian, or adherent of the House of Hanover. Hogg, in his "Jacobite Relics," and others, sometimes give it a retrospective signification, and it is then used as synonymous with Royalist or Cavalier, Whig becoming equivalent to Roundhead, or Puritan, or Parliamentarian. The main interest of the Jacobite struggles, apart from James's campaign in Ireland and Dundee's victory at Killiecrankie, centres in the abortive rebellions of 1715 and 1745; and the best of the lyrics bearing on the struggles of the party are connected with the operations of those rebellions and their results, especially of the latter. But so numerous are the songs dealing with every stage of the contest, that the first volume of Hogg's "Jacobite Relics" is confined to songs previous to the battle of Sheriffmuir, 13th November 1715, and yet his collection does not contain above one-fifth of the lyrics that he might have admitted.

The ill-success of the Jacobites in all their efforts is attempted to be explained by representing them as singers and sentimentalists rather than workers and men of the world, like their opponents the Whigs. But this only half explains the matter. The non-success resulted in great measure from the total incapacity of the Stuarts. Had they had a tithe of the ability of William they must have succeeded, for the people were ten to one against the Revolution,

and the Church to a man was violently active against
the House of Hanover.   We subjoin two remarkable
passages from the life of William, Earl of Shelburne,
bearing directly on this point :—

" It is common to attribute the happiness and comfort which
this country enjoyed from the period of the Revolution till
the commencement of the present reign to the excellence of
our Constitution, to the Whigs, and to a variety of other
causes ; whereas, I conceive the true cause to have been the
existence of a Pretender with a very just right to the throne
upon all Tory and Monarchical principles, and all old pre-
judices, but without sufficient capacity to disturb the reigning
family, or to accommodate himself to the new principles which
have been making a slow but certain progress ever since the
discovery of the press.   The Hanover family never imagined
they would continue, and, as their only chance, threw themselves into the arms of the Old Whigs, abjuring the rights and
the manners of Royalty—in other words, telling the people,
' We are your slaves and blackamoors.' "—Vol. 1, pp. 21, 22.

Again—

" Foreigners attribute all this [national prosperity] to the
English Constitution, which, in fact, was owing to the single
circumstance of a Pretender, who kept the reigning family in
perpetual awe, supported as they were by an immense body
of property among the Tories, a considerable party among the
Lords and Commons, Scotland almost entirely devoted to
them, and a great part of Ireland by means of the Catholics.
This obliged the Hanoverian family not only to be on their
guard, but to support Revolution doctrines and principles,
upon which ground they stood."—Vol. 1, pp. 33, 34.

The Jacobite feeling died hard.   A good deal of
sentimental Jacobitism existed in the country down
to a comparatively late period, and persons perfectly
loyal to the Hanoverian dynasty passed their glasses
over the water-decanter when the toast of " The

King" was given, thus drinking to "the King over the water," even after the death of Henry, Cardinal York, the last legitimate scion of the Stuart family. Dr. Johnson, though a pensioner of George III., was an avowed Jacobite. Indeed, the feeling was hereditary with him, for his father, Michael Johnson, was so decided in his faith on this head that when he was elected a Magistrate of Lichfield he had to take the oath of fidelity and allegiance, and disavow transubstantiation, circumstances carefully minuted in the records of the Corporation. Of himself Johnson said—" Now that I have this pension, I am the same man in every respect that I have ever been ; I retain the same principles. It is true that I cannot now curse the House of Hanover ; nor would it be decent for me to drink King James's health in the wine that King George gives me money to pay for. But, sir, I think that the pleasure of cursing the House of Hanover, and drinking King James's health, are amply overbalanced by three hundred pounds a year." His defence of Jacobitism, though evidently a piece of humour, is singularly ingenious :—" A Jacobite, sir, believes in the divine right of kings. He that believes in the divine right of kings believes in a Divinity. A Jacobite believes in the divine right of bishops. He that believes in the divine right of bishops believes in the divine authority of the Christian religion. Therefore, sir, a Jacobite is neither an Atheist nor a Deist. That cannot be said of a Whig, for *Whiggism is a negation of all principles.*"

Scott, also, though the familiar of "The First Gentleman in Europe," was one of these sentimental Jacobites. He had lived much with persons who had taken a share in the '45, and his chivalrous nature prompted him always to sympathise with those who had staked and lost all on a desperate game, especially where self was sacrificed to loyalty. Accordingly, he is nowhere more happy or more at home than when treating either directly or incidentally of some detail in the history of Jacobitism. In "The Bride of Lammermoor," Frank Hayston of Bucklaw, who had come to the far end of a fair estate, and was being promised a commission in the Irish brigade by Captain Craigengelt, an agent from St. Germains, one of those slippery desperadoes who sold their secrets indifferently to either party, says to his tempter—"And now 1 shall be obliged, 1 suppose, to shelter and shift about like yourself— live one week upon a line of secret intelligence from Saint Germains—another upon the report of a rising in the Highlands—get my breakfast and morning draught of sack from old Jacobite ladies, and give them locks of my old wig for the Chevalier's hair." " Waverley " is full of the '45, and the description of the battle of Prestonpans is a masterpiece. " Redgauntlet " deals with the expiring struggle of Jacobitism in these islands, and the character of Redgauntlet himself is the male type of that of Flora MacIvor in " Waverley." He is the man of one idea, who will stick at nothing to accomplish it. But vile self never steps in. His loyalty is immaculate. Pate Maxwell of Summertrees, or Pate-in-Peril, is a character of quite a different stamp. He is selfish to the backbone, and, though still as malignant a Tory at heart as ever, had contrived to make his peace with the Government. Mrs. Crosbie, the wife of the Provost of Dumfries, is a Tory of a good common-sense type:—" Come, come," said the lady, " we will have no argument in this house about Whig or Tory; the Provost kens what he maun *say,* and I ken what he should *think;* and for a' that has come and gane yet, there may be a time coming when honest men may say what they think, whether they be Provosts or not."

The great store-house of the lyrical poetry of the Jacobites is Hogg's " Relics." " The extent of this literature," says Dr. Murray, " is indeed extraordinary —perhaps unequalled by the polemical songs of any other contest in the history of the world." And he adds—" I know of no contest which has produced such a number of songs equal to those of the Jacobites in defiant resolution, in reckless satire, in subduing pathos, and in exuberant mirth." Many of the tunes also to which they are set are exquisitely beautiful, and are prime favourites at the present day. The songs themselves are a distinct species, in nowise related either to the old ballad or to the modern lyric. They took their rise from a peculiar class of circumstances, by which their structure and sentiment were moulded, and these circumstances having ceased to be similar songs are no longer produced.

The chief historical event in Scotland during the remainder of the life of James in which the Jacobites were engaged was the battle of Killiecrankie, fought on Saturday, 27th July 1689, between the forces of James commanded by Dundee, and the Royal troops commanded by Mackay. The Royal troops were ignominiously routed, but Dundee fell in the moment of victory. His death more than counterbalanced the success of the day. Three accounts of the battle may be consulted with pleasure and profit—that of Sir Walter Scott in the "Tales of a Grandfather," that of Lord Macaulay in his "History of England," and that of John Hill Burton in his "History of Scotland." Admirable as the others are, the last bears away the palm. There are two songs on the subject. The oldest begins thus—

> " Clavers and his Highlandmen
>   Cam down upon the raw, man,
> Who, being stout, gave mony a clout,
>   The lads began to claw, then.
> Wi' sword and targe into their hand,
>   Wi' which they were na slaw, man,
> Wi' mony a fearfu' heavy sigh
>   The lads began to claw, then."

A characteristic verse descriptive of the Highland mode of fighting is the following—

> " Hur skept about, hur leapt about,
>   And flang amang them a', man,
> The English blades got broken heads,
>   Their crowns were cleaved in twa, then ;

> The dark and dour made their last hour,
>   And proved their final fa', man :
> They thought the devil had been there,
>   They play'd them sic a pa', then."

In describing their attack on the Cameronians, the singer says—

> " But her nainsell, wi' mony a knock,
>   Cried, ' Furich,' Whigs awa', man."

The other song on the same subject is given in Johnson's "Museum," as an old song with alterations. The chorus is old; the rest of it was written by Burns—

> " Whare ha'e ye been sae braw, lad !
>   Whare ha'e ye been sae brankie, O !
> Whare ha'e ye been sae braw, lad !
>   Cam' ye by Killiecrankie, O !
> An' ye had been whare I ha'e been,
>   Ye wadna been sae cantie, O ;
> An' ye had seen what I ha'e seen,
>   I' the braes o' Killiecrankie, O.
>
> " I've faught at land, I've faught at sea,
>   At hame I faught my auntie, O ;
> But I met the devil and Dundee
>   On the braes o' Killiecrankie, O."

There is also a rhymed Latin poem on the subject, styled " Prælium Killicrankianum," said to be the composition of a Professor Kennedy of Aberdeen. It is to be sung to the air of the song first quoted—

> " Grahamius notabilis coegerat Montanos,
>   Qui clypeis et gladiis fugarunt Anglicanos :
> Fugerunt Vallicolæ, atque Puritani ;
>   Cacavere Batavi et Cameroniani, &c."

The chiefs of the party never ceased to plot, but by some strange fatality their plots were always futile. Only two circumstances between the victory at Killiecrankie and the setting up of James's standard at Brac-Mar, on the 6th of September 1715, by John, Earl of Mar, deserve note here. The one is the sailing from Dunkirk, on March 1708, of a French squadron, commanded by the Comte de Forbin, having on board Maréchal Matignon and some French troops, with the Chevalier de St. George himself. Though they reached the Firth of Forth, they were compelled by the British fleet, under Sir George Byng, to bear away for France, the Admiral refusing to disembark the Chevalier, though he urgently desired it. The other is the death of Queen Anne on the 1st of August 1714, just when the Tory Ministry firmly believed that she meant to nominate her brother as her successor. The Jacobites were found to be unprepared and irresolute, while the Whigs were firm and unanimous. King George I. was immediately proclaimed king.

The songs which date between Killiecrankie and Sheriffmuir are, as might be expected, grossly abusive of William III. and George I., but display in many instances superlative powers of sarcasm. Unfortunately they sometimes descend to the calling of names. William, as a Dutchman, is generally styled Hogan Mogan, and is occasionally made to express himself in a gibberish which Hogg happily terms " Aberdeenshire Dutch," as in this stanza of "Willie Winkie's Testament"—

> " Take you, beside, dis ragged coat,
>   And all de curses of de Scot,
>   Dat dey did give me vonder vell,
>   For Darien and dat Macdonell.
>   Dese are de tings I fain vold give,
>   Now dat I have not time to live ;
>   O take dem off mine hands, I pray !
>   I'll go de lighter on my vay."

The two things that rendered William most unpopular in Scotland were the English opposition to the Darien colonisation scheme, and the Massacre of Glencoe, both of which are alluded to in the lines quoted. These subjects were too sore not to be repeatedly alluded to. In "The Rebellious Crew" we find—

> " Our Darien can witness bear,
>   And so can our Glencoe, sir ;
>   Our South Sea it can make appear,
>   What to your kings we owe, sir.
>   We have been murder'd, starved, and robb'd,
>   By these, your kings and knav'ry,
>   And all our treasure is stock-jobb'd,
>   While we groan under slav'ry."

Again, in "Charlie Stuart"—

> " On Darien think, on dowie Glencoe ;
>   On Murray, traitor ! coward !
>   On Cumberland's blood-blushing hands,
>   And think on Charlie Stuart."

As a companion to the extract from "Willie Winkie's Testament," we subjoin one from "Geordie Whelp's Testament"—

"Ane auld black coat, baith lang and wide,
    Wi' snishen burken'd like a hide,
    A skeplet hat, and plaiden hose,
    A jerkin, clarted a' wi' brose,
    A pair o' sheen that wants a heel,
    A periwig wad fleg the deil,
    A pair o' breeks that wants the doup,
    Twa cutties, and a timmer stoup."

On the 20th February 1701, William's favourite
horse Sorrel stumbled on a mole-hill in Hampton
Court Park. The King was thrown and broke his
collar-bone. He died early in the following March.
The Jacobite songs contain unfeeling allusions to this
accident—

"But Willie's latter end did come,
    He broke his collar-bone, man."

The famous quarrel-scene in "Waverley," after the
banquet at Tullyveolan, was occasioned by the
drunken laird of Balmawhapple demanding a bumper
"to the little gentleman in black velvet who did such
service in 1702 (it should be 1701), and may the
white horse break his neck over a mound of his own
making."

Gilbert Burnet, Bishop of Salisbury, William's
favourite chaplain and adviser, was an object of
especial detestation to the Jacobite muse. "Bishop
Burnet's Descent into Hell" is not without humour—

"The devils were brawling at Burnet's descending,
    But at his arrival they left off contending;
    Old Lucifer ran, his dear bishop to meet,
    And thus the arch-devil th' apostate did greet:

'My dear Bishop Burnet, I'm glad beyond measure,
This visit, unlook'd for, gives infinite pleasure ;
And O, my dear Sarum, how go things above ?
Does George hate the Tories, and Whigs only love ?'"

The character and antecedents of the First George made him a fair mark for satire. While Electoral Prince he had married his cousin, the Princess Dorothea, who had imprudently permitted some freedoms, which are not supposed ever to have culminated in criminality, to the handsome Swedish Count Koningsmark, who was in consequence put to death somehow—probably strangled—and his body buried under the floor of the Electoral Princess's dressing-room. The Princess herself was removed at once and for ever from her husband's dwelling, and was thenceforth known as the Duchess of Halle. Allusion to Koningsmark's murder is made in the following lines—

"We might ha'e weel kend he wad never do good,
He was aye sae fond o' the knuckling o't ;
At hame, in Hanover, he kill'd, in cold blood,
A pretty young Swede, for the cuckling o't."

A more sordid motive is elsewhere assigned for his making away with the "pretty young Swede"—

"Wae worth the time that I came here,
To lay my fangs on Jamie's gear !
For I had better staid at hame,
Than now to bide sae muckle blame.
But my base, poltroon, sordid mind,
To greed o' gear was still inclin'd,
Which gart me fell Count Koningsmark
For his braw claise and holland surk."

The poverty of the Electoral Court was a favourite theme—

> " Wha the deil ha'e we gotten for a king,
>   But a wee, wee German lairdie ?
> And when we gade to bring him hame,
>   He was delving in his kail-yairdie ;
> Sheughing kail, and laying leeks,
>   But the hose, and but the breeks ;
> And up his beggar duds he cleeks,
>   The wee, wee German lairdie."

George had two mistresses—Madame Schulen-berg, afterwards created Duchess of Kendal, who was as thin and scraggy as a May-pole ; and Madame Kielmansegge, Countess of Platen, afterwards created Countess of Darlington, who was as corpulent and ample as the Duchess was long and emaciated. She was dubbed by the Jacobites "the Sow ;" hence such songs as "The Sow's Tail to Geordie," of which the following is a sufficiently ample specimen :—

> " It's Geordie he gat up to dance,
>   And wi' the sow to take a prance,
> And aye she gart her hurdies flaunce,
>   And turn'd her tail to Geordie."

" At St. James's Palace," says Macaulay, " on the morning of Sunday, the 10th of June 1688, a day long kept sacred by the too faithful adherents of a bad cause, was born the most unfortunate of princes, destined to seventy-seven years of exile and wander-ing, of vain projects, of honours more galling than insults, and of hopes such as make the heart sick." The reference is to the Chevalier de St. George—

James VIII., as his adherents styled him—the Pretender, in the nomenclature of the enemies of his house. The term "Pretender" originated thus:— His mother, Mary of Este, was reported to be pregnant, but by most persons the report was received with derision as a fraud of the Jesuits, who were naturally anxious to exclude the Princess of Orange from the succession. Mary's calculations proved wrong by a month, and when her hour came she was conveyed in a chair from Whitehall to apartments hastily fitted up in St. James's Palace. To secure purity of succession, the great dignitaries of Church and State are wont to be present at a Royal birth. In this instance, when suspicion was rampant, it was more than usually necessary that unimpeachable witnesses should assist, and that those whose interests were thus unexpectedly imperilled should be at hand either in person or by deputy. But such was the fatuous stolidity of James that these most necessary precautions were neglected, and there were circumstances which made it appear as if he had purposely removed those most interested from the scene. The Princess Anne, who had conceived strong suspicions, and who had resolved to be present, had been advised by her father to go to Bath; the Dutch Ambassador should have been invited as the representative of William, the husband of the Princess Mary, but was not; the Primate Sancroft, whose especial duty it was to attend, had been sent to the Tower a few hours before; and the Hydes, the uncles and natural protectors of the two Princesses, were not sent for, though one of them lived within two hundred yards of St. James's. The principal witnesses present of both sexes were Papists, and the report spread that a new-born child had been introduced into the royal bed by means of a warming-pan. Nobody now doubts the genuineness of the descent of James, but the perverse folly of his father procured for the son the title of Pretender, instead of which, however, the Whigs generally called him " Perkin," to which more particular reference will be made under " Whig Songs."

James received the worst possible education, in a sham court, without any of the realities or responsibilities of royalty. His talents, besides, were defective. He is said, however, to have been kind, good-natured, and courteous, and had a noble countenance, with a tall, thin person, whence in the Whig songs he is often styled " the slim young man." The poet Gray describes him as " a thin, ill-made man, extremely tall and awkward, and has extremely the air and look of an idiot." The two sons impressed him more favourably. " They are good, fine boys, especially the younger (Henry Duke of York), who has the more spirit of the two." The elder was Prince Charles Edward, the young Chevalier, who proved himself a man of much greater capacity and resolution than his father. But his education had been strangely mismanaged. He had been brought up a Papist, and had not been taught to abjure one of those errors

I

which had proved so fatal to his ancestors. His features, which those of her present Majesty are said to resemble, evincing their common Stuart origin, were tinged with an expression of melancholy even in the hour of triumph. Dr. Carlyle, who saw the Prince twice after the battle of Prestonpans, as he passed from the Palace to visit his troops, says, " He was a good-looking man, of about five feet ten inches; his hair was dark red, and his eyes black. His features were regular, his visage long, much sunburnt and freckled, and his countenance thoughtful and melancholy." The splendid summer of his Scottish campaign was followed by a dreary winter of sordid, solitary drunkenness, the result, perhaps, of disappointed hopes, and absolute exclusion from a blood-stirring career. During his wanderings among the Highlands and Islands, he was oftener familiar with usquebaugh than with nourishing food, and this, with his short, black pipe, frequently had to supply the place of a meal. So much for the two Pretenders. Dr. William King, Principal of St. Mary's Hall, Oxford, is credited with the authorship of the following pithy epigram :—

> " God bless the King, God bless the Faith's Defender ;
> God bless, no harm in blessing, the Pretender :
> Who that Pretender is, and who that King,
> God bless us all, is quite another thing."

John, Earl of Mar, who displayed the royal standard at Castletown, in Braemar, on September 6, 1715, had been Secretary of State during the last years of

Queen Anne, and had actively promoted the Union
and the passing of the Act of Succession. He was
then, of course, a Whig, but he passed over to the
Tories. On the accession of George I. he was ready
to turn his coat again, but George commanded him
to deliver up the seals, and informed him that he had
no further use for his services. Mar, who was ambitious, and an arch-intriguer, resolved on revenge,
and hastened to Scotland to rouse the clans in favour
of the Pretender. His time-serving character was
well understood. His English footman said of him—
" Let my Lord alone ; if he finds it necessary, he can
turn cat-in-paw with any man in England." And in
" Perkin's Lament " it is said of him—

> " Mar, robbed of place and pension,
> Rebels through fortune's frown."

The first operation of any consequence was the
battle of Sheriffmuir, fought on a common about two
miles from the village of Dunblane, 13th November
1715. The clans were commanded by Mar, who displayed no single qualification of a general—not even
the vulgar one of personal courage. The royal forces
were commanded by the Duke of Argyle, Captain-
General of the troops in Scotland. Mar outnumbered
Argyle nearly as three, some say as four, to one. The
left wing of each army was routed, and fled, so that
there was the singular appearance of a chase going
both north and south. Both sides claimed the victory,
but as Mar was prevented from moving to the west,
and as Argyle retained a position by which he was

enabled to defend the Lowlands, the triumph was substantially Argyle's. The double flight of this confused affray is alluded to in the contemporary ballad—

> " There's some say that we wan, and some say that they
> wan,
> And some say that nane wan at a', man ;
> But one thing I'm sure, that at Sherramuir,
> A battle there was, that I saw, man.
> And we ran, and they ran, and they ran, and we ran,
> And we ran, and they ran, awa', man."

Scott notes a curious incident in connection with this battle :—" Much noble and gentle blood was mixed with that of the vulgar. A troop of volunteers, about sixty in number, comprehending the Dukes of Douglas and Roxburgh, the Earls of Haddington, Lauderdale, Loudon, Belhaven, and Rothes, fought bravely, though the policy of risking such a *troupe dorée* might be questionable. At all events, it marked a great change of times, when the Duke of Douglas, whose ancestors could have raised an army as numerous as those of both sides in the field of Sheriffmuir, fought as a private trooper, assisted only by two or three servants." This *troupe dorée* is thus alluded to in the ballad—

> " Lord Roxburgh was there, in order to share
> With Douglas, who stood not in awe, man ;
> Voluuteerly to ramble with Lord Loudoun Campbell ;
> Brave Ilay did suffer for a', man.

The celebrated Rob Roy, who was a dependent of Argyle's, was present at Sheriffmuir with Mar, in

command of a large body of MacGregors and Mac-
Phersons. But he looked coolly on, and took no
part in the engagement. Not even taunts could
induce him to order his men to charge. Whether
this arose from unwillingness on the part of his men,
or from a desire not to disoblige his patron Argyle—
or, as the ballad hints, from motives of plunder—it
is now impossible to tell. But Rob Roy was always
a diplomatist—

> " Rob Roy there stood watch on a hill, for to catch
>   The booty, for ought that I saw, man ;
> For he ne'er advanced from the place he was stanced,
>   Till no more was to do there at a', man."

" Dialogue between Will Lickladle and Tam Clean-
cogue, twa shepherds wha were feeding their flocks
on the Ochil Hills on the day the battle of Sheriffmuir was fought," is sung to the tune of the " Cameronians' March," and is merely an expanded statement of the incidents mentioned in the foregoing
song. The circumstance of the flight, both north
and south, is thus alluded to—

> " WILL. Now, how deil, Tam, can this be true ?
>   I saw the chase gae north, man.

> " TAM. But weel I wat they did pursue
>   Them even unto Forth, man.
> Frae Dumblane they ran in my own sight,
> And got o'er the bridge wi' a' their might,
> And those at Stirling took their flight ;
> Gif only ye had been wi' me,
> You had seen them flee, of each degree,
>   For fear to die wi' sloth, man.

" WILL. My sister Kate came o'er the hill
    Wi' crowdie unto me, man ;
    She swore she saw them running still
    Frae Forth unto Dundee, man."

Will adds at the close of the song—

    " But Scotland has not much to say
    For such a fight as this is,
    Where baith did fight, baith ran away," &c.

The miserable sequel of Mar's rebellion is well known. Brigadier MacIntosh, having crossed over from Fife to Lothian with 1400 Highlanders, effected a junction with Forster and Kenmure at Kelso. After much disputation and dissent, the Highlanders agreed to accompany Forster into England, the result of which was that the Jacobite forces were blockaded in Preston by Generals Willis and Carpenter, and compelled to yield at discretion. Lords Derwentwater and Kenmure were executed; MacIntosh and Lord Winton effected their escape from the Tower; and the liberation from prison of Lord Nithsdale by the romantic and affectionate ingenuity of his Countess is one of the most touching incidents in history. On the other hand, Mar having fallen back on Perth from Sheriffmuir, was daily experiencing a defection from his ranks, as well of men of rank as of the clansmen. Meanwhile the Chevalier, having landed at Peterhead, proceeded to Perth, which he found was likely to be abandoned. His manifest dejection dispirited his followers, and Argyle having arrived within eight miles of Perth, a retreat was determined on. When the clans reached Montrose, the Chevalier, with Mar, Lord Drummond, and a few others, stealthily embarked in a vessel prepared for their reception and sailed for France. The entire proceedings of the insurrection were a wretched fiasco.

Of a totally different complexion was the rebellion of 1745—as different as was the dejected, spiritless Chevalier de St. George from his adventurous and high-spirited son. It had brilliant gleams of success, and though it resulted disastrously, the actors in it could regard its operations and their share in them with no unpardonable pride. The three most important incidents in it were the battles of Prestonpans, Falkirk Moor, and Culloden or Drummossie Moor. An animated narrative of these battles will be found in " The Tales of a Grandfather." The pusillanimity or defective judgment of Sir John Cope, the commander of the royal forces in Scotland, having left the passage to the Lowlands open, Prince Charles Edward marched southward, and got possession of Edinburgh. Cope, anxious to repair the effects of his blunder, embarked his troops at Aberdeen and landed at Dunbar. The Prince hastened to give him battle, and history does not record a more ignominious defeat than that of Cope at Gladsmuir or Prestonpans. There is no song more popular in Scotland than " Johnnie Cope," with its burden —

" Hey, Johnnie Cope, are ye wauking yet ?
Or are ye sleeping I would wit ?
O haste ye, get up, for the drums do beat,
O fie, Cope, rise in the morning."

There are two sets of the song. The refrain of the second set is slightly different from the above—

"Hey, Johnnie Cope, are ye wauking yet?
Or are your drums a-beating yet?
If ye were wauking I would wait,
To gang to the coals in the morning."

From the second set we quote—

"Cope sent a challenge frae Dunbar:
'Charlie, meet me an' you daur,
And I'll learn you the art of war,
If you'll meet me i' the morning.'

"When Charlie looked the letter upon,
He drew his sword the scabbard from:
'Come follow me, my merry, merry men,
And we'll meet Johnnie Cope i' the morning.'"

Sir John having reached Berwick with the greater portion of his discomfited dragoons in a most disorderly and disreputable condition, he was taken smartly to task by Lord Mark Kerr, of the Lothian family, "A house," says Scott, "which has long had hereditary fame for wit as well as courage." We quote from the first set—

"Says Lord Mark Car, 'Ye are na blate
To bring us the news o' your ain defeat;
I think you deserve the back o' the gate:
Get out o' my sight this morning.'"

This account of the affair, however, does Sir John scant justice. In the course of his flight he made some effort among the stragglers he overtook to regulate the retreat. But Brigadier Fowlks and Colonel Lasselles reached Berwick without once

having looked behind them, and it was to them that
Lord Mark Kerr remarked—"Good God! I have
seen some battles, heard of many, but never of the
first news of defeat being brought by the general
officers before." See letters from Dr. Waugh, 2d
October 1745, referred to by Mr. Burton, vol. viii. p.
457, of "History of Scotland."

Another metrical effusion, "The Battle of Prestonpans," is the production of Mr. Skirving, a Lothian
farmer, father of the eccentric Mr. Skirving, a painter
of some note, one of his productions being the well-
known portrait of Burns. We subjoin the following
lines for the sake of the anecdote connected with
them—

> "Lieutenant Smith, of Irish birth,
>   Frae whom he [Major Bowle] called for aid, man,
> Being full of dread, lap o'er his head,
>   And wadna be gainsaid, man.
>
> "He made sic haste, sae spurred his beast,
>   'Twas little there he saw, man ;
> To Berwick rade, and falsely said
>   The Scots were rebels a', man.
> But let that end, for weel 'tis kend
>   His use and wont's to lie, man ;
> The Teague is naught ; he never faught
>   When he had room to flee, man."

Throughout the whole song there is the same caustic
spirit displayed. Smith, to wipe off the stain of the
lampoon, sent a challenge to Skirving from Haddington. "Gang awa' back," said Skirving to the
messenger, "and tell Mr. Smith that I havena time
to come to Haddington; but tell him to come here,

and I'll tak a look o' him, an' if I think I'm fit to
fecht him, I'll fecht him; and if no, I'll do as he did
—I'll rin awa'."

The brave and pious Colonel Gardiner was cut
down by a Highlander armed with a scythe fixed
on a pole, close by his own park wall. The day
before the battle he invited young Carlyle to dine
with him. Carlyle writes—" He looked pale and
dejected." Speaking of the soldiers of his regiment,
he said—" I'll tell you in confidence that I have not
above ten men in my regiment whom I am certain
will follow me." And so the event proved. The
course of events from Prestonpans to Falkirk may
be briefly stated thus :—Charles having resolved, in
spite of urgent advice to the contrary, to march into
England, soon arrived in Carlisle, and took both the
town and castle, in which he left a garrison. He
proceeded through Lancashire, expecting a rising in
his favour, but only about two hundred of the lowest
populace of Manchester joined his standard. Having
reached Derby, Lord George Murray, much to the
chagrin of Charles, counselled a retreat into Scotland,
which was carried into effect in good order. Being
joined by reinforcements from Perth, Charles attempted to reduce the Castle of Stirling, his troops
now numbering about nine thousand. Meanwhile
the royal troops under General Hawley had reached
Falkirk, and it was resolved to give them battle.
Hawley, who was reputed a natural son of George
II., had conceived a supreme contempt for the

Highland soldiery, and when his troops were before the enemy was wasting his time at Callander House with the Countess of Kilmarnock, who was evidently using her blandishments to make him neglect his duty. When summoned by a messenger to the field, he was in such confusion that he set off without his hat. The forces on each side were about equal, but victory remained with the Highlanders, and Hawley retreated to Edinburgh, with his troops thoroughly demoralised. His base birth is alluded to in the following stanza, and twice in the same song his amorous propensities are made the subject of a jeer. The title of the song is "The Battle of Falkirk Moor."

> "Up and rin awa, Hawley,
>   Up and rin awa, Hawley ;
>   The philabegs are coming down
>   To gie your lugs a claw, Hawley.
> Young Charlie's face, at Dunipace,
>   Has gi'en your mou' a thraw, Hawley ;
> A blasting sight for bastard wight,
>   The warst that e'er he saw, Hawley."

This battle was fought on the 17th January 1746. The rebellion was extinguished at Culloden by the Duke of Cumberland, 16th April 1746, and the hopes of the adventurous young Chevalier for ever quenched. The atrocities that followed the victory procured for the Royal Duke the well-earned epithet of the "Butcher Cumberland." These atrocities are too well known to all patriotic Scotchmen to require recapitulation. A thrill of indignation shot through

the veins of men of all parties.   Witness " The Tears
of Scotland," by Dr. Smollett, who was not a Jacobite.
The last stanza is full of generous indignation—

> " Whilst the warm blood bedews my veins,
> And unimpaired remembrance reigns,
> Resentment of my country's fate
> Within my filial heart shall beat ;
> And, spite of her insulting foe,
> My sympathising verse shall flow.
> Mourn, hapless Caledonia, mourn,
> Thy banished peace, thy laurels torn ! "

There are numerous accounts of the sufferings,
wanderings, hairbreadth escapes, and final getting
off of Charles after the defeat of Culloden ; and the
fidelity of the many poor men who imperilled their
lives to protect his, disdaining to be bribed by thirty
thousand pounds set on his head, has been the theme
of universal praise.   The well-known " Wae's me for
Prince Charlie" is a comparatively modern production—

> " A wee bird cam' to our ha' door,
> He warbled sweet and clearly,
> And aye the o'ercome o' his sang
> Was ' Wae's me for Prince Charlie ! ' "

§ 2. WHIG SONGS.

Our illustrations of the Jacobite struggles, and of
the sentiments from which they arose, and which were
strengthened by them, from contemporary Jacobite
song, would be defective if not supplemented by
illustrations from the lyrical literature of their adver-

saries. Dr. J. Clark Murray says—"It is not surprising that there should have been few songs, and
these few of small poetical merit, on the side of the
Whigs." This can refer only to the Whig songs contained in the first series of the " Jacobite Relics," and
of these Hogg says—" There is not one that I can trace
to be of Scottish original." They possess no great
merit, but are valuable as indicating English, especially London, feeling on a struggle that might have
ended disastrously for the Hanoverian dynasty and
the Whig party. They lack the enthusiasm and
defiant spirit of the Jacobite songs, and are mainly
sarcastic, often mere parodies of popular ditties, and
the composition of men too prosaic to stake life and
fortune for an idea. Of the Whig songs appended to
the second series of the " Relics," Hogg says—" They
are altogether rather respectable, and some of the
true Scottish ones very good." For the best of them
Hogg was indebted to Mr. David Laing. Neither
are Whig songs so scant in number as Dr. Murray
imagines, and as they are less known than their Jacobite brethren, we shall give copious extracts.

In reference to James's losing three kingdoms for
his obstinate attachment to the Roman Catholic
faith, in which obstinacy he was encouraged by his
wife and his confessor, the "Song on the Thirteenth
of January 1696" says—

> " The furious James usurped the throne,
>   To pull religion down, O ;
> But by his wife and priest undone,
>   He quickly lost his crown O.

> To France the wandering monarch trudged
>   In hopes relief to find, O ;
> Which he is like to have from thence,
>   Even when the devil's blind, O."

One of the many fatal blunders of the Stuarts,
from James I. down to Prince Charles Edward, was
their blind belief in the doctrines of the divine right
of kings, and the duty of passive obedience in their
subjects. In the "Tories' Lamentation" occur these
lines—

> "Keep out, keep out Hanover's line,
>   'Tis only James has right divine,
> As High Church parsons cant and whine."

And again, in "The Truth at Last," the pulpit-
physician is represented as saying—

> "Now I do affirm t'ye, these men do design
>   To unking the Queen and keep out the right line,
> Damn passive obedience and our right divine,
>   Which nobody can deny."

Queen Anne was believed by the Jacobites to have
had the intention of establishing her brother on the
throne, and before her death the friends of James
talked openly of his succession, and drank his health
(they were adepts in drinking) publicly as James the
Third. It was believed that he had twice had a
private interview with his sister before her last ill-
ness, having come over in the retinue of the Duke
d'Aumont, who had also been closeted with Anne.
The Duke was an especial bugbear to the Whigs—

" Attend and prepare for a cargo from Dover ;
  Wine, silk, turnips, onions, with the peace are come over,
  Which Duke d'Aumont has brought to make room for a
    rover,
      Which nobody can deny.

"O Lewis ! at last thou hast played the best card ;
  Lay heroes aside, and tricksters reward ;
  Thou hast got by D'Aumont what thou lost by Tallard,
    Which nobody can deny."

He seems to have been of luxurious habits. However, the claret may have been mentioned merely because it was the national beverage of Frenchmen. The reference is in the " Raree Show "—

    " Here be de Duc d'Aumont's whole cellar of claret,
    Burnt by de plot laid as high as de garret."

The Tories had their October and their March Clubs, in which they pledged each other, and drank success to their schemes in mighty ale of the brewings of these two favourite months. The Whigs got up rival clubs, in which beer of a different quality was drunk, but their success was at the best equivocal. In "Hey, Boys, up go we," the Tories are represented as singing—

    " We'll broach our tubs and principles
      Of October passive growth,
    And till our tubs and bottles fail,
      We'll stand and fall by both."

The close of a parody of "The First Psalm" is as follows—

    " So shall not the Pretender's crew ;
      They shall be nothing so,

But as the dust which from the earth
The wind drives to and fro.

" Therefore shall not the Jacobites
In judgment stand upright,
Nor Papishes with Protestants
Come into place and sight.

" For why ?   The friends of Hanover
At Westminster are known ;
And eke the schemes at Bar-le-Duc
Shall quite be overthrown."

The Chevalier de St. George, when obliged to leave
France, was permitted to take up his residence in the
territories of the Duke of Lorraine, who had the
temerity to disregard an application from the British
Government to extrude him from his dominions.
Hence the reference to Bar-le-Duc, formerly the
capital of the Duchy of Bar, in Lorraine.   This explains also the following stanza—

" Here's a health to the King, sound the trumpet and
      the drum,
And let Perkin with all his renegades come ;
Let the Devil and the Pope advance in his train,
We'll soon send him back to sup in Lorraine. "

On the actual breaking out of the rebellion in 1715,
the Whigs, though greatly alarmed, pretended to be
only surprised, and reiterated their stale charge of
spuriousness of blood against the Chevalier de St.
George—

" Sure England's now grown mad, sir,
And Scotland with frenzy possesst,
    Thus to strive against the stream,
    And, deluded by a dream,
To endeavour mighty George to molest.

> A bastard for king they set up, sir,
> Forsooth, by hereditary right ;
>   Though, when all is said and done,
>   He's but a tailor's son,
> And will gain but a halter by 't."

Overlooking the fact that Mar had been deprived of office by George I. immediately on his arrival, and told that his services were no longer required, the Whig song-writers exactly reverse the situation, and represent him as a Judas who forsook his master, in violation of oaths and the sacrament. They also allude to his personal deformity, for, like Richard III., he was as crooked in his person as he was tortuous in his policy—

> " This crooked disciple pretends he will bring
> A Popish Pretender whom he calls a king,
> For which both himself and his master may swing,
>   Which nobody can deny."

Allusion has already been made to the proneness of the Whig muse to parody. One of the best of these is " Perkin's Lament," based on a well-known ballad in Gay's play of " What d'ye call it ? " The irrepressible warming-pan is of course there in all its glory—

> " 'Twas when the seas were roaring
>   With blasts of northern wind,
> Poor Perkin lay deploring,
>   On warming-pan reclined ;
> Wide o'er the foaming billows
>   He cast a dismal look,
> And shivered like the willows,
>   That tremble o'er the brook."

The " Ablution " is a humorous adaptation of the

K

story of Achilles's being dipped in the Styx to render him invulnerable; but the liquor having missed the heel by which he was held during ablution, he received his death-wound in that part of his body. Jemmy, that he might proceed to war in safety, requested His Holiness to dip him in holy water. The Father, having made him strip, fastened a gold collar about his neck, to which a rope having been attached, the ablution was performed, three plunges having been given him. Jemmy went to Scotland, and was in Perth with Mar when Argyle was pressing forward to that city. Both were in high glee because of James's supposed invulnerability—

> " But one cloudy day, as Mar chanced to stray
> With his monarch a space from the rest,
> Of a sudden he cried, 'An ill omen I've spied,
> That foretells we shall sore be distressed.
>
> " 'Round your royal neck quite there's a mark very white,
> Which I fear from the water was kept.
> Achilles just so, though 'twas further below,
> Was in danger of death '—then they wept."

The white mark round the neck was ominous of hanging or decapitation. This discovery of Mar's quite altered the complexion of affairs, and completely damped the courage of the Chevalier, the sequel being the pusillanimous embarkation at Montrose. The " Raree show," in the Somersetshire dialect, is conceived in atrociously bad taste. It lampoons St. John, the Duke of Ormond, Mar, Nithsdale, Derwentwater, and the Pretender himself, of whom, in reference to his supposed deficiency of courage, it says—

> " Zee how he does zit wid vinger in eye,
> And would vor a kingdom not vite, zur, but cry."

" The Right and True History of Perkin " is a long satirical poem, of considerable smartness. It gives the history of Perkin, from the warming-pan to the flight from Montrose, including the negotiations of D'Aumont with Anne for the succession of her brother, the campaign of Mar in Scotland, of Brigadier MacIntosh and Forster in England, and the march of the prisoners taken at Preston to London, to the tune of " Traitors all a-row." Like the most of the Whig songs, it is a very heartless production. It contains a reference to the elevation of Mar to a dukedom—

> " He told 'em they might all for mighty honours look,
> For he that was before a lord was now become a duke."

At the commencement of the insurrection of 1715 Mar felt some embarrassment from the want of a formal confirmation of his authority as generalissimo. This, " given at our court of Bar-le-Duc, the 7th day of September 1715, and in the fourteenth year of our reign," was brought over by Ogilvie of Boyne, and he was said to have in addition brought with him a patent raising Mar to a dukedom.

Argyle comes in for his meed of praise as a resolute and vigilant commander—

> " At the battle of Dumblane,
> Where ye know it was true
> That Mar had many men,
> And the Duke had very few ;

> But the cause it was good,
>   And I tell you true,
>   Heaven fought for Argyle to a wonder."

His advance from Stirling towards Scone, which
caused "each mother's bairn to scamper to Montrose,"
and Mar and the Chevalier "with panic fear" to
embark for France, is also the subject of eulogium.
The pusillanimous flight from Montrose is injuriously
commented on in "Perkin's Last Adventure; or, A
Trip through the Back-Door."

The remaining Whig songs have much greater
interest, as dealing with the more spirit-stirring
incidents of the insurrection of 1745, headed by the
Young Chevalier. In "O, Brother Sandie, hear ye
the News?" his intended descent on Scotland is
announced—

> "The Pope sends us over a bonnie young lad,
>   Who, to court British favour, wears a Highland plaid."

The incident of the Young Pretender landing at
Kinloch-Moidart, 25th July 1745, attended by a
retinue of seven persons, is thus alluded to in "Few
Good Fellows when Willie's awa'." Willie is the
"Butcher Cumberland," in comparison with whom
the other generals engaged to suppress the rebellion
—Cope, Wade, and Hawley—are but as the small
dust in the balance—

> "Then landing in Moidart, a favourite den,
>   By seven attended, no Greeks ye may ken;
>   He nibbled at Britain as did his papa,
>   But weel kend the mouse that the cat was awa'."

Cope's ignominious discomfiture at Prestonpans is got over as deftly as may be—

" But Cope's schemes, both here and at Preston decline,
  By marching the circle and not the straight line ;
  The best were fatigued, and the rest were but raw ;
  Great Gard'ner fell bravely while Will was awa'."

The same song admits that even Hawley's renown had its flaws at Falkirk, while in "The Battle of Falkirk" his misconduct is more circumstantially, though still apologetically, described—

" Five platoons we gave in their face,
  Which beat the bravest out of his place ;
  If Hawley had rallied and come to his stance,
  We had beat our foes to death and to France."

Nothing could be more naïve than the excuse made for the retreat of the Royalist forces to Edinburgh. It was a piece of necessary and far-sighted policy—

" To Edinburgh, then, we posted in haste,
  For fear that the rebels had gone to the east :
  And we in Falkirk, if they had gone there,
  We had been ashamed for evermair."

It is not surprising that the Whig muse is comparatively silent about Culloden. The horrors and atrocities of that day were a disgrace not only to soldiership, but to humanity. The poltroons who fled, without striking a blow, from the field of Prestonpans, with all the malignity of base and little souls, avenged their own disgrace and ignominious terrors on the wounded and dying on Drummossie Moor, on helpless women and children, on old men, who, like Priam, could no longer bear the weight of their armour. The proceedings of that day tarnished the name and fair fame of English soldiery, who comported themselves with the savagery of a Tartar horde. The few references to it are intentionally colourless—

> " As great Nassau the Boyne, brave Cumberland's sword
> Has dinted Culloden in deathless record."

A false and ungenerous fling is made at Charles on the score of personal timidity. The fact is he was rash to foolhardiness :—

> " Charlie may mourn Culloden Muir,
>   Where a' his stoutest friends did fa',
> An' he stood safely in the rear,
>   Amang the first to rin awa'."

After hinting that Culloden had converted many Tories to Whig principles—though, after all, they were not honest Whigs—the singer proceeds—

> " But softly, Sir Perkin, a word in your ear,
> Remember Culloden field, tremble and fear."

Culloden is handled very daintily: the matter would not bear near inspection. The Chevalier is several times advised to turn priest, like his brother Henry Benedict, and get himself elevated to the Cardinalate—

> " For dancing you were never made,
>   Bonnie laddie, Highland laddie ;
> Then while 'tis time leave off the trade,
>   Bonnie laddie, Highland laddie.
> Be thankful for your last escape,
>   Bonnie laddie, Highland laddie ;
> An', like your brother, take a cap,
>   Bonnie laddie, Highland laddie."

Again—

> "But you think that your brother may try us upon it,
> A cardinal's cap looks as fine as a bonnet."

The popularity of the Duke of Cumberland with the Whigs after Culloden is almost incredible, for he was not a man to be loved. Macaulay says, " His nature was hard; and what seemed to him justice was rarely tempered with mercy." Whether he ordered the atrocities that followed Culloden, or merely permitted them, he is equally inexcusable, though an excuse has been attempted. It is said that Lord George Murray, the chief of Charles's staff, issued an order on the morning of the battle to give no quarter to the Royal forces. The Jacobites deny that the Chevalier either sanctioned or knew of this order, though it seems to be established that such a general order was given. Be that as it may, the severities practised by the Hanoverian forces can in no wise be justified. Cumberland, like all his family, was constitutionally intrepid, but his temper was naturally severe. He distinguished himself at Dettingen and Fontenoy; but he lost all the battles he fought except Culloden, and his single victory loaded him with more disgrace than all his defeats. In "Fame, let thy trumpet sound," the following prayer is offered up for the Duke—

> " O grant that Cumberland
> May, by God's mighty hand,
> Make our foes fall.

From foreign slavery,
Priests and their knavery,
And Popish revery,
God save us all.

Of a more lively strain is the following—

"Our Willie is a warlike prince,
The bravest hero e'er ye saw ;
In martial fields he nobly dares,
And justly bears the gree awa.
His coat is of the scarlet red,
An' O but Willie he looks braw ;
An' at his side he wears a sword,
An' briskly wields it best of a'."

Further on it is said—

"He freed us from a foreign yoke,
An' rebel clans has chased awa ;
Where Charlie thought to win a crown
He's gi'en him a cauld coal to blaw."

Here again the non-inventiveness and want of originality of the Whig Muse are apparent. The song
quoted from is built on the lines of "Willie was a
wanton wag," as the following one is on those of
another equally lively and popular ditty—

"Now tune your pipe, and dance your fill,
Wi' mirth and meikle glee, laddie,
For Cumberland is now come down
Frae Rome to set us free, laddie.
Up an' waur them a', Willie,
Up an' waur them a', Willie,
Thou'st done thy best to come in haste,
To save us ane an' a', Willie."

In the case of the Stuarts, it would almost seem

as if Providence had been directly opposed to them.
" The stars in their courses fought against Sisera."
Everything they projected failed, and, in addition to
their own unwisdom and childish obstinacy, their
advisers were, for the most part, plotters and not
statesmen.

CHAPTER IV.

BORDER SONGS AND BALLADS.

SCOTT was just in time to save his valuable collection of the " Border Minstrelsy." When he set out on his raid over hill and dale after old songs and ballads, he went in the spirit of the enterprising mosstroopers, about whom he thought and wrote so much, determined not to turn his face homeward without some spoil. Whether living hard with drunken writers or jolly stock-farmers, he never forgot his object ; and though his collection is of unequal value, and he was sometimes imposed on, carrying off as an antique what was a modern production, the publishing and editing of the " Minstrelsy of the Border " was not the least of the many services he rendered to his beloved " Caledonia, stern and wild." He was a true Borderer in spirit, and had he lived at an earlier day, would have lifted stock with as much energy and as little compunction as old Wat of Harden himself. William of Deloraine of the " Lay of the Last Minstrel," the riever of Westburnflat of the " Black Dwarf," and Christie of the Clinthill and his ruffianly chief, Julian Avenel, of " The Monastery," are de-

picted not only with inimitable truth and spirit, but
with a certain sympathy with those who could back
a horse, wield a lance, and take and hold by the
strong hand what they needed.

"Chevy Chase," already reviewed, is strictly a
. Border ballad. The incident it commemorates resulted naturally from the condition of the Border
community—a condition which arose gradually but
inevitably out of the geographical position of the
district. During the War of Independence, when the
Governments of the two kingdoms were engaged in
internecine strife, the Borderland was the theatre of
continual trouble, and by conquest of territory from
weaker neighbours powerful families grew up—such
as the Douglasses—rivalling in magnificence and
resources the Royal House. To these, in course of
time, was naturally confided the defence of the
several marches, and they formed alliances with other
great families to obtain their assistance and that of
their followers in times of difficulty. Some of these
families possessed lands wrested from England, and
having acquired them by the sword, by which they
found themselves able to retain them, they thought
little of securing a feudal right to them by charter.
This is exemplified in the "Song of the Outlaw
Murray," which has probably no historical basis, but
there could be no better illustration of local feeling.
A king, said indifferently to have been James II.,
James III., and James IV., summons James Boyd,
Earl of Arran, represented as his brother-in-law, to

proceed to Ettrick Forest, held without title from
the crown by the outlaw Murray, and ask him to
come to Edinburgh under promise of safe warrant.
The King addressed the Earl in the following
terms—

> " ' Wellcome, James Boyd,' said the noble King,
>   ' A message ye maun gae for me ;
> Ye maun hie to fair Ettrick Forrest,
>   To you outlaw where dwelleth he.
> Ask him of whom he holds his lands,
>   Or man wha may his master be ;
> Desire him to come, and be my man,
>   And hold you fair forrest of me.' "

Boyd proceeds on his mission, and finds the outlaw hunting in the forest with five hundred men clad
in Lincoln green. Having explained the object of
his visit—

> " ' Thir lands is MINE !' the outlaw said,
>   ' And I ken no king in Christantie ;
> Frae Soudron I this forrest wan,
>   When the king and his men was not to see.' "

This feeling of might constituting right was not
confined to the great territorial proprietors, but
descended to the lowest stratum of society ; and the
freebooter, owning nothing but his horse and lance,
his jack and steel-cap, thought himself justified in
" conveying " to himself, if he could, whatever he set
his heart on. The principal objects of plunder were
horses and cattle, and the chiefs of clans had generally places of security to which they could drive
their booty, and retain it till necessity should send
them out on a new raid. Females of the highest

rank regarded this marauding in the most complacent
spirit. When her larder was exhausted, the Flower
of Yarrow, wife of Walter Scott of Harden, placed
before her six stalwart sons covered dishes containing
only clean spurs, a hint to them to procure in the
usual way a further supply of provisions. A rhym-
ing prayer, chanted by the Borderers when they
were setting out to harry some unfortunate owner
of cattle, is extremely naïve. There is nothing like
what is known as conscience in Border morality—

> " He that ordained us to be born,
> Send us mair meat for the morn :
> Come by right, or come by wrang,
> Christ, let us never fast owre lang,
> But blythely spend what's gaily got—
> Ride, Rowland, hough's i' the pot."

Persons holding sentiments like these were very
troublesome neighbours, as those who had anything
to lose found to their cost. In the humorous " Complaynt " of Sir Richard Maitland of Lethington
" against the Theivis of Liddisdail " it is stated—

> " Of Liddisdail the common thiefis
> Sa peartlie stellis now and riefis,
> That nane may keip
> Horse, nolt, nor scheip,
> Nor yett dar sleip
> For their mischiefis."

These were a lower order of marauders than the
ordinary mosstrooper, if what follows is truth and
not mere exaggerated satire—

> " They spuilye puir men of their pakis,
> Thay leif them nocht on bed nor bakis ;

Baith hen and cok
With reil and rok,
The Lairdis Jok
All with him takis.

" Thay lief not spindell, spoone, nor speit ;
Bed, bolster, blanket, sark, nor scheit ;
Johne of the Parke
Ryps kist and ark ;
For all sic wark
He is richt meit."

John of the Syde, of whom we shall hear further,
Clement's Hob, Will of the Lawis, and Hab of the
Schawis, for " ilk ane o' them has ane to-name," are
also mentioned in terms equally complimentary.

A state of morality like this, permeating all ranks
of the community, is not only dangerous to indi-
viduals, but disgraceful to the Government which
permits it to exist. About 1529 matters had come
to such a crisis on the Borders that James V., the
" King of the Commons," whose energetic suppression
and punishment of violators of the law made his
people say of him that he made " the rush-bush keep
the cow," paid a flying visit to the Borders with an
army of eight thousand men, under the pretext of
hunting, but in reality to suppress turbulence and to
punish misdoers.   The principal culprit was Johnie
Armstrong of Gilnockie, the brother of the chief of
the Armstrongs, who inhabited the " debatable land,"
belonging strictly to neither kingdom.   At the head
of a formidable band of maurauders Johnie levied
black-mail over an extensive district, and his name
was a terror as far as Newcastle.   Though policy

made him attach himself to Scotland, that the richer
territory and populace of England might yield him
tribute, he regarded himself rather as the ally than
the subject of the Scottish King. When James
arrived in Armstrong's neighbourhood, he was met in
the most amicable and confiding spirit by the freebooter at the head of twenty-four well-mounted
gentlemen, richly apparelled—a sight which so
irritated the King that, ordering " the tyrant," as old
Pitscottie calls him, to be taken out of his sight, he
exclaimed, " 'What wants that knave, that a king
should have ? " and ordered him and his followers to
instant execution. Armstrong, after making in vain
many great offers to the King, said very proudly, " 1
am but ane fool to seek grace at a graceless face ; but
had I known, sir, that ye would have taken my life
this day, I should have lived upon the Borders in
spite of King Harry and you both ; for 1 know King
Harry would downweigh my best horse with gold to
know that I was condemned to die this day."
Accordingly Johnie and his followers were hanged
on trees at Carlinrigg Chapel. The trees are said to
have all withered away, in token of the unjust executions of which they had been made the instruments.
Mr. Burton says, "The chronicles and the ballad
literature of Scotland treat the affair with the sadness pertaining to the fall of power—to its fall by
unworthy means."

The copy of the ballad of "Johnie Armstrang"
given in the "Border Minstrelsy," and which is

given also by Aytoun with a slightly modernised
orthography, is taken from Ramsay's " Evergreen."
An inferior version was published by Ritson in his
" English Songs," vol. ii.   One account makes it that
the Armstrongs were decoyed into James's presence
by a friendly letter under the King's own hand.   The
ballad sanctions this statement—

> " The King has written a loving letter,
>   With his ain hand sae tenderlie ;
> And he has sent it to Johnie Armstrang,
>   To come and speak with him speedilie."

This is probably, however, only a vulgar error, the
vulgar being prone to believe that when a popular
hero has come to grief at the hand of superior power
there has been entrapping of one kind or other.   The
bravery of Johnie's appearance is thus described in
the ballad; and it is to be remembered that such
characters, like the modern brigands of Italy,
delighted more in personal finery for themselves, but
especially for their females, than in handsome
furniture and delicate arrangements for eating or
sleeping—

> " Johnie wore a girdle about his middle,
>   Embroidered o'er wi' burning gold,
> Bespangled with the same metal,
>   Maist beautiful was to behold.

> " There hung nine targats at Johnie's hat,
>   And ilk ane worth three hundred pund."

Among the many fair offers made by Johnie to His
Majesty, if he would only grant him his life, were
the following—

> " Full four-and-twenty milk-white steeds,
> Were a' foaled in a year to me,"

with as much English gold as four of their broad
backs could bear;

> " Gude four-and-twenty ganging mills,
> That gang through a' the year to me,"

with as much good red wheat as their hoppers could
bear; to which were to be added four-and-twenty
bold sisters' sons to fight for him to the death, and to
make all the country as far as Newcastle tributary
to him. One of the offers, as given by Pitscottie, is
singular—" Secondly, that there was not ane subject
in England—duke, earl, lord, or baron—but within
ane certain day he should bring any of them to His
Majesty, either quick or dead." The popular view of
Johnie's death closes the ballad—

> " Johnie *murdered* was at Carlinrigg,
> And all his gallant companie ;
> But Scotland's heart was ne'er sae wae,
> To see sae mony brave men die—
> Because they saved their countrie dear
> Frae Englishmen ! none were sae bauld,
> While Johnie lived on the Border-side,
> None of them durst come near his hauld."

It was during this memorable expedition also that
James had Adam Scott of Tushielaw and Cockburn
of Henderland executed—the latter being hanged
over the gate of his own tower. It has generally
been supposed that the touching ballad of " The
Border Widow's Lament " refers to the latter event.
Motherwell first questioned the correctness of this

L

hypothesis, and Aytoun reluctantly adopted his opinion. It seems to be an adaptation from "The Lady Turned Serving-Man," an old English ballad printed in the third volume of Percy's "Reliques." It contains, besides, lines from "Helen of Kirkconnel" and "The Twa Corbies," and is probably nothing more than an ingenious but very beautiful cento. It is a pity that criticism should in this instance so rudely dispel very pleasing and long-established associations. The description of the widow's desolation and of her solitary vigil by the dead is exceedingly pathetic—

> " I sewed his sheet, making my maen,
> I watched the corpse, myself alane ;
> I watched his body, night and day ;
> No living creature came that way.

> " I took his body on my back,
> And whiles I gaed, and whiles I sate ;
> I digged a grave, and laid him in,
> And happed him with the sod sae green."

Says Alexander Smith, "There is no tumult, no complaint, no wild wringing of sorrowful hands, no frenzied appeal to the pitiless Heaven that saw the deed and made no sign. A broken heart indulges in neither trope nor metaphor; the language is simple as a child's, circumstantially relating without any passion or excitement. All lesser feelings are lost and swallowed up in utter desolation and woe."

The Borderers were distinguished by a strange mixture of courage and rapacity, but they were not given to the shedding of unnecessary blood. If they could accomplish their purpose of carrying off their prey, which was for the most part attempted under the cloud of night, they doubled like a fox, their desire being to entirely elude notice. If they were opposed, however, they did not tamely deliver up their spoil, nor pusillanimously turn tail, but did battle valiantly for what, when once captured, they deemed their own. But in cases of feud, revenge was reckoned a virtue, and, in the spirit of the Sicilian vendetta, the victim was tracked from youth to age, and from spot to spot, till the feud was quenched in blood. When they thought that they had been treated injuriously or unworthily, a singular ferocity took possession of them. From the "Campagnes de Beaugé," a French officer who served in Scotland, we gather the following tale of horror. The English, having taken and garrisoned the castle of Fairnihirst, were guilty of the most atrocious excesses of lust and cruelty. In 1549 a band of Frenchmen, with Fairnihirst and his Borderers, carried the castle by escalade, and the English retired into the keep, in which a breach was soon made by mining. The commandant, creeping through the hole, surrendered himself to De la Mothe-Rouge, but a Borderer, having recognised in him the ravisher of his wife, at one blow swept his head four paces from his body, when a hundred Borderers rushed to wash their hands in his blood. The prisoners, after having their eyes put out, were put to death, their limbs being hacked off before the mortal wound was inflicted. When their own

prisoners were slain, they purchased those of the
French, that the game of blood and revenge might be
prolonged. An incident displaying an equally barbarous spirit occurred in 1517. The Regent Albany
inveigled the Lord Home, Warden of the East
Marches, to Edinburgh in 1516, and had him tried
and executed. He appointed Anthony d'Arcey,
Seigneur de la Bastie, to succeed him. The gallant
Frenchman was induced by Home of Wedderburn to
come to the neighbourhood of Langton, where, finding himself in the hands of enemies, he attempted to
escape to the Castle of Dunbar; but his horse having
stuck in a morass, he was overtaken, when Wedderburn struck off his head, and attached it to his saddle-
bow by the long flowing hair.

The Borderers, however, were not without savage
virtues. As a rule, they were faithful to their word,
and when a person had been guilty of perfidy, he was
proclaimed at the first Border meeting, and not unfrequently met his death at the hands of his own
clansmen for the disgrace he had brought upon them.
Prisoners dismissed upon parole either remitted the
ransom-money, or, failing to do so, surrendered themselves to bondage. There was a general reluctance
to shed blood, and to enemies in fair fight, where no
feud existed, and to each other in the daily intercourse of life, their lenity and moderation were exemplary. Their religious feelings seldom mounted
beyond superstition; the Reformation, therefore, was
later in making its way in the Borders than in other

parts of the country. Sunday was a day of amusement and pleasure. It was at a football match on a Sunday in 1600 that the plot for putting to death the Scottish Warden, Sir John Carmichael, was concocted.

The living by plunder, as they did, is not to be regarded as implying a low morality. Men of native generosity and honesty might be freebooters without deterioration to their characters for these virtues. The state of society at that period was such that no man who had live stock was sure of its safety for a night. The rupture of a truce might precipitate a band of mounted marauders on the stables and byres of any "warm" man on either side of the Border, and he who at sundown was wealthy might by morning be a beggar. Hence retaliation presented itself as not only an honourable but an honest procedure. All were not like the Græmes, who

"Found the beeves that made their broth
    In Scotland and in England both."

But however accurate and graphic a description of the Border life of strut and strife may be when given in general terms, it is weak and ineffective compared with an exhibition of individual cases. The Border ballads bring all that rude, hearty life before us in numerous phases with admirable force and humour, and a dramatic power and propriety which leave nothing to be desired. No better introduction to the subject could be found than the "History of Geordie Bourne," as given in the memoirs of Sir Robert Cary,

afterwards Earl of Monmouth, who for a time acted
as the deputy of his father, Lord Hunsdon, Warden
of the East Marches.   It is extracted in the "Minstrelsy of the Border."

In "The Raid of the Reidswire," a copy of which
is in the Bannatyne MS., an account is given of a
fray between the forces of the two Wardens of the
Middle Marches, resulting from the haughty temper
and want of courtesy and common-sense of an important official at a meeting convened for peaceful
purposes, and which nearly embroiled the two
kingdoms in war.   On the 7th of June 1575, a
meeting was held between Sir John Forster and Sir
John Carmichael, the English and Scottish Wardens,
for the redress of some wrongs.   A bill was filed
against an Englishman, whom, according to Border
law, Carmichael demanded to be delivered up to
him.   This Forster refused to do; interspersing his
remarks with reflections on Carmichael's family—

> " Carmichael bade them speak out plainlie,
>   And cloke no cause for ill nor good ;
> The other, answering him as vainlie,
>   Began to reckon kin and blood :
> He raise and raxed him where he stood,
> And bade him match him with his marrows ;
>   Then Tynedale heard them reason rude,
> And they loot off a flight of arrows."

The fray thus begun, the Scots were soon overpowered by the force of numbers, the Warden himself being " bair through the breiks," and brought to
the ground.   But just then a body of Jedburgh men

arrived on the field, and completely turned the fortune of the day, which was accomplished the more easily that the Tynedale men having got among "the merchant packs," the English were in some disorder. The Scots pursued their assailants two miles; twenty-five English were killed; and the Warden and several men of high rank were taken prisoners and sent to the Regent Morton at Dalkeith. This untoward occurrence equally incensed Elizabeth and embarrassed Morton. It required much skilful diplomacy and moderation of action to set matters right between the two kingdoms.

In "Jamie Telfer" there is a spirited account of a foray, the pursuit, the combat, the rescue of the booty, and the retaliation. The English were the aggressors. The captain of Bewcastle led the freebooters, whom a guide directed to Jamie Telfer's of Dodhead, in Selkirkshire. They soon loosed the kye and ransacked the house, despite the prayers and threats of Jamie, the captain adding insult to injury. Jamie ran ten miles afoot to Stob's Ha', the residence of "Auld Gibby Elliot," who inquired—

"'Whae's this that brings the fray to me?'"

Jamie despondingly replied—

"'It's I, Jamie Telfer o' the fair Dodhead,
    And a harried man I think I be!
There's naething left at the fair Dodhead
    But a waefu' wife and bairnies three.'

"'Gae seek your succour at Branksome Ha',
    For succour ye'se get nane frae me!

Gae seek your succour where ye paid black-mail,
    For, man ! ye ne'er paid money to me.'"

From these bitter words of old Elliot we learn
that it was customary for the less powerful proprietors to pay black-mail to the more powerful,
that they might assist them to recover after a raid.
Jamie proceeds with a heavy, heavy heart to Coultart
Cleugh, the home of Jock Grieve, his brother-in-law.
Here and at all his places of call he makes precisely
the same complaint. Jock mounts Jamie on "a
bonnie black," and he next proceeds to William Wat's
at Catslockhill. Wat and his two sons mount, and
accompany him to Branksome Ha', when the bauld
Buccleuch gave orders to "warn the water, braid and
wide"—that is, to alarm those who lived along its
side. The summons having been promptly obeyed,
the Scots, led by Willie, probably a natural son of
Buccleuch's, and accompanied, among others, by the
redoubtable Wat o' Harden and his sons, set off in
hot pursuit. They soon come up with the captain
driving the kye, and request him to deliver them up,
but he haughtily refuses. The battle then commences, and it is described with Homeric spirit and
minuteness. Willie is slain, and the Scots, roused
to fury by the death of their leader, urge on the
attack so vigorously that thirty-two of the English
fall, and the captain receives a critical wound that
unmans him for life. Meanwhile Watty Wudspurs
urges them to improve their victory by adding the
captain's kye to Jamie's. So, proceeding to Stane-

girthside, they burst the door, let loose the kye, and drive them to Dodhead along with those they have recovered—

> " When they cam to the fair Dodhead,
>   They were a welcome sight to see !
> For, instead of his ain ten milk kye,
>   Jamie Telfer has gotten thirty and three.

> " And he has paid the rescue shot,
>   Baith wi' goud and white monie ;
> And at the burial o' Willie Scott
>   I wat was mony a weepin e'e."

The ballad is the composition of a true poet.

" Christie's Will " gives a very amusing portraiture of the lawlessness, recklessness, and, at the same time, gratitude for favours done, of these Ishmaelites of the Borderland. Christie's Will was William Armstrong, a lineal descendant of the famous Johnie Armstrong, executed by James V., and, like him, resided in the Tower of Gilnockie. Will, being confined in Jedburgh Jail for the theft of two colts, was liberated at the instance of the Earl of Traquair, Lord High Treasurer. Shortly after, an important case, in which Lord Traquair was deeply interested, was to be decided in the Court of Session, and it was thought that it would be decided against him by the casting vote of Sir Alexander Gibson, Lord Durie, the presiding Judge. At the instance of Traquair, Christie's Will kidnapped Lord Durie on Leith Sands, conveyed him to the Tower of Graham, in Annandale, and imprisoned him three months in a solitary apartment,

where he never saw a human face, his food being
conveyed to him through an aperture in the wall.
The case having gone favourably for Traquair, Will
muffles Lord Durie, conveys him to Leith Sands, and
sets him down on the very spot where he had "lifted"
him.   His family had in the meantime gone into
mourning; a successor had been appointed to him;
and his unlooked-for return, while it gave pleasure
to some, was unwelcome to others.   That Lord Durie
was kidnapped is matter of history, and is reported
in "Forbes's Journal of the Session," Edinburgh
1714.

There are three ballads that bear a remarkable
family likeness, "Archie o' Ca'field," "Jock o' the
Side," and "Kinmont Willie."   In each a prison is
broken and a prisoner released, his limbs loaded with
irons; in each the rescuers escape by the skin of their
teeth, as it were, swimming a brimming river in sight
of their pursuers, who are too wise or too timorous
to imitate them, and then taunting them from the
farther side.   Archie o' Ca'field, one of three brothers,
is lying in Dumfries Jail, condemned to die.   The
younger of the other two expresses sadness at the
impending fate of his "billy," while the elder callously
observes that whether he were merry or sad their
brother could not be bettered unless they had thirty
men to aid them; ten to hold the horses' heads, ten
to watch, and ten to break the prison.   But "mettled
John Hall, the love of Teviotdale," avers that he
could bring about a rescue if assisted only by other

eleven. They take horse, and on arriving at Murraywhate they light down speedily—

> " ' A smith ! a smith ! ' Dickie he cries,
>   ' A smith, a smith, right speedilie,
> To turn back the caukers of our horses' shoon !
> For it's unkensome we wad be.' "

In time they arrive at Dumfries port; five hold
the horses, five watch, and mettled John Hall and
Dickie, the younger brother, undertake the task of
liberation. This accomplished, John Hall carries
Archie on his back down the Tolbooth stair and puts
him, fetters and all, on the black mare's back. After
riding wearily the live-long night, they arrive once
more at Murraywhate, when Dickie again calls for a
smith to file the irons from his brother. Before,
however, this could be accomplished, Lieutenant
Gordon is down on them with a hundred men in his
company. They mount in hot haste and gallop to
Annan Water, which was flowing like the sea. The
younger brother wishes to exchange horses with the
elder till they swim the water. But Ca'field refuses
with brutal indifference, averring that it was better
to lose one than all. Dickie, therefore, attempts the
" weil " with his little black mare, " young and very
skeigh," and burdened with two men, one of them
heavily ironed. His gallantry is rewarded by his
arriving safely at the other side—

> " ' Come thro', come thro', Lieutenant Gordon !
> Come thro' and drink some wine wi' me !
> For there is an alehouse here hard by,
> And it shall not cost thee ae penny.' "

Gordon declines, but asks for his irons, which John Hall sportively says will be good shackles to his plough. Archie taunts his late keeper by asking him to cross and drink some wine with him.

"Jock o' the Side" first appeared in the "Hawick Poetical Museum," 1784. The hero was an Armstrong, son of Lady Downie, and nephew to the Laird of Mangerton. Liddesdale having ridden a raid, Jock is taken prisoner and lodged in Newcastle Jail. Lady Downie appeals to her brother, and not in vain—

> "'Ne'er fear, sister Downie,' quo' Mangerton,
> 'I have yokes of owsen, twenty and three ;
> My barns, my byres, and my faulds a' weel filled ;
> I'll part wi' them a' ere Johnie shall die.
>
> "'Three men I'll send to set him free,
> A' harnessed wi' the best o' steel ;
> The English louns may hear and drie
> The weight o' their braidswords to feel.'"

These three are the Laird's Jock, the Laird's Wat, and an English fugitive outlaw named Hobbie or Halbert Noble. Ca'field thought thirty-one men necessary to break the Tolbooth of Dumfries, but Mangerton, of higher courage, deemed three sufficient to herry Newcastle Jail, though one of these, "the Laird's saft Wat," was but a craven. As in the previous ballad, the horses were to be shod the wrong way, and the three were not to seem like gentlemen,

> "But look like corn-cadgers ga'en the road."

Neither were they to show their armour, but they were to be arrayed like country lads—

"Wi' branks and brecham on each mare."

To enable them to scale Newcastle wall, they cut, by the light of the moon, a tree with fifteen nogs on each side. This proved to be three ells too short, so they had to force the gates. They wrung the neck of the porter, and deprived him of his keys. Reaching the jail, they call on Jock, who is in quite a doleful mood, as one who should die to-morrow. They cheer him up, and tell him to work within, and they would work without and soon set him free. Forcing the doors, the Laird's Jock got the prisoner on his back loaded with

"Full fifteen stane o' Spanish iron."

Outside the gates the prisoner is set on horseback, and made the subject of wanton jokes—

"'O Jock! sae winsomely ye ride,
    Wi' baith your feet upon ae side;
Sae weel ye're harnessed and sae trig,
    In troth ye sit like ony bride!'"

When they came to Cholerford the Tyne was running like a sea. Wat the craven loses heart, but cheered on by Jock, they swam safely over, just in time to escape from twenty men in pursuit from Newcastle. The land-sergeant would not take the water, but requested them to leave the fetters. These, however, Jock said he would retain to make shoes to his mare, as he had bought them right dearly.

"The reality of this story," says Scott, "rests solely upon the foundation of tradition." Not so the stirring event commemorated in "Kinmont Willie." It

is recorded in Spottiswoode's " History of the Church,"
and in a contemporary MS., which is quoted in the
" Border Minstrelsy." The ballad was much improved
by passing through the hands of Scott. Kinmont
Willie, or Willie Armstrong, a descendant of Johnie
of Gilnockie, was, in direct violation of the Border
laws, captured by the English, on Scottish ground,
too, and conveyed prisoner to Carlisle Castle. The
Warden of the West Marches, Sir Walter Scott of
Buccleuch, wrote to Salkeld of Corby Castle, the
deputy of the English Warden, Lord Scroope, to deliver up his prisoner, taken in violation of the truce :
but without effect. Buccleuch resolved to release
Willie, but, as there was peace between the countries,
with as little violence as possible. He collected a
troop of two hundred horse—some accounts say
about three hundred—though according to the ballad
there were only forty. The facts and the poetic
narrative differ so little that we shall follow the
ballad. Ten men formed the van, with hunting
horns and bugles ; ten, " like Warden's men arrayed
for fight," came with Buccleuch ; ten came like a
mason gang, carrying ladders long and high ; and ten
came like broken men. The first man they met after
they crossed the debatable land was " the fause
Sakelde," who questioned each band in turn. The
mason lads said they were going to herry a corbie's
nest—an allusion to his own castle of Corby.
Encountering the broken men, led by Dickie o'
Dryhope, " who had never a word of lear "—

" ' Why trespass ye on the English side ?
Row-footed outlaws, stand !' quo' he ;
The never a word had Dickie to say,
Sae he thrust his lance through his fause bodie."

This is a poetic fiction, for Salkeld was in Carlisle
Castle. They crossed the Eden at Staneshawbank,
where they left their horses, and proceeding quietly
to the Castle, placed their ladders against the wall,
when Buccleuch was the first to mount. So says
the ballad. The fact, however, is that the ladders
being too short they forced an entrance by the
postern with mining instruments, while Buccleuch
took a position between the postern and the city gate
to secure the retreat of his own men from the
castle—

" Wi' coulters and wi' fore-hammers,
We gar'ed the bars bang merrilie,
Until we cam' to the inner prison,
Where Willie o' Kinmont he did lie."

Willie's courage had oozed out at the near prospect of death, and he bids them give his service to
his wife and bairns, and all good fellows that speered
for him—

"Then Red Rowan has hent him up,
The starkest man in Teviotdale ; "

But Willie bids Rowan halt till he should take
farewell of Lord Scroope, which he does melodrama-
tically, promising to pay him for his lodgings the
next time he met him on the Border side—

" Then shoulder high, wi' shout and cry,
We bore him down the ladder lang,

At every stride Red Rowan made
   I wot the Kinmont's airns played clang !

" 'O mony a time,' quo' Kinmont Willie,
   'I've ridden a horse baith wild and wud,
But a rougher beast than Red Rowan
   I ween my legs have ne'er bestrode !

" 'And mony a time,' quo' Kinmont Willie,
   'I've pricked a horse out ower the furs ;
But sin' the day I backed a steed
   I never wore sic cumbrous spurs ! ' "

They make good their retreat to the Eden, flowing
" frae bank to brim," which they swim just as Lord
Scroope came up with a thousand men, horse and
foot, at whom Buccleuch flung his glove, and asked
him to visit him in Scotland if he disliked his visit
to merry England. Elizabeth was greatly offended
at this exploit, and insisted that the perpetrator of it
should be put into her hands. After some negotia-
tion, Buccleuch went voluntarily to England, where
he was treated with honour and soon dismissed.

In the ballads illustrated, Scotland and Scotsmen
generally come off victorious. But all the Border
ballads are not of this strain ; for example, the
humorous " Dick o' the Cow," and the savage " Fray
of Suport."

The Border life was one of great excitement.
People inured to rapine and violence do not readily
settle down into peaceful and law-abiding ways.
The radical cure is extirpation. Buccleuch led to
Holland a legion formed of the most desperate of the
Border rievers, and the Graemes of the debatable

land were transported to Ireland. Of Buccleuch's legion few ever saw their native land again ; and the Græmes were prohibited to return under the pain of death. But the hardy, daring, and enterprising spirit of the old marauders has not died out among their descendants. Instead of lifting their neighbours' cattle, they are now sedulously raising stock for themselves ; instead of enriching themselves by sword and spear, thousands of looms are bringing wealth to the district. The old wild spirit still breaks out at fairs and trysts, and Dandie Dinmont and Jock o' Dawston Cleugh return from Staneshaw-bank or other gathering, where they still combine business and conviviality with broken heads and bruised bones, come by in a dispute about their respective marches, or something less intelligible. The character wears well. It is the old self-assertive, rug-and-rive one, sweetened and toned down to modern tastes.

CHAPTER V.

§ I. LOVE AND COURTSHIP.

THE name of the love-songs of Scotland is legion. They date from a remote period, and their number is being constantly added to, for the humbler classes of Scotchmen, especially in rural districts, are so saturated with the spirit of their country's Muse, that they hasten to chronicle in verse any access of passion, pleasing or the reverse, and thus live their bliss over again, or lull the demon of disappointment to rest. The great master of Scottish song in this department is Burns, whether he describes the over-mastering passion of two humble lovers who are to each other all and all, whom no thought of world's gear ever fashes, and whose passion, warm as tropic suns, is pure as the virgin snow on the mountain-top, or the more questionable intercourse of a couple of warm-blooded rompers, enamoured of moonlight walks "amang the rigs o' barley." Exquisitely tender and passionate examples of the former class may be found in "My Nannie, O," and in "Mary Morison;" while of the latter class there is absolutely no end. What courtier ever described with greater grace and delicacy the titled beauty whom he sought to win, than does this country lad, this simple ploughman, the maiden of low degree whose daily task it was to do the roughest of country work?

> " Her face is fair, her heart is true,
>   As spotless as she's bonnie, O ;
>   The opening gowan, wat wi' dew,
>   Nae purer is than Nannie, O."

In " Mary Morison " he writes—

> " How blithely wad I bide the stoure,
>   A weary slave frae sun to sun,
>   Could I the rich reward secure,
>   The lovely Mary Morison."

The same self-denying feeling finds expression in " The Bonnie Lass o' Ballochmyle," inspired by a lady of high birth, whom he had encountered in her brother's woods on the banks of the now classic Ayr—

> " Oh ! had she been a country maid,
>   And I the happy country swain,
>   Though sheltered in the lowest shed
>   That ever rose on Scotland's plain,
>   Through weary winter's wind and rain,
>   With joy, with rapture, I would toil ;
>   And nightly to my bosom strain
>   The bonny lass o' Ballochmyle."

To return to " Mary Morison," according to Hazlitt, one of those songs " which take the deepest and most lasting hold of the mind "—

> " Yestreen, when to the trembling string
>   The dance gaed through the lighted ha',

> To thee my fancy took its wing—
> I sat, but neither heard nor saw ;
> Though this was fair, and that was braw,
> And yon the toast of a' the town,
> I sighed, and said amang them a',
> ' Ye are na Mary Morison.'"

The song concludes with two lines of peculiar delicacy. Adjuring Mary to accord him pity if she cannot accord him love, he says—

> "A thought ungentle canna be
> The thought o' Mary Morison."

This shows the native chivalry of Burns; it shows also the original purity of his soul, ere he was corrupted by intercourse with the world, and before the fame of his genius, and his bewitching social qualities, had made him be sought out by all sorts and conditions of men. The two songs referred to were written at Lochlea, when he was not much above twenty. Though outside of our plan to notice the songs of Burns, it would be indefensible to pass over entirely the love-songs of the greatest master in that line, ancient or modern—it would be like exhibiting "Hamlet" with the part of *Hamlet* left out.

The finest compliment ever paid to the sex is his song of " Green Grow the Rashes "—

> " What signifies the life o' man,
> An 'twere na for the lasses, O.

> " Auld Nature swears the lovely dears
> Her noblest work she classes, O ;
> Her 'prentice han' she tried on man,
> An' then she made the lasses, O."

In this song, as in so many others, Burns improved an old ditty to the same air; but he transmuted lead into gold, out of a sow's ear making a silk purse. The conceit in the last verse resembles a passage in "Cupid's Whirligig," a comedy published in 1607, which it is probable Burns never saw. There is no greater nuisance than your hunter-up of parallel passages. If we were to credit some of these wooden pedants, there is scarcely an original idea, image, or expression in the "Paradise Lost."

The Scottish love-song has a distinctive character, being generally a story, while its English analogue is a sentiment. It is for the most part the production of a person in the humbler walks of life, who, when swayed by a fervent and pure passion, lavishes on its object all beauty and loveliness, and associates what is fairest and purest in her with whatever is fairest and sweetest in the scenes of their meeting—in the stars above them, in the flowers under their feet, in the hoar hawthorn under which they sat, and in the gurgling stream which, as it flowed past them, kissed its pebbled bed. The English love effusion, on the other hand, is generally the production of an individual of the higher and more cultured ranks, and is characterised by fancy rather than by passion, by courtliness rather than by warmth, by reticence rather than by impetuous candour, by conceit rather than by the unfettered language of the heart. The Scottish lover is absorbed in his love, takes his fellows into his confidence, and publishes the name of the beloved. The English lover is self-possessed, and disguises the loved one under a classic name. This unnatural practice was imitated by some Scottish songsters, chiefly those of higher rank, who imitated their brethren of the South. Such were William Crawford of Auchinames, William Hamilton of Bangour, Lord Binning, and others. In a word, the English Muse is cold and stately—the Scottish, warm and natural; the English Muse refined and graceful—the Scottish, dealing with its subjects dramatically, occasionally too familiar, and sometimes coarse.

One characteristic of the humble singer must not be overlooked. He often creates the charms which he celebrates. We have seen what a sweet picture Burns draws of his Nannie. It is the quintessence of beauty and purity. "Nannie" was Agnes Fleming, the daughter of a farmer in Tarbolton parish, and not at all a beauty, though, like "Bonnie Jean," she had a good figure and carriage. But passion clothes its object in

"A light that never was on sea or shore ;"

and the first flush of youthful affection is eminently enthusiastic and unselfish. It has transformed many an essentially prosaic character into a poet for the nonce, and some of these single-birth songs are among the finest we have. It is not the being of flesh and blood that walks by his side or is enfolded in his arms that the youthful lover sees, but an ideal,

fancy-born, and coloured with the hues of heaven.
"Years, that bring the philosophic mind," cool his
enthusiasm; but amid the triumphs of after-life,
when his soul may have been sated with riches, and
every ambitious longing gratified, he looks back with
regret to the bright dreams of his golden prime.
The sexual passion has been refined and idealised
by the vast collection of songs that treat it as pure
and sacred.

The earliest love-song we possess is entitled "A
Song on Absence," preserved in the Maitland MS.,
and by both Pinkerton and Maitland ascribed to
James I. of Scotland. The orthography of the subjoined lines is modernised—

> " As he that swims, the more he ettle fast,
>   And to the shore intend,
>   The more his feeble fury, through wind's blast.
>   Is backward made to wend ;
>   So worse by day
>   My grief grows aye ;
>   The more I am hurt,
>   The more I sturte.
>   O cruel love ! but deid thou has none end."

The royal singer, if James be really the author,
sighs for death as a termination to his pains, but finds
a solace to his grief in the exercise of his poetic gifts.

In our ballad literature many love-tragedies are
recorded. Among those specially deserving of notice
are "The Lass of Lochroyan" (one of the ballads
which Mr. Chambers asserts to have been tampered
with), on which Burns based his song of "Lord

Gregory;" "Willie and May Margaret;" "The Dowie Dens of Yarrow," &c. The author of the ballad last mentioned must have been a poet of the highest order. "Helen of Kirkconnel" is known to every one.

Of the songs expressing the feelings of lovers suffering from an unrequited affection, those of the male generally breathe resentment rather than sorrow. In "Fient a crum of thee she faws," by Alexander Scot, the Scottish Anacreon, who flourished during the reign of Mary, we find the following naïve lines—

> " Return thee hameward, heart, again,
>   And bide where thou was wont to be ;
> Thou art ane fule, to suffer pain,
>   For luve of her that luves not thee."

Sir Robert Ayton of Kinaldie, Fifeshire—a gentleman of the bedchamber to James I. of England, and private secretary to his Queen and to the Queen of Charles I., a friend of Ben Jonson and of Hobbes of Malmesbury, and buried in the south aisle of the choir of Westminster Abbey, where there is a marble and copper monument to his memory—also expresses, in pure and forcible English, his resentment at the fickleness of an unfaithful fair one—

> " Yet do thou glory in thy choice,
>   Thy choice of his good fortune boast ;
> I'll neither grieve, nor yet rejoice,
>   To see him gain what I have lost :
> The height of my disdain shall be
> To laugh at him, to blush for thee ;

> To love thee still, but go no more
> A begging at a beggar's door."

This cavalier way of treating a lady recalls some verses of the great Marquis of Montrose, not, however, to be interpreted literally, but allegorically, as referring to the unwavering loyalty due by the state to its King by right divine—

> " Like Alexander I will reign,
>   And I will reign alone ;
> My thoughts shall ever more disdain
>   A rival on my throne.
>
> If in the empire of thy heart,
>   Where I should solely be,
> Another do pretend a part,
>   And dares to vie with me ;
> Or if committees thou erect,
>   Or go on such a score,
> I'll sing and laugh at thy neglect,
>   And never love thee more."

It is comparatively easy for a man, immersed in affairs, his thoughts prevented from being morbidly concentrated on one theme by the distractions furnished by the battle of life, to shake himself free of any painful feeling originating in unreciprocated affection, for few are of such fragile tissue as the milksop hero of " Barbara Allan." But it is entirely different in the case of a woman. She has centred her affections on a single object, the possession of which is the one aim of life, and if she loses it, to her

> " The bare heath of life presents no bloom."

The heroines of song and ballad too often give

their lovers the last proof of affection, and when they
are deserted, there remains for them nothing but the
slumber of the grave. This is finely illustrated in
" Waly, waly up the bank," the deserted one in this
case being a traduced and discarded wife, and not a
ruined maid—

> " I leaned my back unto an aik,
> I thoucht it was a trusty tree ;
> But first it bowed, and syne it brak,
> Sae my true love did lichtly me.

> " O wherefore should I busk my heid,
> Or wherefore should I kame my hair ?
> For my true love has me forsook,
> And says he'll never love me mair.

> " Now Arthur's seat shall be my bed,
> The sheets shall ne'er be fyled by me :
> Saint Anton's well shall be my drink,
> Since my true love has forsaken me.

> " Martinmas wind, when wilt thou blaw,
> And shake the green leaves aff the tree ?
> O gentle death, when wilt thou come ?
> For of my life I am weary.

> " Oh, oh, if my young babe were born,
> And set upon the nurse's knee,
> And I mysel' were dead and gane,
> For a maid again I'll never be ! "

" Auld Robin Gray," the finest of all modern
Scottish ballads, embodies an affecting love-tragedy,
but it is so familiar that to quote would be a work
of supererogation. It is the production of Lady Ann
Lindsay, daughter of the fifth Earl of Balcarres.

There is also a comic, or at least a humorous, side
to the lyrical histories of disappointed love on both

sides, as in Mrs. Grant of Carron's " Roy's Wife of Aldivalloch "—

> " O, she was a canty quean,
>   Weel could she dance the Highland walloch ;
> How happy I had she been mine,
>   Or I been Roy of Aldivalloch ! "

And in " My Heart's my ain "—

> " 'Tis nae very lang sinsyne
>   That I had a lad o' my ain ;
> But now he's awa' to anither,
>   And left me a' my lain.
> The lass he's courting has siller,
>   And I hae nane at a' ;
> And 'tis nocht but the love o' the tocher
>   That's ta'en my lad awa'.
> But I'm blyth that my heart's my ain,
>   And I'll keep it a' my life,
> Until that I meet wi' a lad
>   Who has sense to wale a good wife."

Many songs express the exultant feelings of lovers who are happy in the objects of their choice and in their unswerving fidelity. These are as healthful and refreshing as a mountain breeze.

The harmony between our Scottish love-songs and the varying aspects of external nature has been already alluded to, and numerous scenes over the length and breadth of our land have become classic from their association with happy humble loves.

Before proceeding to notice in detail the specialties of a Scottish rustic courtship we shall give two quotations, as modernised by Allan Cunningham, from Alexander Montgomery (fl. 1570), author of " The

Cherry and the Slae," an amatory poet of birth and
scholarship, who delighted in strange measures, in
conceits, in allegory, and in idle learning. Had he
written in simple ballad measure and in his native
Doric, his genius might have caused him to be ranked
as one of our purely national poets. But he seems
to have considered departure from the ordinary form
of verse a merit, and the merit by so much the greater
as that departure was more complete. His admiration
of the sex was not so much passionate and absorbing
as chivalrous and calculated; and such love as he did
or could bestow must be carefully differentiated from
that of the honest rustic, whose heart-history is for
the time the Alpha and Omega of his existence.
Montgomery has sufficient self-possession and equa-
nimity to tag on the dead bones of classical mythology
to his otherwise admirable lyrics, thus divesting them
of all human interest. In the following quotations
" but " means " without "—

> " Without love would be strife,
>   Nor kindness could endure ;
> Without love what is life ?
>   A pain that nought can cure ;
> But love, where is delight ?
>   A dool that nane now dree ;
> But love, how could I write
>   My sang sae sweet and free ? "

Take this by way of contrast—

> " But freedom, what is life ?
>   The night without the moon ;
> But freedom, what is love ?
>   A light that's saunted soon.

> A kiss is but a touch,
>   Too pleasant far to last ;
> Oh ! lasting joys for me—
>   I'd rather be free than fast."

From both of these extracts it appears that Montgomery was too self-conscious to reach the ideal of abnegation exhibited by the lover of rural life.

As "ilka land has its ain lauch," so in every country there are variations in the mode of courting, and some of the Scottish customs are curious, and to foreigners seem bizarre. Much of the courtship of our rustics is, from the deficiency of house accommodation, conducted under the canopy of heaven, or what shelter is most convenient. But of this anon. A touching instance of a modest rural courtship is presented in the "Cotter's Saturday Night." Jenny, woman grown, the eldest hope of the cotter, in service at a neighbouring farm, visits the paternal homestead on Saturday night. The priest-like father is giving high-toned moral lessons to his offspring—

> "But, hark ! a rap comes gently to the door ;
>   Jenny, wha kens the meaning o' the same,
> Tells how a neebor lad cam' o'er the moor,
>   To do some errands, and convoy her hame.
> The wily mother sees the conscious flame
>   Sparkle in Jenny's e'e and flush her cheek,
>   With heart-struck anxious care inquires his name,
> While Jenny hafflins is afraid to speak ;
> Weel pleased the mother hears it's nae wild, worthless rake."

The bashful youth is introduced, talks to the father of horses, pleughs, and kye, while the mother is

> " Weel pleased to think her bairn's respected like the lave."

Then follow two magnificent stanzas—the apostrophe to happy love and the imprecation on the seducer. Our Fifth James was a less bashful wooer than Jenny's blate inamorato. But the national manners had been very much modified in the direction of decorum between the time of James V. and Robert Burns. There was anciently a directness of conversation—a tendency, with Burton, to call a spade a spade—which did not really argue a lower moral tone than that of our more reticent age. We don't know even if much of our literature—the sensational novel, for instance—is not, from its insidious suggestiveness, and its stifling hotbed atmosphere, more dangerous to morals than the frank and daring outspokenness and the healthful breeziness of our old roughly-humorous songs. What in speech is now to us indelicacy was a habit of the age, and did not affect its morality. If James is really the author of " The Gaberlunzie Man " and " The Jolly Beggar "— and opinion is divided on the matter—these songs must in the course of transmission have been considerably modified—

> " The pawky auld carle cam' ower the lee,
>   Wi' mony guid-e'ens and days to me,
> Saying, ' Guidwife, for your courtesie,
>   Will ye lodge a silly puir man ? '

> " The nicht was cauld, the carle was wat,
>   And down ayont the ingle he sat ;
> My douchter's shouthers he 'gan to clap,
>   And cadgily ranted and sang."

This was not a prearranged meeting for courtship,

and it shows the freedom of former times, that the auld wife, evidently from the context possessed of considerable rustic wealth, should permit such familiarities between the pawky auld carle and her daughter. Both the songs ascribed to James are full of dramatic incident, and present vigorous images of humble and rural life. We are losing, if we have not already lost, the art of composing songs so fresh and lively, so merry and humorous, so directly the inspiration of a healthy full-blooded nature.

Rustic courtship, being conducted for the most part out of doors, might seem to strangers a dangerous practice, and doubtless it favoured intrigues. But fathers and mothers, now pillars of the Kirk and honoured matrons, had managed their love-affairs in the same style, and regarded the custom as harmless. In the "Flowers of the Forest" occur these lines in reference to this mode of courting—

> " At e'en, at the gloamin', nae swankies are roamin',
> 'Bout stacks wi' the lasses at bogle to play."

Assignations were generally held in some pleasing natural scene, as on the lea-rig, at thorny bush or birken tree, with laverocks whistling in the air; on the corn-rigs bonny, or amang the rigs o' barley; amang the broom o' the Cowdenknowes, or low down in the broom, that had a greener twig, a gaudier flower, and diffused a rarer fragrance to the landward beauty, because her love was waiting there for her; or amang the birks of Aberfeldy, gladdened by the

song of birds, by flower-crowned cliffs, by the mur-
muring of streams, the roaring of waterfalls, and the
fragrance of the leafy wood. It was on the banks
of the Fail, beside the Castle of Montgomery, that
Burns had his last solemn affecting interview with
his Highland Mary—most affecting from the depth
and purity of the passion, and from the solemnity
of the rites with which, ere they parted for ever,
they ratified eternal fidelity. Other scenes, now
classic through song inspired by love, will readily
suggest themselves to one but slightly acquainted
with our lyric treasures, as Maxwelton Braes, Kelvin
Grove, Gala Water, the thrice-classic Yarrow, and
the Bonnie Wood o' Craigielea. Lovers fanning the
flame of passion amid scenes of such freshness and
beauty must have been dead to " all impulses of soul
and sense "—to sight, sound, and fragrance—if their
love was not intensified and hallowed by the environ-
ments in which it found scope for its indulgence.

When the youthful lover wished to have an interview with a maiden with whom he had no assig-
nation, and who, it might be, did not even know him
personally, he availed himself of the services of a
third party, known as a *black-foot*. Burns, who was
a very general lover indeed, employed as his *black-
foot*, when he lived at Lochlea, John Lees, a Tarbolton shoemaker, who, when he had asked the girl
out, got his *congé* from the poet in these terms—
" Now, Jock, ye may gang hame." Burns himself,
who was passably good-natured, and could readily

sympathise with a love-sick swain, sometimes acted
the part of middle-man himself, though his more
appropriate *rôle* was rather that of the lion than of
the jackal. When the young woman was got out of
doors, the pair would retire to the barn for conversation, the girl not being at all squeamish, or troubled
with superfluous fears. She trusted to her own
good sense and robust frame for protection, and
seldom scrupled to favour any good-looking lad, even
though a stranger, with an interview, longer or
shorter. There was something amounting almost to
adventure in these midnight love rambles of the
farm-youth. He had often miles to walk to the
home of his mistress, over trackless moors studded
with moss-hags and quagmires, any one of which,
from a false step, or an obscuration of the moon,
might become his grave. Neither was any in-
clemency of weather able to damp his ardour, or
prevent his keeping his tryst—

> " The westlin wind blaws loud and shill,
> The night's baith mirk and rainy, O ;
> But I'll get my plaid, and out I'll steal,
> And owre the hills to Nannie, O."

And in the oldest extant form of the " Lee-rig " we
find—

> " Although the night were ne'er sae wet,
> And I were ne'er sae weary, O,
> I'll rowe thee o'er the lee-rig,
> My ain kind dearie, O."

Many of our finest lyrics have been suggested
by these adventurous nocturnal expeditions. The

N

dangers of the way, natural and supernatural—for the road was often haunted—were forgotten quite when he met with his mistress, and she proved kind. But sometimes, with the waywardness of her sex, she proved capricious, and sometimes he had to encounter the wiles and stratagems of rivals, who had recourse occasionally to violence. Says Cunningham—" It may be well if to a warm heart and a persuasive tongue he adds a strong arm and good courage, for many a handsome maiden would think her charms unworthy of song if they brought but a solitary admirer.   In humble life, as well as in high, there is an archness and a coquetry which is soothed and gratified by variety of admiration." There is no more exacting coquette than the beauty of the barn and byre, of the hay-field and the corn-rig. By the way, it was on the corn-rig that Burns first experienced the electric thrill of passion. It was in his fifteenth year, when his partner in the harvest field was a bewitching creature a year younger than himself, who was equally smitten with the future poet. In returning from the shearing they loitered behind the rest of the labourers; her voice thrilled his heart-strings like an Æolian harp; and when he picked out the thistles from her hand his heart beat a furious ratan.

There were recognised seasons in which the youth of both sexes came into free and public intercourse, when feasting, song, and dance added wings to the leaden hours of night. These were Hallowe'en, the sheep-shearing festival, and the Kirn, or harvest-home. On these interesting occasions old and young met together on the most cordial terms. Age felt the old fires live in its ashes from association with happy youth, and youth was sobered and subdued into cheerful modesty and decorum by the presence and the counsels of hoary age. There was formerly a rustic festival, now from the march of civilisation completely obsolete except in name—the Rocking— a gathering in some ample farm-kitchen of the daughters of the neighbouring farmers and their sweethearts, when the females spun "tow" or lint on their rocks or distaffs. Analogous to this is the American Quilting-bee. These meetings were cherished by the youthful Scottish peasantry as saints' days are by pious Catholics. In his "Epistle to J. Lapraik," an old Scottish bard, Burns happily describes such a scene of mingled industry and mirth—

> " On Fasten-e'en we had a rockin',
>   Ta ca' the crack and weave our stockin' ;
> And there was muckle fun and jokin',
>   Ye needna doubt ;
> At length we had a hearty yokin'
>   At sang about."

The Kirn, or harvest-home, was a scene of greater revelry. In "Scotch Drink" Burn says—

> " That merry night we get the corn in,
>   O sweetly then thou reams the horn in ! "

In Burns's district sheep-shearing festivals would be few and far between, as Kyle is agricultural, and not pastoral. As to the rites, ceremonies, supper,

and other attributes of Hallowe'en, it is unnecessary
to speak. The Scotchman who has not the " Hallow-
e'en " of the Ayrshire bard by heart is a species of
traitor to his nationality.

In pastoral districts several interesting processes
brought the sexes together under favourable auspices,
and of these they gladly availed themselves. Among
them were the ewe-buchting, and the wauking of the
fauld. Lady Grizzel Baillie has a fragment, the
first stanza of which runs thus—

" O, the ewe-buchtin's bonnie, baith e'ening and morn,
   When our blithe shepherds play on the bog-reed and horn ;
   While we're milking, they're lilting, baith pleasant and
       clear—
   But my heart's like to break when I think on my dear."

" The Ewe-Buchts," first published in Ramsay's
" Tea-Table Miscellany," and inserted by Percy in
his " Reliques," is a lyric of much merit—

" Will ye go to the ewe-buchts, Marion,
   And wear in the sheep wi' me ?
   The sun shines sweet, my Marion,
   But nae hauf sae sweet as thee."

To prevent the lambs that had been weaned from
returning to their dams, it was customary for the
shepherd, with one of the female domestics of the
farm, to watch the fold, or ewe-bucht, during the
entire night. In the mild and genial July season
this was accounted no hardship. On the contrary,
especially if the watchers stood to each other in the
relation of sweethearts, the occasion was eagerly

embraced and improved to give full vent to and
strengthen their loves. The "Gentle Shepherd"
opens with one of Ramsay's most successful songs, of
which the subject is this pastoral vigil—

> " My Peggie is a young thing,
>   Just entered in her teens ;
> Fair as the day, and sweet as May,
> Fair as the day, and always gay :
> My Peggie is a young thing,
>   And I'm nae very auld,
>   And weel I like to meet her at
>   The waukin' o' the fauld."

§ 2. MARRIAGE—THE PRELIMINARIES.

Marriage in a man's life is an episode, in a woman's
the *Ultima Thule* of her hopes. Among the upper
ranks it is frequently preceded by a tedious and
sometimes vexatious disposition of settlements, but
is hedged about by no such impediments in the case
of the humbler classes, with the accidents of whose
union, as illustrated by song, we have here mainly to
do. Not that they rush blindly into matrimony, or
without the salutary prologue of a committee on ways
and means. The national temperament is too canny
for that. But there are different appraisements of
ways and means. A youthful couple, radiant with
mutual affection, blessed with health, hope, and courage, and who have hitherto been able to fight the
battle of life " for their ain hand," foresee no difficulty
in continuing the struggle successfully when their

resources are united, and higher incitements have
supervened to nerve them for the combat. The
humblest have some goods and chattels, which they
enumerate with becoming pride, and when these are
comparatively valuable the enumeration is made
with humorous exultation. And there is a delight-
ful unselfishness exhibited on the part of the stronger
sex. Far from acting the part of a fortune-hunter,
the expectant bridegroom makes the most of his own
possessions, fully satisfied if he shall gain the un-
dowered object of his passion. An honest contempt
for the mean-spirited suitor whose object is pelf is
everywhere rampant, and finely illustrated in " Jenny's
Bawbee."

In " The Courtship of Jock the Weaver and Jenny
the Spinner," a song popular a century and a half
ago in the parishes of Beith, Kilbirnie, and Dalry, in
Ayrshire, Jock vaunts his means of keeping a household in a rather *outré* fashion—

> " I've bocht Boulie Willie's lume, my lassie ;
>   Although she be aul' she's hard at the bane ;
> Four-and-twenty year I may ride on the limmer :
>   Ye thocht that I was puir, but ye're fairly mista'en."

Other sorry chattels are catalogued with equally
sturdy pride, and, of course, disparaged with true
feminine contradictoriness, and affectation of independence ; yet Jenny clinches the bargain after this
manner—

> " Sae tak' your plaid about you, Johnnie,
>   And come your ways up by our house at e'en ;

For I like a lad that's brisk and bonnie,'
    Though ye're no sae rich, my Johnnie lad, as ye
        wad seem."

The curious song of " The Wooing of Jenny and
Jock," contained in the Bannatyne MS., furnishes an
amusing list of what may be called " the bride's flit-
ting." The mother in her pride of heart makes the
enumeration, partly to show that her daughter has
solid attractions, and partly to show, no doubt, that
she comes of a thrifty and industrious race, and
therefore a " tocher-guid " in herself—

" My bairn, she says, has of her awin
    Ane guse, ane gryce, ane cock, ane hen,
Ane calf, ane hog, ane foot-braid sawin,
    Ane kirn, ane pin, that ye weel ken ;
Ane pig, ane pot, ane raip there ben,
    Ane fork, ane flaik, ane reel, ane rock,
Dishes and dublers nine or ten ;
    Come ye to woo our Jenny, Jock ? "

Jock is not only a lad of mettle—he is a lad of
exquisite humour, in whom life is so rampant that it
is impossible to be ailing in his company. After the
marriage is completed, he turns to the complacent
mother, and, telling her that her daughter is not
thrown away, as it is well known that he has enough
of his own, enumerates in turn some of his " guids
and gear."

" I have ane helter, ane eik, ane heck,
    Ane cord, ane creel, and als ane cradle,
Five fidder of rags to stuff ane jack,
    Ane auld pannel of ane laid saddle,

> Ane pepper poek, made of a paidel,
>   Ane spounge, ane spindle wanting ane knock,
> Twa lusty lips to lick ane ladle,
>   To gang together Jenny and Jock."

Several of the songs have a very business-like air.
The swain wishes no shilly-shallying; he gives an
inventory of his possessions, and wishes the day to be
named offhand.   An amusing instance of this occurs
in " I hae laid three herring in saut," of which there
are versions and counterparts in English dating as far
back as the time of Henry VIII.   The burden of
them all is, " I cannot come every day to woo," and
the idea on which they are based is, that having more
goods than he can consume himself, the wooer wants
some kind-hearted " Joan " to share them with him.
They have been even burlesqued—the lands and
tenements of the original version dwindling into a
rent-roll of twopence-halfpenny from house and
land in Kent, paralleled in the Scotch travesty by a
lairdship in the Merse, extending to the nineteenth
part of a goose's grass.   The earliest known Scottish
form occurs in Herd's collection—

> " I hae laid three herrin' in saut—
>   Lass, gin ye'll tak' me, tell me now ;
> I hae brewn three pickles o' maut ;
>   And I canna come ilka day to woo.
> I hae a wee calf that wad fain be a cow—
>   Lass, gin ye'll tak' me, tell me now ;
> I hae a gryce that wad fain be a sow,
>   And I canna come ilka day to woo."

This seeming indifference, however, is merely an

artifice in the way of rustic bargain-making, a *ruse*
being considered a legitimate concomitant of everything in that department. We subjoin two characteristic examples of this. The first is from "The
Ewe-Buchts," published in Ramsay's "Tea-Table
Miscellany," 1724. The beautiful air to which it is
sung is given in "Orpheus Caledonius," 1725.

> "I've nine milk ewes, my Marion,
> A cow and a brawny quey ;
> I'll gie them a' to my Marion,
> Just on her bridal-day.
> I'm young and stout, my Marion ;
> Nane dances like me on the green :
> *And, gin ye forsake me, Marion,*
> *I'll e'en gae draw up wi' Jean.*"

A similar appeal is made in "Jockie said to
Jenny," but we have here in addition Jenny's very
wise and natural reply—

> "I hae gowd and gear ; I hae land eneuch ;
> I hae seven good owsen gangin' in a pleuch—
> Gangin' in a pleuch, and linkin' ower the lea ;
> *And, gin ye winna tak' me, I can let ye be.*"

And so on with his other possessions. The
sensible Jenny replies—

> "Jenny said to Jockie, 'Gin ye winna tell,
> Ye shall be the lad, I'll be the lass mysel' ;
> Ye're a bonnie lad, and I'm a lassie free—
> Ye're welcomer to tak' me than to let me be.'"

A singularly humorous description of a rustic
wooer setting out on matrimonial thoughts intent is
given in "Muirland Willie," which appeared in the

"Tea-Table Miscellany" and in "Orpheus Caledonius." Willie, who was a lad of mettle, and
determined to have Maggie for his bride, sets out on
his grey yaud, which he pricked on with pardonable
elation, equipped with dirk and pistol. His warlike
guise is thus accounted for by Burns—"This lightsome ballad gives a particular drawing of those
ruthless times when thieves were rife, and the lads
went a-wooing in their warlike habiliments, not
knowing whether they would tilt with lips or lances.
Willie's dirk and pistols were buckled on for this
uncertain encounter, and not for garnishing and
adorning his person." On coming to her father's
door, he announces his purpose in the most direct
and business-like manner, and objects to any lengthened palaver. The father, equally practical, gives
him full permission to try his fortune, hinting that
his daughter is not likely to gloom on such a proper
lad. Willie at once lets them know that he is a man
of substance, possessing three oxen in a plough, two
"guid-gaun yauds," or work-horses, and other gear,
besides land held from the laird that would keep
them in peats and lang-kale. The maid arrayed
herself in her best, and blinkit bonnily on her wooer,
who gallantly advanced, and with rustic freedom and
spirit "grippit her hard about the waist"—

> "'To win your love, maid, I'm come here ;
> I'm young, and hae eneuch o' gear ;
> And for mysel ye needna fear,
>   Troth try me when ye like.'

> He took aff his bannet and spat in his chew,
> He dichtit his gab, and he pried her mou',
>   With a fal, dal," &c.

No rustic maid could resist such bluntness and ardour. Willie had conquered, but Maggie prudently referred him to her father, who is asked with consummate coolness and candour what he will give with his daughter. This was an unusual course, but the father was a man of sense and of the world, and he answered at once—

> "'Now, wooer,' quoth he, 'I haena mickle,
>   Put sic as I hae ye'se get a pickle;'"

and he proceeds to enumerate the items of the tocher-guid that he will equip his daughter withal—

> "'A kilnfu' o' corn I'll gie to thee,
>   Three soums o' sheep, twa guid milk-kye;
>   Ye'se hae the weddin' dinner free;
>   Troth, I dow do nae mair.'
>   'Content,' quoth Willie, 'a bargain be't;
>   I'm far frae hame; make haste, let's do't,'
>   With a fal, dal," &c.]

The free wedding dinner was in contradistinction to the penny pay-wedding, where each guest contributed his quota to the expenses of the festivity, the surplus accruing to the "young folk" to help them to a start in the world.

Still, though the raptured lover is in general content with the person of his beloved, and ready to sing—

> "I'll tak thee, sweet May, in thy snood,"

"acres of charms" are not to be despised, and she who is so endowed has little to fear on the score of admirers. This is put with much cynical force in "Tibbie Fowler," a fragment of which was given by Herd, but the song first appeared complete in Johnson's "Museum." Tibbie Fowler seems to have been an actual personage, who lived in Leith, and was married to a son of Logan of Restalrig, the conspirator. If the heroine of the song was the person who was married to George Logan, whose house was in the Sheriff Brae in Leith, she was, as Nisbet states in his "Heraldry," a daughter of Ludowick Fowler of Burncastle. Logan, the father, was "ane godles, drunkin, and deboshit man," whose connection with the Gowrie conspiracy, when established, caused his bones to be exhumed and exhibited in Court. Sentence of forfeiture was then pronounced against him, and his estates passed from his family, most of them falling to the Earl of Dunbar. If the name was proscribed, as stated by Logan in the second volume of his clans, it is strange that his son should have been allowed to wear it. Be this as it may, the Tibbie Fowler of the song was richly endowed with pelf, and consequently with lovers—

> " Ten cam' east, and ten cam' west ;
>   Ten cam' rowin' ower the water ;
> Twa cam' down the lang dyke-side :
>   There's twa-and-thirty wooin' at her.

> " There's seven but and seven ben,
>   Seven in the pantry wi' her ;

> Twenty head about the door :
> There's ane-and-forty wooin' at her ! "

There is a naïve commentary on this, evidently
from one of the softer sex—

> " Be a lassie e'er sae black,
>   Gin she hae the penny siller,
> Set her upon Tintock tap,
>   The wind will blaw a man till her.

> " Be a lassie e'er sae fair,
>   An' she want the penny siller,
> A flee may fell her in the air,
>   Before a man be evened till her."

The " lassie e'er sae fair " does not half believe this
herself.

Lovers like Jock and Muirland Willie, with their
brisk gallantry and plain, outspoken ways, succeed
with the sex as they deserve. A woman, like a well-
broken horse, likes to find her master. On the other
hand, the sneak, though ever so " braw a young lad,"
is fated to meet with defeat and disaster, as in the
case of " The Brisk Young Lad," who came awooing—

> " But I was baking when he came,
>   When he came, when he came ;
> I took him in and gie'd him a scone,
>   To thowe his frozen mou'.

> " I set him in aside the bink,
>   I gae him bread and ale to drink :
> And ne'er a blythe styme wad he blink,
>   Until his wame was fou."

Consequently when this " cauldrife wooer," having
been shown out, befyled himself by falling into " the

deuk-dub before the door," the mirth of the guidman, the guidwife, the town neighbours, and of the fair baxtress herself, knew no bounds.

Among the plenishings expected to be provided by the bride were blankets, sheets, and bed furniture in general. Young women were in the habit of spinning wool and lint for this purpose in anticipation of marriage, and the " beiner" she was in these articles the greater credit to her thrift and foresight. Hence may be understood the chagrin of the bride in " Woo'd and married and a'," which appeared first in Herd's Collection—

> " The bride cam' out o' the byre,
>   And, O, as she dighted her cheeks !
> Sirs, I'm to be married the night,
>   And have neither blankets nor sheets ;
> Have neither blankets nor sheets,
>   Nor scarce a coverlet too ;
> The bride that has a' thing to borrow,
>   Has e'en richt muckle ado."

In Alexander Ross's song with the same title, the complaint is made seriously against the bride that " she neither kent spinning nor carding."

The practice of " asking the consent "—that is, of the expectant bridegroom formally asking the daughter from her parents — gave rise to many ludicrous scenes, especially where the lover was one of the bashful sort. In proportion to the intensity of his passion was his perturbation. But the generality of lovers approached the auld folks with perfect assurance, the whole affair having been long tacitly understood. Another practice, now entirely in disuse, at least in urban districts, was what was called "foot-washing"—the ceremony of washing the feet of the parties affianced in the house of the bride, when there was usually a festival. The ceremony was observed somewhat after this fashion: —The bridegroom and bride having stripped their shoes and stockings, the jolly guests smeared their feet and legs with oil or grease, which they next rubbed over with soot till the legs of the candidates for matrimony vied with those of blackamoors. They then applied a detergent in the shape of soap and coal-cinders, not with the greatest tenderness. The victims bore the operation with patience and good-humour and the rest of the night was devoted to song and the dance, with a due intermixture of John Barleycorn. The practice is said still to exist among some of the mining population. The "best man" and "best maid" were generally chosen so that they should be mutually acceptable; and not unfrequently their meeting and acting together on such occasions resulted in marriage. It was the duty of the best man to give in the "cries"—that is, to furnish the session-clerk of the parish with the information necessary to enable him to make out the banns for proclamation. According to the rank of the parties proclamation was made at one, two, or three times. Three is the legal number, and proclamation thrice was cheap; twice, about two, and once, about three times dearer. The increased prices were fines for irregular procedure. The greater proportion of proclamations was at three times, and the marriages of the commoner people were usually celebrated towards the close of the week, mostly on Friday night. Few marriages were celebrated in May, a prejudice inherited from the Romans. The best man had several duties to perform in addition to standing by the side of the bridegroom while the ceremony was being performed. He was expected to present the bride with a ring, and where machines were used, to hire the same and pay for them. These were hard lines, but we believe they are now considerably relaxed, parties paying for their own vehicles.

§ 3. THE MARRIAGE.

A Scottish rustic marriage is generally a very humorous affair. There is no puling or weeping on the part of the bride and her female friends. The *summum bonum* of a woman's wishes has been attained, and her satisfaction is not attempted to be concealed. A Scottish marriage is also a very simple affair. We do not refer to the curt and rude ceremony performed of yore by the blacksmith of Gretna Green, or to the declaration before a Justice of the Peace, or to the mutual acknowledgment of each other as husband and wife before witnesses, or to the grotesque procedure of being bedded and having the fact properly attested, or to the thousand-and-one other ways in which, in the opinion of our neighbours south of the

Tweed, a man may be fixed for life in the bonds of matrimony in Scotland against his will, and even without his knowledge. The ceremony is not performed in the church, but in the house of the bride's parents. The clergyman having satisfied himself that the "cries" or banns have been duly proclaimed, makes a short address on the institution and obligations of marriage, bids the parties join hands, asks them if they take each other for husband and wife, offers up a short prayer, and the whole affair is over. The putting of a ring on the bride's finger by the bridegroom is not usual. The ceremony is generally performed in the evening, and immediately after, enjoyment, boisterous and unsophisticated, is seriously set about. The marriage supper, previously set out, is now eaten; and in many cases Mess John himself blesses the viands, and by his presence restrains somewhat, but only somewhat, the irresistible glee of the wedding guests. Sometimes he pawkily retails an anecdote or a joke suitable to the occasion, and bordering as nearly on indecorum as his cloth and character will permit. After supper dancing commences, and if there is not much grace, there is great vigour. The proceedings are very humorously and very happily sketched in "Muirland Willie:"—

> "The bridal-day it came to pass,
>   With mony a blithesome lad and lass;
> But siccan a day there never was,
>   Sic mirth was never seen.
> This winsome couple straikit hands;
> Mess John tied up the marriage bands.

o

" Sic hirdum-dirdum, and sic din,
     Wi' he o'er her, and she o'er him ;
 The minstrels they did never blin'
     Wi' mickle mirth and glee ;
 And aye they bobbit, and aye they beck't,
 And aye they reeled, and aye they set."

This song seldom fails, or at least seldom failed,
to be sung at country weddings. Of late, however, we
are getting more genteel and less Scottish, and are
remodelling our national customs after the English
fashion, which is surely a senseless blunder. We
should rather retain them complete in form and
colour where they are harmless.

The marriage supper in the case we are supposing
—that of an ordinary rustic marriage—usually consists, in these degenerate days, of tea, with trimmings
more or less substantial. But in the brave days of
old it was different. Scottish fare of the most substantial kind, not only multifarious, but hetero-
geneous, was placed on the groaning board. In the
" Blythsome Bridal," ascribed to Francis Sempill of
Beltrees, who survived till about the year 1685, and
who is also credited with the authorship of " Maggie
Lauder," " Hallow Fair," and " She raise and loot me
in," the constituents of the marriage supper are
detailed with a humour and minuteness absolutely
amazing, and in a dialect which, not only to an
Englishman, but to many a living Scotchman, is a
fountain shut up and a book sealed. It is not to be
supposed that such a miscellaneous collection of
dainties and viands ever decked a single table, but

the author overflows with good humour and merriment, and revels in the idea of the mountains of good cheer which his memory and his imagination suggested to him. After enumerating lang-kale and pottage, bannocks of barley meal, and good salt-herring to relish the ale, he proceeds —

> "And there will be fadges and brachan,
>   Wi' fouth o' guid gabbocks o' skate,
> Powsoudie, and drammock, and crowdie,
>   And caller nowt-feet on a plate ;
> And there'll be partans and buckies,
>   And speldins and haddocks enew,
> And singit sheep-heads and a haggis,
>   And scadlips to sup till ye spew.

> "And there'll be lapper-milk kebbucks,
>   And sowens, and farles, and baps,
> Wi' swats and weel-scraped painches,
>   And brandy in stoups and in caups ;
> And there'll be meal-kail and castocks,
>   Wi' skink to sup till ye rive ;
> And roasts to roast on a brander,
>   Of flukes that were taken alive.

> " Scraped haddocks, wilks, dulse, and tangle,
>   And a mill o' guid sneeshin' to prie ;
> When weary wi' eatin' and drinkin',
>   We'll rise up and dance till we dee."

Sempill was a wag of the first water, overflowing with animal spirits, and full of resources. In the fifth number of the "Paisley Repository" an amusing anecdote is told of him, as to how he first puzzled and incensed and then propitiated an officer of Cromwell's, who commanded the English forces by which Glasgow was at the time garrisoned. The

authorship of this song has been claimed by Mark
Napier for Sir William Scott of Thirlstain, ancestor
of the present line of the Lords Napier, on the
authority of Francis, ninth Lord Napier, to whom the
tradition had come down directly from father to son,
from the son of Sir William himself. However, the
weight of testimony preponderates in favour of
Sempill. Joanna Baillie has paraphrased the song
with more success than could have been anticipated.
She has preserved to a surprising degree the spirit
and vivacity of the original, which, in a process of
transmutation, are apt to evaporate. The offensive
nicknames so characteristic of the old Scottish rural
life are eliminated, and the *faux pas* of Kirsh, who
came to the South for manners, is consigned to the
oblivion it deserves. "The Blythsome Bridal" appeared first in Watson's "Collection of Scottish
Poems," 1706, side by side with "Christ's Kirk on
the Green."

Supper over, the dancing began, distinguished, as
has been said, less by grace than by vigour. The
dances were the good old dances of the country, gone
through with wonderful precision of ear, every change
of position being accompanied with an ear-splitting
"hooch," which made the rafters ring. The barn
was the usual *salon*, cleared of encumbrances for the
nonce, and lighted up by tallow candles in tin
sconces. The dances may be described as Burns
described those of the witches in "Alloway's auld
haunted kirk"—

"Nae cotillon brent new frae France,
But hornpipes, jigs, strathspeys, and reels
Put life and metal in their heels."

A most admirable and lifelike presentment of this
portion of the wedding festivities is given in "Willie
was a Wanton Wag," first published in the "Tea-
Table Miscellany," with the initials "W. W." These
are said to denote William Walkingshaw of Walkingshaw, in Renfrewshire, whose era is not precisely
known, but, from his fondness for alliteration, it was
probably prior to the time of Ramsay. In the index
of Johnson's "Museum" the name of Walkingshaw
as the author is inserted on the authority of Burns;
and the "Harp of Renfrewshire" homologates the
statement. Genealogists, however, have discovered
that there was no William in the family; and Mr.
Laing is inclined to believe that "W. W." means
Wanton Willie, a sobriquet of William Hamilton of
Gilbertfield, the friend and correspondent of Allan
Ramsay. Be this as it may, the lyric is exceptionally excellent, full of originality, of pawky humour,
amusing drollery, and dramatic propriety of character.
Willie's good humour, frankness, and gallantry are
first described, and some characteristic hints are
given as to his dress, which corresponded with the
freedom and brilliancy of his character—

" And was not Willie weel worth gowd ?
He wan the love o' grit and sma' ;
For after he the bride had kissed,
He kissed the lassies haill-sale a'.

> Sae merrily round the ring they rowed,
>   When by the hand he led them a',
> And smack on smack on them bestowed
>   By virtue of a standing law."

After Willie had exhausted himself by bobbing at
the ring, he advised the bridegroom to take his
place, who, nothing loath, consented. But the mag-
netism which in Willie irresistibly attracted the
fair had no place in the composition of the bridegroom—

> " Then straight he to the bride did fare,
>   Says, ' Weel's me on your bonnie face !
> With bobbing Willie's shanks are sair,
>   And I am come to fill his place.'

> " ' Bridegroom,' says she, ' you'll spoil the dance,
>   And at the ring you'll aye be lag,
> Unless like Willie ye advance ;
>   Oh, Willie has a wanton leg !
> For wi't he learns us a' to steer,
>   And foremost aye bears up the ring ;
> We will find nae sic dancing here
>   If we want Willie's wanton fling.' "

Mr. Cunningham's criticism on this song of songs
is equally just and genial :—" Willie is, indeed, the
first and last of his race: no one has imitated him,
and he imitated none. He is a surpassing personage,
an enthusiast in merriment, a prodigy in dancing ;
and his careless graces and natural gifts carry love
and admiration into every female bosom. The
eulogium of the bride equals a certificate of character
by the parish minister; his rapidity in communicating pleasure seems as quick as the diffusion of light ;

and yet all this, so welcome to the bride, and so agreeable to the lasses in general, costs him no effort —to please is natural to him : his careless ease and buoyant happiness of manner, his wanton leg and roguish look, become him as fruit becomes the tree, or light the moon. The very 'tag' at his shoulder has something talismanic about it."

There is a song called "The Shepherd's Wife," preserved by Herd, which is more free in its sentiments and expressions than the taste of our times would sanction. It enumerates the allurements with which the shepherd's wife sought to bring her husband home, each rising in seductiveness till the climax is reached. Together with "Bab at the Bolster," more commonly written and pronounced "Babity Bowster," it was a favourite chant or bridal song in less squeamish times than ours. "Bab at the Bolster" was a chant accompanying a peculiar dance and marching of couples in a ring, which took place when the festivities were about to close. The marriage guests took their seats round the dancing apartment, or, joining hand in hand, male and female alternately, formed a circle which continually revolved, surrounding one of the guests armed with a bolster, for which, as being more convenient, a white pocket-handkerchief is generally substituted. The party forming the centre of the circle sings some such doggerel as this—

" Wha learned you to dance,
Babity Bowster, Babity Bowster !

Wha learned you to dance,
    Babity Bowster, brawly?

" My minny learned me to dance,
    Babity Bowster, Babity Bowster ;
My minny learned me to dance,
    Babity Bowster, brawly."

The person with the handkerchief gyrates with
the circle, and makes coy but delusive advances to
several of the persons composing it, till at last he or
she suddenly spreads the handkerchief on the floor
before the favoured one, who is bound to kneel on
the handkerchief too. A hearty smack is given, the
male making it as pronounced as possible, while the
fiddler humorously pretends to cover the salute by
a ludicrous squeak of his instrument. The prefer-
ences given in this primitive dance generally indicate
the state of feeling, and the knowing ones are keenly
observant, and draw the proper inferences. When
a person has performed his *rôle*, he steps out of the
circle, and the several couples as they are released
promenade round with arms entwined, and thus there
is much scope for flirtation, all in the way of
business, and without exciting censorious remark.
After this, " Auld Lang Syne " is sung, and the
parties disperse.

The ceremonies noted are the usual ones, and
seldom is any of them dispensed with. There were
others which are now becoming, or have already
become, obsolete, but which deserve a passing notice.
Of these, one was a dramatic representation, con-

sisting of pantomime, acting, dancing, music, and
song. The verse was entirely satiric, and sometimes
evinced much rude power. Cunningham describes
one of these representations, entitled " The Wooing
of the Maiden." Moving in time to the tune which
gave its name to the entertainment, a youth and
maiden entered the dancing apartment, each loaded
with superfluous finery, that of the maiden being
of antique fashion. After a short pantomime, in
which they appear to be highly enamoured of each
other, the maiden sang a song in praise of wealth,
and the happiness it imparts to the married life,
extolling at the same time the wisdom and discretion
of mature years, herself now falling into the sere and
yellow leaf. The youth, on the other hand, replied
in a strain that set youth, health, and true love
above all other considerations, especially the sordid
one of marrying for money, and, selecting a young
and beautiful but tocherless maiden, made panto-
mimic love to her, which irritated the more mature
and better-dowered virgin. With alternations of
pantomime and satiric verse, the contest ended
advantageously to her who had acres of charms.
There were other dramatic personations of a similar
character at harvest-homes, otherwise called kirns
or maidens.

An interesting and exciting observance was the
" Broose," or horse-race for the bride's handkerchief,
generally ridden on the taking home of the bride,
while the tune to which the " Battle of Sheriffmuir "

was afterwards adapted was played. The tune, which is very old, was called originally " She's yours, she's yours, she's nae mair ours," for which was after-wards substituted the title of " John Paterson's Mare." In " The Auld Farmer's New-year Morning Salutation to his Auld Mare Maggie," Burns refers to this marriage race—

> " When thou was corn't, and I was mellow,
> We took the road aye like a swallow ;
> At Brooses thou had ne'er a fellow
>   For pith and speed ;
> But every tail thou pay't them hollow
>   Whare'er thou gaed."

As the Broose was generally ridden by well-mounted young farmers, tolerably mellowed with the national beverage, it was a spectacle greatly enjoyed. When the bride reached the threshold of her future home, she was, at least in the South of Scotland, like her Roman sister, lifted over it, lest she should stumble—a premonition of ill luck ; and a farle of oat-cake, or a sweet-cake baked for the pur-pose, was broken above her head—a sort of silent invocation that she might always have abundance of the staff of life. These rites are borrowed from classic antiquity.

The marriages of the humbler classes generally take place on Friday evening. This breaks the week as little as possible, and gives the parties Saturday to recover from the effects of their joviality. This is the " old wedding-day," often wisely devoted to an expedition to some interesting locality, either in

vehicles or on foot. On the Sunday comes the
"kirking." The newly-married pair appear in their
pew in their wedding garments, which, being often
distinguished more by show than good taste, make
the parties the observed of all observers for one day
at least. With Monday come the cares and the
duties of everyday life, when junketing and holiday-
making must cease, stock taken of ways and means,
and plans laid to make the pot boil.

§ 4. THE MARRIED LIFE.

The songs bearing on the married state are numerous, and for the most part the effusions of persons in
humble life; consequently they treat of the feelings generated by the conjugal relation in the sphere
where they are put to the severest test by the inevit-
able hardships that wait on "puirtith cauld." And
yet it is an honourable testimony to the national
character—to its innate worth and solidity—that the
purple light which irradiated the hopeful morning of
love shines on undimmed through the disillusioned
day, and beams with mellow splendour in the calm
eventide. The Malthusian doctrine of the undesir-
ableness of a numerous progeny, as constituting so
many unwelcome guests at the scanty board, has no
place in this primitive philosophy. It is simply
ignored. On the contrary, the olive branches are
thankfully received, are recognised as gifts from
benignant Heaven to sweeten the poor man's lot,

and to draw closer the bonds of goodwill and affection
between the happy parents. Labour is not felt to be
a curse, but rather a blessing, and is submitted to the
more cheerfully that it enables them to preserve an
honourable independence, and provide, unaided by
the cold hand of Charity, for themselves and theirs.
"The Boatie Rows" gives appropriate expression to
these sentiments—

> " O weel may the boatie row
> That fills a heavy creel,
> And cleads us a' frae head to feet,
> And buys our parritch-meal.
>
> " When Sawnie, Jock, and Janetie
> Are up and gotten lear,
> They'll help to gar the boatie row,
> And lighten a' our care.
>
> " And when wi' age we're worn down,
> And hirpling round the door,
> They'll row to keep us hale and warm,
> As we did them before."

A people cherishing such sentiments can never be
slaves; and it will be a dark day for Scotland should
the operation of the poor-law ever extinguish this
sturdy spirit.

Nothing could express more truthfully what a pure
loyal woman should feel on the return of a long-absent
husband than the jubilant exclamations of the sailor's
wife in "There's nae luck about the house." There
is not the slightest trace of selfishness; her own joy
and happiness have indeed culminated, but all her
thoughts and arrangements are " to pleasure our guid-

man, for he's baith leal and true." When she has
satisfied herself that Colin has arrived, she hastens
to greet him at the shore, not without giving orders
that everything should be arranged for his comfort in
such fashion that his humble home might seem to
him after his wanderings a true haven of rest—

> " Rise up and make a clean fireside,
>   Put on the mickle pat ;
> Gae little Kate her cotton gown,
>   And Jock his Sunday's coat ;
> And mak' their shoon as black as slaes,
>   Their stockins white as snaw ;
> It's a' to pleasure our guidman—
>   He likes to see them braw.
>
> " Sae sweet his voice, sae smooth his tongue ;
>   His breath's like cauler air ;
> His very fit has music in't,
>   As he comes up the stair.
> And will I see his face again ?
>   And will I hear him speak ?
> I'm downricht dizzy wi' the thoucht :
>   In troth I'm like to greet."

The last line is exquisite; she does not weep,
though on the verge of it—recalling to us Wordsworth's—

> " Thoughts that do often lie too deep for tears."

It would be singular were this song, so vividly
picturing wifely feeling on a most interesting occasion,
not the composition of Mickle after all, but of Jean
Adams, the elderly spinster and Crawford's Dyke
schoolmistress.

Burns's "John Anderson my Jo, John," is known

and admired "from Indus to Peru." The aged dame
recalls to herself and her helpmate the days of their
golden prime with complacency unmingled with
regret. On the altar of her heart the flame of love
still burns, less fiercely but not less intensely than in
the days of youthful passion; and having climbed
life's hill together, and now approaching its foot, her
consolation is, that as their lives were pleasant their
deaths will not be divided. Two lines of the older
version deserve to be quoted for their charming *bon-
homie*—

> " Yet weel I mind you on a day
>   The pride o' a' the parochine."

A similar sentiment occurs in "Johnie's Grey
Breeks." The humble pair are neither young nor
old, but at that stage of life when the battle is fiercest,
and heart and hope not so high as of yore. Johnie's
grey breeks, that once fitted him most finely, are now
worn threadbare, and wider than they wont to be.
Yet thus sings his faithful mate—

> " But gin I had a simmer's day,
>   As I hae had right monie, O,
> I'd make a web o' new grey
>   To be breeks to my Johnie, O.

> " For he's weel wordy o' them,
>   An better, gin I had to gie,
> And I'll tak' pains upo' them,
>   Frae faults I'll strive to keep them free.

> " For when the lad was in his prime,
>   Like him there warna monie, O," &c.

Still the national thrift peeps out, as will be seen
in other songs of the married life—

> " But he maun wear the auld pair
>   A wee, though they be duddy, O."

For example, in the fine old ballad, " Tak' your auld
cloak about ye," thrift is the burden of the song of
" Bell, my wife." The guidman is requested to get
up in a season of unutterable discomfort—of cold
winter rain, with biting blasts, and snow-clad hills—
to save Crummie's life. He pleads the thinness of
his cloak, worn for thirty years, and now scantly
worth a groat, as an excuse to have a new one, and
introduces some commonplaces, as threadbare as his
cloak, on the folly of excessive thrift. But Bell
meets his arguments gallantly, and routs him utterly
by an unanswerable appeal at once to "auld langsyne" and the present moment—

> " ' Guidman, I wat it's thretty year
>   Sin' we did ane anither ken ;
>   And we hae had atween us twa
>   Of lads and bonnie lasses ten :
>   Now they are women grown and men,
>   I wish and pray weel may they be ;
>   If you would prove a guid husband,
>   E'en tak' your auld cloak about ye.'
>
> " Bell, my wife, she lo'es na strife,
>   But she would guide me if she can ;
>   And, to maintain an easy life,
>   I aft maun yield, though I'm guidman :
>   Nocht's to be gain'd at woman's hand,
>   Unless ye gie her a' the plea ;
>   Then I'll leave aff where I began,
>   And tak' my auld cloak about me."

Admirable practical philosopher! This ballad cannot be of later date than the sixteenth century, as it is quoted by Iago in Act ii., sc. 3, of "Othello." It appeared first in Ramsay's "Tea-Table Miscellany," and Percy gave another version in the "Reliques" from his ancient folio MS. It is in the English idiom, but scarcely of equal excellence with the Scottish version. It contains an additional stanza, thus—

"O Bell, why dost thou 'flyte and scorne'?
　Thou kenst my cloak is very thin;
It is so bare and overworne,
　A cricke he thereon cannot renn:
Then Ile noe longer borrowe nor lend,
　'For once Ile new apparel'd bee,
To-morrow Ile to town and spend,'
　For Ile have a new cloake about mee."

The portions within inverted commas are restorations by Percy. In his "Scottish Songs," 1794, Ritson published from a MS. of Charles I.'s time in the British Museum a song with the title, "Dame, do the thing whilk I desire." This "dame" so far resembles the "wife" of the preceding song, that she will do only what she likes herself, and simply from self-will; but otherwise the conditions are entirely reversed. *She* is the sluggard and the waster, therefore the production belongs rather to the region of satire than to that of the poetry of ordinary life as it should be; but unfortunately the "dame" has had, and will have, too many sisters to keep her in countenance. She refuses to rise and make herself "boune"

for the market; objects to " bake her bread by any
man's shins "—that is, to take her pattern in rising
from her neighbours ; and, generally, advises her husband and her neighbours to mind their own affairs,
hinting that his importunity for her rising proceeds
from his desire to " be at the tother can."

> " ' Guidwife, ye maun needs tak' a care
>   To save the geare that we hae won ;
> Or lay away both plow and car,
>   And hang up Ring [the dog] when a' is done.
>   Then may our bairns a-begging run,
> To seek their mister in the myre.
>   Sae fair a thread as we hae won !
> Dame, do the thing whilk I require.
>
> " ' Guidman, ye may weel a-begging gang,
>   Ye seem sae weel to bear the pocke ;
> Ye may as weel gang sune as syne,
>   To seek your meat amang guid folke.
>   In ilka house ye'll get a locke,
> When ye come whar your gossips dwell.
>   Nay, lo you luik sae like a gowke,
> I'll do but what I list mysell.' "

The imperiousness of the Scottish housewife is a
favourite theme with song-writers. Generally the
guidwife gives excellent economic reasonings for her
persistence, and the husband, after a faint show
of resistance, yields her the day. In the " North
Country Garland " (1824), a collection of old songs
by Mr. Maidment, there is one, " My wife shall hae
her will," in which the reasonableness and propriety
of feminine supremacy in matters domestic are
frankly admitted, but certain sly suggestions are

introduced, which no right-hearted woman with a
grain of humour in her composition could resist—

> " If my dear wife should chance to gang
>   Wi' me to Ed'nburg toun,
>   Into a shop I will her tak',
>   And buy her a new gown.
>   But if my dear wife should hain the charge,
>   As I expect she will,
>   And if she says, ' The auld will do,'
>   But my word she'll hae her will."

And so on with regard to other matters of laudable
ambition with the ordinary run of well-to-do house-
wives.

The spirit of mutual concession is well illustrated
in a humorous lyric preserved by Herd, " My wife
has ta'en the gee." The husband is the narrator,
and he tells how that some good fellows called on
him—

> " And they would have me down
>   To drink a bottle o' ale wi' them,
>   In the neist burrows-town."

Of course, the session was considerably later than
was laid down in the programme, and the husband.
returning at an unconscionable hour, visibly influenced
by John Barleycorn, found his wife vehemently in-
dignant. Recognising the justness of her wrath and
his own folly, he promises amendment, and thus
ended the hurlyburly—

> " When that she heard, she ran, she flang
>   Her arms about my neck ;
>   And twenty kisses in a crack;
>   And, poor wee thing ! she grat.

> ' If you'll ne'er do the like again,
> But bide at hame wi' me,
> I'll lay my life, I'll be the wife
> That never tak's the gee.' "

Sometimes the guidwife, herself above the suspicion of a dram, finds a ready and kindly excuse for the frailties of her lord—

> " Twa score and ten has cooled his bluid,
> And whiles he needs a drap to warm him ;
> But when he tak'st to do him guid,
> He whiles forgets, and taks't to harm him.

> " When twa hae wrought and twa hae fought
> For thretty years sae leal thegither,
> A faut or flaw is nought ava,
> They may weel gree wi' ane anither."

Occasionally both parties agree in their love of the can ; but in " Todlin Hame," according to Burns " the first bottle-song that ever was composed," there are no indications of squalor, poverty, ill-temper, and brutal quarrelling, owing perhaps to the merely occasional inroads on sobriety, or it may be to the fact that the tipple is ale, unsophisticated, and not that new whisky, loaded with fusel oil, that maddens the brains of the dwellers in the Saltmarket and Cowgate, and fills newspapers with reports of outrages on wives, too often to the extent of murder.

> " My kimmer and I lay down to sleep,
> And twa pint-stoups at our bed's feet ;
> And aye when we wakened we drank them dry—
> What think ye o' my wee kimmer and I ?

> " Leeze me on liquor, my todlin dow,
> Ye're aye sae guid-humoured when weetin' your mou' !

> When sober sae sour, ye'll fecht wi' a flee,
> That 'tis a blithe nicht to the bairns and me,
>   When todlin hame, todlin hame,
>   When, round as a neep, ye come todlin hame."

So much for one side of the picture of married life as represented in Scottish song; the other side, so far as there *is* another side, must likewise be noticed.

The national character is too vigorous and practical for the happiest of wives to be represented as insipid, or the fondest of husbands as weakly uxorious. Consequently when collisions occur, the tactics of the disputants deserve careful study, being often inspired by a grotesque humour, and sometimes displaying high strategic genius. A most amusing instance of this is "Get up and bar the door," of unknown authorship, which appeared in Herd's Collection (1769). The narrative is the quintessence of liveliness, the humour rich and genial, the characters sharply defined, the dramatic propriety without a flaw, and the denouement irresistibly ludicrous. The time is Martinmas, when "the wind blew cauld frae east to west, and blew into the floor;" the scene the kitchen, where the operation of pudding-making had been going on, the *mart* for winter consumpt being evidently just slain; the knot to be unloosed —*dignus vindice nodus*,—the barring of the door; and the original *dramatis personæ*, the guidwife and the guidman.

> " They made a paction 'tween them twa,
>   They made it firm and sure,

> That whaever spak' the foremost word
>   Should rise and bar the door."

Two gentlemen appear on the scene "at twelve
o'clock at night." To no question they put can they
obtain an answer, and they proceed to the crucial
test, so far as concerns the guidwife, of eating first
the white puddings and syne the black, but without
effect. The guidman, however, is not so heroically
stoical, for when the one traveller presents his knife
to the other, suggesting that he should shave therewith the auld man, the boiling pudding "bree"
being handy to form a lather, himself meanwhile to
snatch a kiss from the guidwife, he had lighted on
the last straw that broke the camel's back—

> "O, up then started our guidman,
>   And an angry man was he ;
>   'Wal ye kiss my wife before my face,
> .   And scaud me wi' puddin' bree !'
>
> " Then up and started our guidwife,
>   Gied three skips on the floor ;
>   'Guidman, ye've spoken the foremost word,
>   Get up and bar the door.'"

Another instance of female strategy, practised all
the world over now as of old, as could be attested
by legions of facile husbands, may be found in the
galloping lyric, "I'll gar our guidman trow." The
giddy-pated fair one, secure of her influence over
her weaker half, boasts of the tactics she will employ
to compass first "a bonnie side-saddle," and then
"twal bonnie gowd rings." Her *dernier ressort* for

reaching the climax of her foolish desires she thus
jubilantly describes—

> " I'll gar our guidman trow
>   That I'm gaun to die,
> If he winna fee to me
>   Valets twa or three,
> To bear my train up frae the dirt,
>   And ush me through the town ;
> Stand about, ye fisher jauds,
>   And gie my gown room."

" Our guidman cam' hame at e'en " furnishes
another instance of an honest man's being ruthlessly
hoodwinked by the superior ingenuity of his wife.
It first appeared in Herd's Collection. Though
evidently of Scottish origin, there are English
variations of it. The audacious coolness and men-
dacity of this strong-minded female is beyond
description laughable. By dint of sheer " brass "
she makes the " auld, blind, dotard carle " trow that
a riding-horse is a milk-cow; that a pair of jack-
boots are water-stoups; that a sword is a parridge-
spurtle; that a powdered wig is a clockin'-hen; that
a greatcoat is a pair of blankets; and, finally, that
" a sturdy man " is a milkmaid. As now sung, the
last verse is radically modified, certainly for the
worse, the " sturdy man " being metamorphosed into
" our cousin Mackintosh frae the North Countrie."
This is done to save the reputation of the ready-
witted virago; but the song loses half its humour and
point by representing the lady as catering for the

safety of a Jacobite in trouble, instead of trying to
conceal the presence of a gallant. As there is a copy
of the English version in the "Roxburghe Collection,"
its date is not later than the seventeenth century,
and it can therefore have no connection with either
of the Jacobite rebellions of 1715 and 1745. The
comment of "the puir blind body," "But lang-
bearded milkmaids saw I never nane," jumps
surprisingly with that of Sir Hugh Evans in the
"Merry Wives of Windsor," when Falstaff issues
from Ford's house disguised as the Fat Woman of
Brentford : "I like not when a 'oman has a great
peard."

"Ever alake my auld guidman," a song of uncertain date preserved by Ramsay, professes to be
an account by an accidental eye-witness of a quarrel
between a man and his wife. "It is written," says
Cunningham, "in the free and overflowing manner
of the olden times—dramatic, humorous, and sarcastic, hovering on the very borders of indelicacy
without being indelicate, and involving a very serious
and indecorous question without any breach of
decorum." The nature of it may be easily surmised.
The auld guidman, probably in his lifetime an
object of frequent objurgation, is tauntingly cast in
the teeth of his successor, one of those stolid un-
impressionable personages whose native self-com-
placency is heightened by the consciousness of
solvency, and who regard money as a cure for all the
ills that flesh is heir to—

"The auld guidman that thou tells of,
  The country kens where he was born,
Was but a pair silly vagabond,
  And ilka ane leuch him to scorn ;
For he did spend and mak' an end
  Of gear that his forefathers wan ;
He gart the puir stand frae the door :
  Sae tell me nae mair of thy auld guidman."

To an elaborate catalogue of the charms of " winsome
John," his blinking een, rosy face, flaxen hair, swan-
white skin, and tall and comely person, he replies—

" Why dost thou pleen ? I thee mainteen ;
  For meal and maut thou disna want ;
But thy wild bees I canna please,
  Now when our gear 'gins to grow scant.
Of household stuff thou hast enough ;
  Thou wants for neither pot nor pan ;
Of siclike ware he left thee bare :
  Sae tell me nae mair of thy auld guidman."

However, she returns to the charge, and fairly routs
him by an irritating and invidious contrast of the
merits of the two : "Thy courage is cauld, thy colour
wan," &c. And so we are not surprised at the
announcement, " I trow the wife the day she wan."

Different phases of this feeling of matrimonial dis-
content on the wife's side are exhibited, the most
audacious being that in

" O, an ye were dead, guidman !
  And a green turf on your head, guidman ;
Then I wad wair my widowheid
  Upon a ranting Highlandman."

[The screaming of this stanza at the top of her
voice by the half-seas-over wife of John Mucklewrath,

the vulcan of Cairnvreckan, forms an incident in one
of the most interesting and dramatic chapters in
" Waverley," and had a disastrous influence on the
fortunes of that rather insipid hero.] She makes no
secret of her preference for the man of the mountains.
Of all the good things about the house—food for daily
use, and the cattle that constitute their rustic wealth
—the guidman's portion is small, John Highlandman
coming in for the lion's share.   Of the six horses in
the stall the husband is assigned one, but of the six
" kye " in the byre he is to have none.   Is there a
humorous hint here that the means of taking himself
off to make room for his betters will not be grudged
him ?   However, John Highlandman might have
turned out a Tartar, and given her such a taste of his
quality in the capacity of husband that she might ere
long have changed her tune to " Ever alake, my auld
guidman."   An analogous instance occurs in " My
Auld Man " (Ritson's " Scottish Songs," 1793).   A
wicked wife of Cupar never ceased to sing, " Oh, when
will ye die, my auld man ? "   Her wish was granted
in due time, and she stoutly declared that she would
never mourn for an old man.   The sequel is in-
structive—

" Within a little mair than three-quarters of a year,
        She was married to a young man then,
    Who drank at the wine, and tippled at the beer,
        And spent mair gear than he wan.

" O black grew her brows, and howe grew her een,
        And cauld grew her pat and her pan ;

And now she sighs, and aye she says,
    'I wish I had my silly auld man!'"

These songs express the feeling on the woman's
part, when she is not mated to her mind. The portraiture is in each case full of vigorous character, and
the dame is represented, as nearly as decorum will permit, as being dissatisfied because her husband is old
—"a dozent drone," and lacking the ardour of youth.
On the other hand, where the husband is introduced
as dissatisfied with his wife, his objections are quite
presentable on the score of modesty : they proceed
either from her being drunken, quarrelsome, or lazy,
or it may be a portentous mixture of all three. It is
not the capricious desire for a younger and more
beautiful helpmate that moves him, and no charge
of infidelity is ever advanced. The heroine of " Hooly
and Fairly " (Yair's " Charmer," 1751) was blest with
a husband of easy temper, who, as long as she should
drink hooly and fairly, and without trenching on his
share—would have borne with her humours—nay, if
she had confined herself to parting only with " her
ain things " for the sack and canary which she daily
quaffed, no complaint would have been made. But
first she drank the two cows, then her husband's
grey mare, and next her own apparel. Her husband's
habiliments followed in course, being " laid in wad "
piecemeal, till he could not make a becoming appearance among his gossips at kirk and market—

    " A pint wi' her cummers I wad her allow ;
    But when she sits down, she gets herself fou,

And when she is fou she is unco camstarie—
Oh, gin my wife wad drink hooly and fairly!

" When she comes to the street she roars and she rants,
    Has nae fear o' her neibours, nor minds the house wants ;
    She rants up some fule-sang, like, 'Up your heart,
        Charlie !'—
    Oh, gin my wife wad drink hooly and fairly !"

All husbands were not equally indulgent, for in
" My wife's a wanton wee thing," the husband gives
his wife proper, and, it is to be hoped, wholesome
chastisement for having sold her petticoat and drunk
it, and refusing to be guided by her liege-lord—

" She mind't na when I forbade her,
    She mind't na when I forbade her ;
    I took a rung and I clawed her,
    And a braw guid bairn was she !"

An effectual cure for laziness is suggested in " The
Weary Pund o' Tow." The husband had bought his
wife " a half a pund o' tow;" but the spinning proceeds so very leisurely that he exclaims—

" I think my wife will end her life
    Afore the tow be spun."

The cure is thus archly intimated—

" But if your wife and my wife
    Were in a boat thegither,
    And yon other man's wife
    Were in to steer the ruther ;
    And if the boat were bottomless,
    And seven mile to row,
    I think they'd ne'er come hame again
    To spin the pund o' tow !"

The philosophy of the whole matter is admirably summarised in the following lines—

" He that gets a guid, guid wife,
    Gets gear eneuch, gets gear eneuch:
And he that gets an ill, ill wife,
    Gets cares eneuch, gets cares eneuch.
A man may spend, and hae to the end,
    If his wife be ought, if his wife be ought ;
But a man may spare, and aye be bare,
    If his wife be nought, if his wife be nought."

On the whole, there is much reason for national congratulation on the tone and sentiment that pervade the songs bearing on the married life. The relation between the sexes is thoroughly sound and healthful. Pruriency seldom shows its leprous face. Manly endeavour, and womanly co-operation ; tenderness that never becomes mawkish, and confidence that knows it is not misplaced ; a practical mode of dealing with life, that secures comfort, self-respect, and independence ; a courage that never blenches amid the untoward accidents that may be the lot of any one ; and a good-humour and elasticity of spirit, of which it may be said, in the words of the Wise Man, " that they do good like a medicine "—these are the characteristics that we find prominent in this department of national song.

We feel that our remarks on the songs and ballads illustrative of the married life, would be incomplete were we to make no illusion to a certain class of them that represent it as by no means that Elysium which it is fondly imagined to be by love-sick boys and

girls. There can be no fitter introduction than to
quote a stanza of a parody on " Bide ye yet," by Miss
Jenny Graham, a maiden lady of Dumfries, who while
pacing earth's dull round, had evidently never been
solicited by a " winsome marrow "—

> " Alas ! my son, you little know
> The sorrows that from wedlock flow ;
> Farewell to every day of ease,
> When you have gotten a wife to please.
>> Sae bide ye yet, and bide ye yet,
>> Ye little ken what's to betide ye yet ;
>> The half of that will gane ye yet,
>> If a wayward wife obtain ye yet."

Miss Jenny's opinion of her own sex, and of the
chances of domestic felicity, contrast oddly with those
of the heroine of "My heart's my ain," who thus
sings—

> " For though I say't mysel,
> That should nae say't, 'tis true,
> The lad that gets me for a wife
> He'll ne'er hae occasion to rue."

But it is male evidence that we want, and we
shall first take that of " The Carle of Kellyburn
Braes." The original traditionary verses no longer
exist, but they were modified by Burns and inserted
in Johnson's Museum, and further retouched by
Cunningham with the aid of some versions still floating about Nithsdale in his time. This carle had a
wife who was the plague of his days. In his deep
distress he was accosted by the devil, who asked him
how he fenned, when he replied that he had a wife to
whom his Infernal Majesty was a saint—

" ' It's neither your stot nor your staig I shall crave,
    (Hey, and the rue grows bonnie wi' thyme),
But gie me your wife, man, for her I must have,
    And the thyme it is withered, and rue is in prime.'

" ' O welcome, most kindly,' the blithe carle said,
    (Hey, and the rue grows bonnie wi' thyme),
' But if ye can match her ye're waur than ye're ca'd,
    And the thyme it is withered, and rue is in prime.' "

Satan having got the auld wife on his back, carried
her home " to his ain hallan-door," and ordered her to
go in, shotting his speech meanwhile with a few
complimentary expletives.   In the clap of a hand he
turned out fifty chosen fiends on her guard—

" But the carline gaed through them like ony wud bear,
    Whae'er she got hands on cam' near her nae mair."

The fiends were so alarmed that they cried for
help to their master, as she was likely to ruin them
all.   Satan swears by the edge of his knife that he
pitied the married man, and thanks Heaven that he
was not in wedlock, but only in Tartarus, to put it
mildly.   He then carried the old woman back to her
husband, and remarked, when he gave delivery of her,
that though he had been a devil for the most part
of his life, he had never known truly what Tartarus
was till he met with a wife.   Cunningham's version
contains one or two superior touches.   The old man's
glee at the surprise his Satanic Majesty would get
from the tantrums of his wife, and his certainty that
he would not keep her long, are well conceived.   But
his glee was of short duration, for—

"In sorrow he looked up, and saw her and said,
'Ye're bringing me back my auld wife, I'm afraid.'"

On this song Dr. J. Clark Murray remarks, "One might almost be justified in surmising that a faint trace of the pre-Christian origin of the story is retained in the conception of the devil, which bears a similarity to the conception with which we are familiar in the Norse tales." And he subjoins the following quotation from Dasent's "Tales from the Norse"—"Whenever the devil appears in these tales, it is not at all as the arch-enemy, as the subtle spirit of the Christian's faith, but rather as one of the old Giants, supernatural, and hostile indeed to man, but simple and easily deceived by a cunning reprobate, whose superior intelligence he learns to dread, for whom he feels himself no match, and whom finally he will receive in hell at no price."

It has been remarked that the idea of taming a shrew, so familiar from Petruchio's subjugation of Catharine, has not many counterparts in the lyrical poetry of Scotland. On the contrary, where conjugal differences arise, the grey mare generally proves herself the better horse. An amusing instance of this is exhibited in "The Honeymoon," the title given by Ritson to a strange old ballad, preserved in a volume of miscellaneous poetry among the Cotton Manuscripts in the British Museum. Mr. Laing suggests the title "Ane Ballat of Matrimonie," but Ritson's title is in itself a satire, and deserves to be retained. "The poem," says Aytoun, "is evidently of Scottish origin; but I suspect that the transcriber has altered many words, so as to render it more easily intelligible to the English ear." Two young people had not been fully three days married when the husband asked his wife to work, which she peremptorily refused to do, vowing to God that she would not work for him—

> "'An' if thou wilt not work,' quoth he,
>   'Thou drab, I shall thee drive!'
> 'I would to God, thou knave,' quoth she,
>   'Thou durst that matter pryve.'
> The gudeman for to beat his wife
>   In hand apace he went—
> He caught twa blows upon his head
>   For every one he lent
>   Indeed;
> He never blan, beating her then—
>   Till baith his eyes did bleed."

The humour of the thing is that all the while the battle lasts, in which she is infinitely and out of sight the winner, she is crying for mercy, and while he is boasting what he will do, he is being most unmercifully mauled, and can scarcely squeeze his valorous threats from a throat which his beloved's hand has nearly closed. She kissed his mouth with her fist as fast as it could wag, though all the while she was fearful, and nothing bold; and when she had him on his back, standing over him, she cried him mercy, at the same time peeling the bark from his face with her "ten commandments." The neighbours, alarmed by the hurlyburly, pressed to the door, which was firmly fastened. However, they heard the wife exclaim, "Out, alas!" while her prostrate husband swore that he would anon beat her still better than he had done. Dreading that he would kill her outright, they implored him to "stint and leave his strife."

> "'Nay, nay,' quoth he, 'I shall her teach,
> How she shall be sae short
> With me'—
> Yet on his face she laid apace,
> And cried him still, 'Mercie!'"

Sorely pitying the injured woman, her neighbours cried to the gudeman, "For shame! no more!" but he ordered them about their business, as he was not a person to cease chastising his wife for them—

> "'Let her,' quoth he, 'another time
> Not be with me sae bauld;
> For surely an owght I were,
> To bide her taunt or check.'—
> But he could scant the same declare,
> She held so fast his neck
> In a band;
> 'Alas!' quoth she, 'will ye kill me?
> Sweet husband, hauld your hand!'"

No bowels could stand this longer. So the neighbours broke up the door, when the gudewife got out of sight apace for shame, and the gudeman, well-blown about the face, began to stand upright, full of joy for his timeous release. The pair still continued to act in character, for the wife repaired to her chamber manifesting dread, and the husband made merry, swearing that had they not come he would have slain her there and then.

Q

In the whole range of our ballad literature there
is nothing more thoroughly humorous than "The
Wife of Auchtermuchty," which is preserved in the
Bannatyne MS., and is supposed to be the production
of a Sir John Moffat, a "Pope's Knight," and was
therefore probably composed about 1520. It has
suffered no alteration or corruption. A copy printed
by Mr. Laing and the version given by Herd contain
additional matter, which fits so well into the Bannatyne copy that it is probably genuine. The story
has a theme common to many literatures. The
husband, or farmer, of Auchtermuchty is depicted in
the ballad as not unmindful of creature comforts, for
he was one—

> " Wha weel could tipple out a can,
>   And neither lovit hunger nor cauld."

Returning home from the plough, wearied, wet,
and cold, for the day had been foul for wind and rain,
he found his wife comfortably seated at the fire, enjoying herself "with a fat soup"—

> " Quoth he, ' Where is my horse's corn ?
>   My ox has neither hay nor stray :
> Dame ! ye maun to the pleugh the morn,
>   I shall be hussy gif I may.'
> ' Husband,' quoth she, ' content am I
>   To tak' the pleugh my day about ;
> Sae ye will rule baith calves and kye,
>   And all the house, baith in and out.'"

So she gives him the particular instructions suggested to her by experience, such as to sift, and
knead, and to "look that the bairns fyle not the bed,"

and to keep the goslings safe from the hawk. Before going to bed, but surreptitiously, of course—

> "She kirned the kirn, and skimmed it clean,
> Left the gudeman but bledoch bare,"

that is, butter-milk; and rising betimes, took a hearty breakfast, while she did not neglect to provide herself with a double luncheon in her lap. After she had loosed the oxen and proceeded to her ploughing, the gudeman arose, and soon his sorrows and disasters began. Of the seven goslings which he called forth to feed, the greedy gled licked up five; the calves broke loose and sucked the kye, and attempting to redd them with a rung "an illwilly cow brodit his buttock till it bled." In his attempts at spinning he fared no better, and proceeding to the kirn—

> "He jumlit at it till he swat;
> When he had fumblit a full lang hour,
> The sorrow a scrap o' butter he gat."

Of course not. The sow drank his butter-milk, and, aiming a blow at her, he dashed out the brains of the two remaining goslings. He next set the kiln on fire in attempting to kindle it; and proceeding to take up the bairns, the first he got in his arms was in what in common parlance is called a mess; but the description in the ballad brings the whole scene, with its picturesque discomfort, before our eyes. His experience of the first took away his desire to intermeddle with the others. Thinking to wash the foul sheets "on a stane"—an old-fashioned mode of washing which preceded the invention of the patent washing-machine—the burn, which was great of spate, carried them away. The poor man's patience was completely worn out; the last straw had broken the camel's back—

> " Then up he gat on a knowe-head,
>   On her to cry, on her to shout ;
> She heard him, and she heard him not,
>   But stoutly steered the stots about.
> She drave all day until the night,
>   She loosed the pleugh, and syne cam' hame ;
> She fand all wrang that should been right ;
>   I trow the man thought right great shame."

He resigns his office, confessing that had he been gudewife for twenty days he would have wrecked the house. The wife, proud of her triumph, refuses to release him from his household duties, but her husband, with an oath, tells her she may be blithe to get them yet.

> " Then up she caught a meikle rung,
>   And the gudeman made to the door :
> Quoth he, ' Dame ! I shall hauld my tongue,
>   For an' we fight, I'll get the waur ! '
> Quoth he, ' When I forsook my pleugh,
>   I trow I but forsook mysell :
> And I will to my pleugh again,
>   For I and this house will ne'er do well.' "

There is a popular humorous song based on " The Wife of Auchtermuchty," entitled "John Grumlie." Cunningham found it a favourite with the peasantry of Nithsdale. It is not equal in humour, graphicness, or artistic merit to the original.

No. 37 of Dasent's "Tales from the Norse" has for

title "The Husband who was to mind the House."
It closely resembles "The Wife of Auchtermuchty,"
but is much inferior, being farce instead of comedy,
and for the sake of exaggerating the husband's mis-
adventures making them improbable. Mr. J. S.
Roberts, in a note to "The Wife of Auchtermuchty,"
in his edition of "The Legendary Ballads of England
and Scotland," states that "in Mr. John Harland's
'Ballads and Songs of Lancashire, chiefly older than
the Nineteenth Century,' a very interesting volume,
there is a fragment of a ballad called 'The Tyrannical
Husband,' many of the incidents of which are identical with those in the Scottish ballad."

It says something for the native manhood of
Scotchmen that in scenes of domestic embroilment
the popular Muse generally gives the wife the victory.
The husband, quite conscious of being metaphorically
the head of the house, and no less conscious of his
superior physical powers, makes for the door when
his wife, the weaker vessel, seizes the meikle rung.
He knows that apparent defeat is real victory; and
that were he in earnest to try conclusions, and fight
the matter out to the bitter end, his victory would
be his own humiliation. Good-nature also seems to
be constitutional with him, though he is as testy and
irritable a mortal as need be.

Lord Cockburn refers somewhere to the terrible bacchanalianism prevalent in his earlier years. To hold a tight hand over the bottle was what few hosts would have done. On the contrary, they circulated the wine only too briskly, and it was difficult for a man of any geniality to avoid imbibing too copiously. It was a savage species of hospitality, incident to high health and spirits and not too much refinement. Lord Cockburn mentions an amusing incident that happened to himself. The bottle was going its round so briskly among an after-dinner company, that, to prevent himself from being eventually overpowered, he feigned intoxication and disappeared under the table. A hand immediately commenced to fumble about his throat, the owner of which explained that he was the person whose duty it was to unloose the neckerchiefs. This was a charitable arrangement; for men of full habit and tight voluminous neckcloths might have, like the old Laird of Dumbiedykes, "sughed away," while attempting to sing "Deil stick the Minister," or some equally unorthodox canticle, if not too far gone.

The many anecdotes of the fondness of our countrymen for John Barleycorn in his various shapes may be taken *cum grano salis*. They express the grim humour of a people defending, by the

readiest and wittiest reasons that occur to them,
what they believe in their hearts to be objectionable.
Of this class is the remark of the old Highland laird,
more addicted to the use of the national beverage
than was wholesome or decorous, when warned that
whisky was a slow poison, to the effect that, if it was
a poison, it was very slow, for he had been using
it daily for seventy years, and was still tolerably
hearty. The reply of the Highlander to his minister,
who was insisting that whisky was a bad thing,—
"Yes, especially *bad* whisky,"—has a stolid look
about it, but it is just possible that it may be the
perfection of ready humour. The ongoings of some
of the legal luminaries of last century read like
romances. Lord Newton found his intellect cleared
and his judgment steadied by the absorption of six
bottles of claret. De Quincey speaks both of opium
and of wine, not in over-doses, producing the same
effect on himself. After an experiment of this kind
in stimulants or sedatives his mind became, like the
infant world of Ovid—

"Ponderibus librata suis."

Lord Newton's being found sleeping in the
morning among the paraphernalia of the sweeps,
among which he had tumbled over-night in a state
of unconsciousness, was over-doing the matter. It
was gilding refined gold, painting the lily, and—

"Wasteful and ridiculous excess."

But he had a sound brain and stomach, for M.

Simond, in his "Tour in Scotland," published in 1811, describes his surprise on finding in the morning in a clear-headed Judge of the Parliament House, free from all traces of excess, Newton, with whom he had had a fierce debauch the night before.   Lord Hermand bitterly bewailed the degeneracy of the times, when he found the rising race unwilling or unable, or both, to keep him company over his protracted cups.   On circuit he would cool his brain by bathing his head and hands in cold water after an entire night's symposium, and proceed to the bench to dispose of the most serious cases affecting life and property.   His remark about the conduct of a youth who had murdered his companion in what was originally a friendly dispute, intoxication having been pleaded by his counsel as an extenuation of the crime, " If he did that when he was drunk, what would he not do when he was sober," was perfectly natural, and without the least affectation.   Jamie Balfour, who could run when he could not stand, was another specimen of these Titanic topers.   His portrait in Leith Golf-house represented him in the act of singing his favourite song, with the appropriate gesture—

> " When I hae a saxpence under my thoom,
>   Then I get credit in ilka town ;
>   But aye when I'm poor they bid me gang by,
>   Oh, poverty parts guid company !
>   Todlin hame, and todlin hame,
>   Couldna my love come todlin hame."

Alexander Gibson Hunter, a Forfarshire laird, and

for a time the partner of Archibald Constable, was another of those convivialists whose exploits appear fabulous to the more sober generation that now is. He writes to Constable on 30th August 1804:—"Our turtle dinner turned out admirably well. I cut a most distinguished figure; ate seven plates of calipash and two of calipee, besides about three of the fins. We had four kinds of Madeira and claret till half-past eleven. Yesterday plenty of venison and moorfowl at Haggart's, with red champagne, hock (vintage 1727), and excellent claret till half-past ten, with Sir A. Don, Major Maitland, &c." Brechin Castle, the seat of Mr. Maule, afterwards Lord Panmure, was a favourite howff of Hunter's. He had Longman the publisher there with him once. He says:—"Maule was, as usual, very attentive; we had a strong party to dinner, and a good drink till ten or so, but nobody completely pounded; Longman did very well." But not so well next day; for going to Balnamoon, he got his orderly system upset, on which Hunter remarked—"Those Englishers will never do in our country. They eat a great deal too much and drink too little; the consequence is, their stomachs give way, and they are knocked up, of course."

Our bacchanalian songs are among the best ever penned.

> "O gude ale comes, and gude ale goes;
> Gude ale gars me sell my hose,
> Sell my hose and pawn my shoon;
> Gude ale keeps my heart aboon.

> "I had six owsen in a pleuch,
>   And they drew teuch and well eneuch ;
> I drank them a' just ane by ane ;
>   Gude ale keeps my heart aboon."

In the song of " The Miller," which appeared in the
" Charmer" in 1751, and is attributed to Sir John
Clerk of Penicuik, a Baron of the Scottish Court of
Exchequer, who died in 1755, there is a pretty pic-
ture of rustic comfort—

> " In winter time, when wind and rain
>   Blow o'er the house and byre,
> He sits beside a clean hearthstane,
>   Before a rousing fire :
>
> " O'er foaming ale he tells his tale,
>   Which rows him o'er fu' happy ;
> Who'd be a king, a petty thing,
>   When a miller lives so happy ? "

A very rollicking effusion is " Hey for the mill and
the kiln ;" and its refrain, " While the happer said
tak' it, man, tak' it," is an open, fair confession which
scorns a lie. But the hierophant of this species of
lyrical composition is Burns. And here, again, for
intelligible reasons, we must for a space violate our
original plan. What innocent enjoyment has not
" Auld Langsyne " given to tens of thousands of old
and young, of male and female joyous revellers !

> " And surely ye'll be your pint-stoup,
>   And surely I'll be mine :
> And we'll tak' a richt guid willie-waught,
>   For auld langsyne."

It was an astute remark of an Irishman at a Burns
Festival gathering in America, that the stipulation

for a return of the pint-stoup revealed the nationality
of the songster. An Irishman would never have
thought of such a condition. "Willie Brewed a Peck
o' Maut" is the *ne plus ultra* of happy effort in this
line—

> " It is the moon, I ken her horn,
>   That's blinkin' in the lift sae hie ;
> She smiles sae sweet to wile us hame,
>   But by my faith she'll wait a wee !
> For we are na fou ; we're no that fou—
>   But just a wee drap in our e'e.
> The cock may craw, the day may daw,
>   But aye we'll taste the barley bree."

In " Death and Dr. Hornbook " the stanza—

> " The clachan yill had made me canty ;
> I wasna fou, but just had plenty ;
> I stachered whyles, but yet took tent aye
>   To clear the ditches,
> And hillocks, stanes, and bushes kent aye
>   Frae ghaists and witches,"—

is, like Wanton Willie himself, "without a clag."

The jolly rustic is the incarnation of canty good-
humour, and too "comfortable" to care even for
ghaists, though not forgetful of their existence.

In two of his poems Burns has outdone himself—
in " Scotch Drink " (especially in this), and in " The
Author's Earnest Cry and Prayer to the Scotch
Representatives in the House of Commons." He
writes with a will, and his verses "rattle in their
ranks " with glorious vigour and freedom—

> " O thou, my Muse ! guid auld Scotch Drink ;
>   Whether through wimplin' worms thou jink,

> Or, richly brown, ream o'er the brink,
>   In glorious faem,
> Inspire me, till I lisp and wink,
>   To sing thy name!"

The apostrophe to John Barleycorn is superb—

> "On thee aft Scotland chews her cood,
> In souple scones, the wale o' food!
> Or tumblin' in the boiling flood
>   Wi' kail and beef;
> But when thou pours thy strong heart's blood,
>   There thou shines chief.

> "Food fills the wame and keeps us livin';
> Though life's a gift no' worth receivin',
> When heavy dragged wi' pain and grievin';
>   But oiled by thee,
> The wheels o' life gae down-hill scrievin',
>   Wi' rattlin' glee."

Admirable for its humanity is the following—

> "Aft clad in massy siller weed,
> Wi' gentles thou erects thy head;
> Yet humbly kind in time o' need,
>   The poor man's wine,
> His wee drap parritch, or his bread,
>   Thou kitchens fine."

The rest of the poem is equally fine; and the stanza in which he ascribes his inspiration to whisky, the soul of plays and pranks, is especially noteworthy for its plain-spoken vigour. The concluding lines, in which he invokes Fortune, and professes that his wishes from her are limited to—

> "Hale breeks, a scone, and whisky gill,
> And rowth o' rhyme to rave at will,"

have been much admired. The other poem, which

may be regarded as a sequel to the foregoing, is not
less vigorous. Its postscript is especially so. These
pieces seem to have come from the bard at a single
heat, and to have been conceived and composed
very much as they at present appear. Burns never
surpassed them. The phraseology is particularly
happy. The vernacular came to his pen in his early
efforts with such readiness and propriety, that to alter
a word would spoil a whole poem.

In his epistles to his brother bards the prospect of
a meeting is always attended with an anticipation of
a modicum of his favourite beverage. To Lapraik he
writes—

> "The four-gilled chap we'se gar him clatter,
> And kirsen him wi' reekin' water."

But probably these symposia were like Barmecide's
feast; for though he addressed to Pitt the promise
that on certain conditions he would—

> "Drink his health in auld Nanse Tinnock's
> Nine times a week,"

the bard was, on the evidence of Nanse herself, a very
infrequent visitor at her hostelry. In an unquotable
verse in his "Lines on Meeting with Basil, Lord
Daer," he mentions among his bacchanalian exploits
his having been at drucken writers' feasts, slokened
his drouth with mighty squireships of the quorum, and
occasionally exceeded to no small extent with godly
priests. This poetical exaggeration reminds one of Dr.
Carlyle's Autobiography. In his time there was a race

of jolly parsons, especially in the Lothians, who lived
on familiar terms with the country gentry and the
conspicuous members of the legal profession, affected
clubs, and loved a glass of sound claret. The Doctor
himself was a professed *bon vivant*, and his social
charm must have been very great; for, according to
Lord Cockburn, though he never exhibited much talent
in any capacity, he possessed extraordinary influence
with his brethren, and with the best society of the
day both in Scotland and England. As to Church
matters, he was very *Moderate* indeed. In fact, he
prided himself on his sound sense, freedom from
enthusiasm—or, as he termed it, fanaticism—and
knowledge of the world. His economics as to in-
stituting weekly dinners, where good claret and good
conversationalists should assist, were highly diplomatic. When Principal Robertson and he were once
on a time visiting at Lord Bute's at Mountstuart,
there happened to be set before them a remainder of
some superlative claret, which the divines imbibed
with much gusto. Unfortunately it went done. On
this Carlyle took Robertson aside and cautioned him
not to exhibit any falling-off in his potations, lest it
should be attributed to the inferior wine on the table.
These men had sound heads and stomachs, and gave
a wide berth to weak-headed babblers who could not
carry their liquor discreetly. They never forgot that
they were clergymen, and above all gentlemen. The
incident in "Waverley" of the Baron of Bradwardine
retiring with his guests, after a solemn dinner at Tully-

Veolan, to wind up the day's proceedings by a debauch in Luckie Macleary's change-house, is happily illustrated by a passage in Cockburn's "Memorials of his Times." When a boy, he happened to be with his father, who was Convener of the County, in a humble roadside inn, when the Duke of Buccleuch and the chief landed dignitaries of the neighbourhood—all owners of luxurious houses—arrived to have a relaxation of a similar kind over steaming punch. They put young Cockburn in the chair, and the Duke drank his health as the young Convener—"May he be a better man than his father. Hip, hip, hurrah!" &c., &c. The high jinks of Pleydell and his cronies, in "Guy Mannering," were only somewhat more elaborate and less natural than the proceedings of the distinguished topers on this occasion.

A strange custom of last century in Edinburgh was that of ladies and gentlemen of high rank repairing to oyster-cellars, mere *laigh shops* or *dives*, to regale themselves with raw oysters and porter, set on a coarse table in a dingy room lighted with tallow candles. Much of the conversation was what would be deemed to-day improper—in fact, naughty. After the oysters and porter were despatched, brandy or rum-punch was introduced, and a dance was got up, in which oyster-women of known disreputable character were sometimes allowed to mix. As late as 1824, Lord Melville, the Duchess of Gordon, and other persons of rank, renewed the experiences of their youth by having a frolic in an oyster-cellar. Luckie

Middlemass's tavern in the Cowgate was the favourite
scene of these questionable meetings.   Robert Fer-
guson, who loved frolic not wisely but too well, says
of this favourite resort—

> "When big as burns the gutters rin,
>   If ye hae catched a droukit skin,
>   To Luckie Middlemist's loup in,
>   And sit fu' snug,
>   Owre oysters and a dram o' gin,
>   Or haddock lug."

The convivial literature of Scotland is rich and
racy, and quite *sui generis*.   It might imply that, as
a nation, we were more given to the bottle than others.
In one sense this has a semblance of truth, for spirit-
drinking nations are more demonstrative over their
cups than muddle-headed beer-drinkers or placid
wine-bibbers.   But that is the worst of it.   In France
at the present day, drunkenness is largely on the
increase, brandy being preferred by many to wine,
and the favourite absinthe is more deleterious even
than whisky.   It is for the credit of every people, as
of every individual, to have a reputation for sobriety.
In this country our reputation is worse than our
desert, but, on the whole, sobriety is on the gaining
side.   It is not long since the usual sequel of a
dinner-party was a debauch, but this has been altered
entirely.   Convivial literature will never die; and
the time may come when sober gentlemen over some
innocuous tipple will be found joining hilariously
in "Auld Langsyne" or "Willie Brewed a Peck o'
Maut."

In " Peblis to the Play " we have a graphic picture
of tavern life in the reign of the First James of Scotland, 1424–36. The party of merry-makers having
retired to the tavern to dine and dance—

> " Ay as the goodwife brought in
>   Ane scorit upon the wauch,
> Ane bade ' Pay !' Another said ' Nay,
>   Bide while we rakin our lauch !'
> The goodwife said, ' Have ye nae dread,
>   Ye sall pay at ye aucht.'
> A young man stert upon his feet
>   And he began to lauche
>   For heyden
>   Of Peblis to the Play.
>
> " He gat a trencher in his hand,
>   And he began to count.
> ' Ilk man twa and ane happenie ;
>   To pay thus we were wont.'
> Another stert upon his feet,
>   And said, ' Thou art o'er blunt
> To take such office upon hand ;
>   I vow thou servite ane dunt
>   Of me !'
>   Of Peblis to the Play."

This gives rise to a tavern brawl, which is described
with infinite humour. The indignation of the good-
wife at the person scoring the items on the wall to
check her reckoning, and her remark that they should
pay just what they owed, as she would not cheat
them, are both very natural.

Another phase of national conviviality must be
noticed. In his " Traditions of Edinburgh," after
describing the bacchanalianism of the last century,
Robert Chambers adds—

R

" It is hardly surprising that habits carried to such an extravagance among gentlemen should have in some small degree affected the fairer and purer part of creation also. It is an old story in Edinburgh that three ladies had one night a merry meeting in a tavern near the Cross, where they sat to a very late hour. Ascending at length to the street, they scarcely remembered where they were, but as it was good moonlight they found little difficulty in walking along till they came to the Tron Church. There, however, an obstacle occurred. The moon, shining high in the south, threw the shadow of the steeple directly across the street from the one side to the other, and the ladies, being no more clear-sighted than they were clear-headed, mistook this for a broad and rapid river, which they would require to cross before making farther way. In this delusion they sat down upon the brink of the imaginary stream, deliberately took off their shoes and stockings, kilted their lower garments, and proceeded to wade through to the opposite side ; after which, resuming their shoes and stockings, they went on their way rejoicing as before ! "—" Traditions of Edinburgh," p. 158.

An anecdote is subjoined, on the authority of an ancient nobleman, to the effect that the officers of the Crown having procured some important intelligence affecting the Jacobites during the rising of 1715, resolved to forward the same to London by a certain man of rank. Those interested having scented the affair, two tall, handsome ladies, in full dress, and wearing black velvet masks, accosted the messenger on his way to the Canongate to take horse. He proposed to treat them to a pint of claret at an adjoining tavern, an offer which the ladies reciprocated. After a heavy debauch of several hours, the gentleman sank beneath the table, when he was at once robbed of his papers. For the honour of

Scottish womanhood, however, it is only fair to
mention that the robbers were believed at the time
to be young men disguised in women's clothes. In
a note there is a quotation from a curious paper in
the "Edinburgh Magazine" for August 1817, from
which it appears that at the period in question,
"though it was a disgrace for ladies to be seen drunk,
yet it was none to be a little intoxicated in good
company." Similar testimony is given by Mr.
Burton—"Hist. of Scotland," vol. vii. p. 93.

"The bacchanalian song still asserts its supremacy, but
the feats it records are all performed by the male sex. In
the Scotland of the seventeenth century, what is so often
called the gentle, and might in later times be called the sober,
sex, indulged to some considerable extent in hard drinking,
and its feats were celebrated in genial rhyme."

Some specimens of the songs in which this feature
of the national character is exhibited we shall by-
and-by adduce. Meanwhile we may remark, that the
treatment of such cases in song is wholly humorous,
and suggests nothing of the repulsiveness, vulgarity,
and utter demoralisation characteristic of the female
who indulges at the present day. The thirsty heroine
of song is by no means repulsive to a healthily
constituted mind. There is a fund of life and
geniality about her that is irresistible. Even her
husband narrates his domestic *désagrémens* with a
roguish twinkle in his eye. Though forced to confess of
the "wanton wee thing" that—

"She selled her coat, and she drank it ;
She selled her coat, and she drank it ;

> She rowed hersel' in a blanket ;
> She winna be guided by me ; "

he is reconciled to the circumstance from the
fact that he "took a rung and clawed her" till she
became "a guid bairn." The guidwife of "Hooly
and Fairly," referred to previously, seems to have
been fastidious in her potations, for she drank
nothing but sack and canary ; yet though she
beggared her husband of his substance, that good-
natured, long-suffering man was more affected by her
unfair mode of drinking than by her wasting of his
goods—

> " First she drank Crummie, and syne she drank Gairie,
>   And syne she drank my bonny grey marie,
>   That carried me through a' the dubs and the lairie—
>   Oh, gin my wife wad drink hooly and fairly !
>
> " She drank her hose, she drank her shoon,
>   And syne she drank her bonnie new goun ;
>   She drank her sark that covered her rarely—
>   Oh, gin my wife wad drink hooly and fairly !
>
> " My Sunday's coat she's laid it in wad,
>   And the best blue bonnet e'er was on my head ;
>   At kirk and at mercat I'm covered but barely—
>   Oh, gin my wife wad drink hooly and fairly ! "

He is, besides—unfortunately, perhaps, both for
himself and his wife—a man of peace, averse to
wrangling and strife, and willing to allow her what
Horace calls "the gifts of a moderate Bacchus."
She, however, is a virago, who keeps the purse, and
scrimps her facile husband—the "grey marie,"
whether "bonny" or not, being unquestionably the

better horse. "Todlin' Hame" presents an instance in which there is no over-reaching, scrimping, or wrangling. The pair imbibe on a principle of perfect equality, using measures of equal capacity, and doubtless containing beverages of equal potency—

> " My kimmer and I lay doun to sleep,
>   And twa pint-stoups at our bed's feet," &c.*

These female bacchanalians are from the humbler walks of life; not the squalidly poor, indeed, but people with such rustic wealth as a couple of cows and a good grey mare. And it is usual to associate this habit with the humbler class of females only. In Dunbar's "Twa Maryit Wemen and the Wedo," however, the three compotators who "wauchtit at the wicht wyne," were of the higher class; for—

> " Kemmit was their cleir hair, and curiouslie sched
>   Attour their schoulderis doun schyre, schyning full bricht ;
>   With kurches cassin thame aboue, of krisp cleir and thin,
>   Thair mantillis grein war as the grass that grew in May
>   sesoun,
>   Fastnet with thair quhyt fingaris about thair fair sydis !"

If some of our medical journals are to be trusted, there is an insidious habit gaining ground among many matrons of higher and middle life and their daughters of consuming much surreptitious sherry, medicinally, of course, and with the sanction of the family physician, who no doubt finds his account in prescribing a medicine so much to the patient's mind. The craving and believed necessity for this

* See *ante* p. 227.

stimulus proceed from a depressed condition begot
of idleness and listlessness, and entirely differentiate
the recipients from the females of song, who are full
to overflowing of vitality and geniality, their excesses
being occasional, and mere episodes in a laborious
life. There is nothing dreamy about them; they
proceed to the work in hand with the same spirit of
thoroughness and heartiness with which they perform
their ordinary avocations, and get as much joviality
out of the occasion as good liquor and high health
and spirits can extract. Nor with all the plainness
of speech of these bacchanalian chronicles is good
taste violated; they are redeemed from vulgarity by
the finest humour, and transferred to the region of
genuine comedy. The topers are not soakers, like
their modern representatives, who are quite insipid,
and entirely devoid of the game or "go" which
characterised their sisters of old. In the "Antiquary" Scott gives us a presentment of a gossiping
female party whose tipple was "sinning water"—a
corruption of cinnamon water—fortified, no doubt,
by sterner stuff. Mrs. Mailsetter, Mrs. Shortcake,
and Mrs. Heukbane, the wives of the postmaster and
of the chief baker and chief butcher of Fairport, are
shown up, as far as Scott's good nature would allow
him, to our conceptions of the vulgar "cosy" party
of ignorant, uneducated females, whose husbands are
possessed of a little substance, and whose symposia
are apart from their husbands' knowledge.

"Andro and his Cutty Gun," printed in the "Tea-

Table Miscellany," was a great favourite with Burns,
who described it to Mr. George Thomson as the
work of a master. Elsewhere he describes it as
" a spirited picture of a country alehouse, touched
off with all the lightsome gaiety so peculiar to the
rural muse of Caledonia." It seldom fails to be sung
at rustic bridal-parties and house-heatings—

> " Blithe, blithe, and merry was she,
> Blithe was she but and ben ;
> And weel she lo'ed a Hawick gill,
> And leuch to see a tappit-hen."

A Hawick gill was a measure peculiar to that district,
and equivalent to half-a-mutchkin. Authorities
differ as to the capacity of a " tappit hen," so named
from the resemblance of the knob on the top of the
measure to a crested fowl. According to Mr. Chambers, it implies a quart-measure, but according to the
author of " Waverley " it contained at least three
English quarts. Mr. Burton says, " The brief air
devoted to this blithe toperess was wanted for a
fairer spirit, and Burns addressed to a reigning beauty
of his day the well-known—

> ' Blithe, blithe, and merry was she,
> Blithe was she but and ben ;
> Blithe by the banks of Earn,
> But blither in Glenturit Glen.' "

With all deference to the opinion of the historian
of Scotland, and with all respect for the muse of
Burns, his song by no means equals its prototype.
The loss of it would be a matter of little moment;

the loss of the older one would cause a serious gap
in the convivial poetry of Scotland :—

" She took me in, she set me down,
    And hecht to keep me lawin-free,
But, cunning carline that she was,
    She gart me birle my bawbee.

" We lo'ed the liquor weel eneuch,
    But, wae's my heart, my cash was done
Before that I had quenched my drouth,
    And laith was I to pawn my shoon.
When we had three times toomed our stoup,
    And the neist chappin new begun,
In started, to heeze up our hope,
    Young Andro wi' his cutty gun.

" The carline brought her kebbuck ben,
    Wi' girdle-cakes weel toasted brown ;
Weel does the canny kimmer ken
    They gar the scuds gae glibber down."

The next verse contains an expressive monosyllabic
word, perfectly harmless, but which Mr. Chambers
considers naughty, for he expunges the line and sub-
stitutes another for it, which has the double merit of
getting quit of the homely word and making nonsense
of the verse.

The "canny kimmer," to make her ale more in
demand, brings her bebbuck ben—that is, her cheese
—with well-toasted girdle-cakes. According to
Burns, who may be presumed to have despatched a
quantity of them in his day, "these oatmeal cakes
are kneaded out with the knuckles, and toasted over
the red embers of wood on a gridiron. They are remarkably fine, and a delicate relish when eaten warm

with ale. On winter nights the landlady heats them,
and drops them into the quaigh to warm the ale."
The blessing of the hero of "Todlin Hame" falls on
the guidwife because—

> "She gi'es us white bannocks to relish her ale."

Every country and condition of society has its own
relish for its liquor. The Spaniard and Italian relish
their wine with olives, while the homely Englishman
of old made his ale more palatable by dropping into
it a roasted crab. Lever's military heroes spur their
flagging appetites with broiled bones and devilled
kidneys; while the humble Scot given to toping is
too often in the same category with Hugo Arnot of
facetious memory—*like his meat*—for he devours
raw speldrins with his whisky. In "Twelfth Night,"
to Sir Toby Belch's famous query to Malvolio—"Dost
thou think, because thou art virtuous, there shall be
no more cakes and ale?" the clown responds—"Yes,
by Saint Anne; and ginger shall be hot i' the mouth
too." Sir Toby's cakes and ale correspond exactly to
the "girdle-cakes" and "scuds" of the song under
review. The toperess proceeds with her narrative—

> "We ca'ed the bicker aft about,"

nor did they cease till they were completely upset—

> "And aye the cleanest drinker out
> Was Andro wi' his cutty gun.
>
> "He did like ony mavis sing,
> And, as I in his oxter sat,

> He ca'ed me aye his bonnie thing,
>   And many a sappy kiss I gat.
> I hae been east, I hae been west,
>   I hae been far ayont the sun ;
> But the blithest lad that e'er I saw
>   Was Andro wi' his cutty gun."

The author, whoever he was, was a man of true genius. He has handled a subject having all the elements of vulgarity and pruriency without being in the least degree vulgar or prurient, and with such spirit and liveliness that the whole scene is before us. Well might Burns ask Thomson, "Are you not quite vexed to think that those men of genius, for such they were, who composed our fine Scotch lyrics, should be unknown ? It has given me many a heartache."

In the prologue to "The Wife of Bath," Chaucer makes that very astute and managing female avow her love of wine—

> " Then couthe I daunce to an harpé smale,
>   And synge y-wys as eny nightyngale,
> When I had dronke a draught of sweeté wyn.
> Metellius, the foulé cherl, the swyn,
> That with a staf byraft his wyf hir lyf
> For sche drank wyn, though I had been his wyf
> Ne schuld he nought have daunted me fro drink."

The unknown Scottish lyrist has represented his toperess enjoying the caresses of the gallant Andro without suggesting anything indelicate, which is more than can be said of the father of English poetry in the passage just quoted, at least in its sequel

The late Charles Kirkpatrick Sharpe so greatly
admired the following picture of feminine joviality
that he printed some copies of it, with the music,
for presentation to his friends—

> " There were four drunken maidens
>   Together did convene,
> From twelve o'clock in a May morning
>   Till ten rang out at e'en,
>   Till ten rang out at e'en,
>   And then they gie'd it ower.
> And there's four drunken maidens
>   Doun i' the Nether Bow.
>
> " When in came Nelly Paterson,
>   With her fine satin gown :
> ' Come, sit about, ye maidens,
>   And give to me some room,
>   And give to me some room,
>   Before that we gie't ower.'
> And there's four drunken maidens
>   Doun i' the Nether Bow.
>
> " When peacock and pigeon,
>   And hedgehog and hare,
> And all sorts of fine venison,
>   Was well made ready there,
>   And set before the maidens
>   Before they gie'd it ower.
> And there's four drunken maidens
>   Doun i' the Nether Bow," &c.

We remember no similar lyrical literature belonging to England. In "Martin Chuzzlewit" there is a
female compotation narrated in prose, which from
certain adjuncts has become classical. The compotators are Mrs. Gamp and Betsy Prig, in the apartment of the former. Their tipple is poured from a

teapot; the pair are ineffably vulgar, and Betsy Prig
tries to overreach her hostess by helping herself,
unconsciously as it were, to more than her share
of the banquet. There is no joviality, nor geniality;
nothing but sordid soaking, characteristic perhaps of
the age and vocation of the pair. How unlike the
boisterous merriment and *abandon*, the geniality and
exuberant vitality of the heroine of "Andro and
his Cutty Gun!" And the drinking has been preceded, *more Anglico*, at least according to Scotch
opinion or prejudice, by gross feeding.

The heroines of the last two songs quoted are
unmarried. The "four drunken maidens" are
necessarily so, and we infer as much of the heroine
who nestled so cosily in Andro's "oxter." Marriage
would—at least should—put an end to such unpro-
fitable daffin. Indeed, the guidwife with the cares
of a family on her head has not only, as a rule, no
inclination for dissipation herself, but is apt to inter-
fere with that of her husband. This sometimes elicits
censorious remarks, not from the husband himself,
but from his drouthy cronies—

> " There's Johnie Smith has got a wife,
>   Wha scrimps him o' his cogie ;
> If she were mine, upon my life,
>   I'd douk her in a bogie."

The doings of ladies of high rank during last
century in the oyster-cellars of Edinburgh, noticed
above, may appear incredible to ladies of the present
day, who hear them for the first time. But of their

literal truth there is not the slightest doubt. To-day the least coarse form of these orgies would not be tolerated for a moment, and any female, however high her rank, who should patronise it, would find herself at once in Coventry. But manners may change for something more decorous, without it being a necessary corollary that the morals are improved. The safety and comparative harmlessness of these frolics lay in their openness. There was no attempt at conceal-ment, and no consciousness of indecorum. Wherever there is premeditated and cautiously-guarded secrecy, there is criminality, more or less, and a sowing of the seeds of possible shame and grief.

CHAPTER VI.

ROMANTIC SONGS AND BALLADS.

It is not unusual to class Romantic and Legendary songs and ballads under the same head. But there is a difference: Legendary poems contain a supernatural element, and deal with popular superstitions; while Romantic poems have for their subject some striking event, of a heroic or tragic cast, and for the most part purely imaginary. The Romantic ballad literature possesses high poetical merit, and of seven Scottish ballads of this class named by Mr. Chambers, that accomplished critic of the old national literature says that their publication by Dr. Percy did more to create a popularity for the " Reliques " than all the other contents of the book. Unfortunately, these seven are challenged by Mr. Chambers as being spurious antiques, unable to give a good account of themselves. Percy printed them either "from a manuscript copy sent from Scotland," or "from a written copy that appears to have received some modern corrections," or from copies of ballads printed at the instance of Lady Jean Home, or of Sir David Dalrymple, or from some equally suspicious source. We might admit, without impugning their genuineness and antiquity, that they may have received, and probably did receive, some amendments and refinements.

Romantic songs and ballads appeared early in British literature, and they at once acquired unbounded popularity. The oldest Scottish romantic poem is the Sir Tristrem of Thomas the Rhymer, discovered in the Advocates' Library by Ritson, and edited and published by Scott in 1804. The subject of Sir Tristrem was exceedingly popular. He is supposed to have been one of the Knights of the Round Table, and his exploits have been celebrated in French, Italian, Spanish, and German. Raynouard informs us that a romance of Tristrem and Yseult once existed in the language of the troubadours; while the Welsh annals refer to a romance on the same subject of a much earlier date, and represent the hero as belonging to authentic history. Continental Romanticists make Sir Tristrem a native of Bretagne, but the Rhymer assigns his birth to Cornwall, and makes no reference to the history of King Arthur. The cycle of Arthurian romance is of high antiquity and deep interest, and has recently acquired exceptional importance and prominence from its having been taken by Mr. Tennyson as the basis of some of the finest, most polished, and most musical poetical compositions in the English language—

> " What resounds,
> In fable or romance, of Uther's son
> Begirt with British and Armoric knights."

The Border seems to have been the cradle of Romantic fiction in Britain, and the pre-eminence of Scottish poetry in this department must be ascribed in great measure to the exertions of those wandering minstrels who sang in bower and hall the exploits, triumphs, and defeats of imaginary, or at least traditional heroes, and the beauty, love, constancy, or infidelity of their mistresses or wives. Carlisle, the Carduel of the Arthurian romances, and the favourite residence of the King himself, was at that time included in Scotland; his " Round Table " was between Carlisle and Penrith; his "Seat" was at Edinburgh; Galloway belonged to Sir Gawain; and Merlin was buried at Drumelyier on the Tweed. There is, besides, a strong dash of romance in the Scottish character, which could hardly fail to be reproduced in the popular poetry. Even the stern and somewhat repulsive form in which Scottish superstitions developed themselves, though partly due to the sterile and savage aspect of the country, was also the result of the high-strung romantic temperament of the people, still as rampant as of yore.

" Romantic " may be opposed to " Prosaic." A prosaic man moves in a rut, lives conventionally, and would recoil from doing anything that might be considered eccentric as he would from contact with a leper. He is one of what are called " safe men," and nobody would ever dream of his setting the Thames on fire. The romantic man, on the contrary, despises conventionalities, hews out a path for himself, and, while not unfrequently looked on as a dangerous character, is one of those whose enterprise keeps society from stagnating. A prosaic man will submit to conditions of restraint and monotony that would fret a romantic man to death, for he must be free and unfettered as the winds of heaven. The War of Independence; the struggles and ultimate triumphs of the Reformers, who did not, like their brethren of England, accept a reform made to their hand by the sovereign, but modelled theirs after their own design, allowing no interference therewith; and, above all, the Jacobite struggles, from which the English Jacobites, from the more prosaic nature of the English character, kept aloof, are all proofs of the inherently romantic character of the Scot. The sacrifices made by the several denominations who have hived off from time to time from the National Church, are further proofs, if further were needed, of this peculiar trait.

"Hardyknute," once a general favourite, and perhaps still so, is now known to be spurious; and "Sir Patrick Spens" we have already dealt with as an historical ballad. "Gil Morrice," a second edition of which appeared in 1755, had an advertisement prefixed to it setting forth that the preservation of the poem was owing "to a lady who favoured the printers with a copy, as it was carefully collected from the mouths of old women and nurses;" and "any reader that can render it more correct or complete" was requested to favour the public with these improvements. Owing to the success of Home's tragedy of

" Douglas," which was brought out on the Edinburgh stage in 1756, and the composition of which was suggested by " Gil Morrice," the ballad acquired great popularity. Percy adopted it into his " Reliques," with four additional verses which had been produced and handed about in MS. These were evidently some of the improvements advertised for, and formed part of " ingenious interpolations," admitted by the Bishop himself to have been introduced in the process of revisal. Their style is florid, and does not at all resemble that of the genuine old ballad. In Percy's MS. collection there was a very old, imperfect copy of this ballad, having the leading features the same —namely, a baron killing, under the influence of jealousy, a young man who had sent a message to his lady to grant him an interview in the greenwood, and who was not a gallant plotting an intrigue, but a son by a former connection, whose existence she had kept concealed from her husband. Percy permitted Mr. Jamieson to transcribe the old imperfect copy referred to above, which he published in his " Popular Ballads and Songs." In 1827, Mr. Motherwell, in his " Minstrelsy," gave a version taken from the recitation of a woman, then seventy years of age, who had carried it in her memory from her youth. Probably her version, though divested of many modernisms, and altered into something really resembling the genuine old ballad, was an unconscious transformation by the common people of the highly ornate printed version of 1755 into what better pleased ears

accustomed to the measure and diction of our old
poetry. Aytoun's version is founded on that of
Motherwell, and contains some stanzas from the old
imperfect version published by Jamieson; while
others, transferred from " Lady Maisry," are eliminated. The indiscretion of the messenger, who
divulged his mission before the " bauld baron," could
not be checked by the lady, though she stamped with
her foot and winked with her eye, and though the
bower maiden, to screen her mistress, asserted that
the message was to her; for—

> " Trifles light as air
> Are to the jealous confirmation strong
> As proofs of holy writ ;"

and so Gil Morrice was done to death as he sat
gaily singing in the greenwood, " kaiming his yellow
hair." Instead of " Gil Morrice," " Childe Maurice "
should, perhaps, be substituted as the more correct
title. From the resemblance of parts to " Hardyknute " and " Sir Patrick Spens," Mr. Chambers
fixes on Lady Wardlaw as the author of the improved revisal.

" Edward, Edward," printed by Percy in the
" Reliques," from a copy sent to him by Sir David
Dalrymple, Lord Hailes, is also challenged as a
modern fabrication by some person of culture, and
as of no older date than 1700. It is strikingly
melodramatic, and consists of a dialogue between
a youth who has killed his father, and his mother,
on whom he imprecates the curse of hell for the evil

counsels which she had given him. The phraseology
as given by Percy is undoubtedly modern. Divested
of its grotesque orthography, the first stanza runs
thus—

> " ' Why does your brand sae drop wi' blude,
>   Edward, Edward ?
>   Why does your brand sae drop wi' blude,
>   And why sae sad gang ye, O ?'

> " ' O, I hae killed my hawk sae gude,
>   Mither, mither :
>   O, I hae killed my hawk sae gude,
>   And I hae nae mair but he, O.'"

Mr. Motherwell has given a ruder version of the
same ballad, still current in Scotland, entitled " Son
Davie," and Professor Aytoun conjectures that this
is the original one, which Lord Hailes altered into
the more polished " Edward" before sending it to
Percy. This, however, may be an erroneous supposition, for it is easy to find reasons in support of
a foregone conclusion.

" The Jew's Daughter," a Scottish ballad, printed
by Percy from a MS. copy sent from Scotland, and
founded on the practice attributed to the Jews of
crucifying or otherwise murdering Christian children,
is challenged by Mr. Chambers as belonging to what
he designates the Wardlaw group on very slender
grounds. These are not so much parallel expressions
as the general style. He cites one parallel passage—

> " She rowed him in a cake of lead,
>   Bade him lie still and sleep ;
>   She cast him in a deep draw-well,
>   Was fifty fadom deep."

He adds, "This must remind the reader of Sir Patrick Spens—

> " Half ower, half ower to Aberdour,
> It's fifty fathom deep."

A hypothesis must be shaky indeed when recourse is had to such very slender buttressing.

Percy printed " Gilderoy " " from a written copy that seems to have received some modern corrections." The versification is remarkably smooth, and Professor Aytoun says that the corrected copy was the work of Sir Alexander Halket, Lady Wardlaw's brother. This was an unfortunate statement, for Mr. Chambers shows that Lady Wardlaw had no brother, and that no Sir Alexander Halket appears in her family history. It was adapted from a rude street ditty, commemorating the hanging in 1636 of Patrick Macgregor, commonly called Gilderoy, and containing, according to Percy, " some indecent luxuriances that required the pruning-hook." Wonderful stories are told of this wild cateran, such as his having picked the pocket of Cardinal Richelieu while celebrating high mass in the Church of St. Denis, Paris, having by a significant gesture taken the King, who noticed the attempt on his Eminence, into his confidence, who was too much of a gentleman to betray him; his having carried off, with consummate assurance, a trunk of plate from the house of the Duke of Medina-Celi at Madrid; and his having attacked Oliver Cromwell and two servants while travelling from Portpatrick to Glasgow, and shooting the Protector's horse, which fell upon him and broke his leg. He placed Oliver on an ass, tying his legs under its belly, and dismissed him to seek his fortune. Such an aspiring spirit could scarcely fail of coming to grief in the long-run; and we find that, for theft, and for being a common cateran, he was hanged at the Cross of Edinburgh in the year above mentioned. His lieutenants graced the woody along with their chief, who, in consideration of his higher rank, was accommodated with a more exalted gibbet than his coadjutors. His sorrowing widow thus comments on the misfortune that befell her dear—

> "Wae worth the louns that made the laws,
>   To hang a man for gear ;
> To reive of life for sic a cause
>   As stealing horse or mear !
> Had not these laws been made sae strict,
>   I ne'er had lost my joy,
> Wi' sorrow ne'er had wat my cheek,
>   For my dear Gilderoy.
>
> "If Gilderoy had done amiss,
>   He might have banished been ;
> Ah, what sair cruelty is this,
>   To hang sic handsome men ! "

We have already analysed "Edom o' Gordon." It remains, therefore, to notice only two of the seven of those suspicious ballads that, according to Mr. Chambers, gave the "Reliques" the greater part of their popularity—"Young Waters" and the "Bonny Earl of Murray." Percy gave "Young Waters" "from a copy printed not long since at Glasgow, in

one sheet octavo. The world was indebted for its
publication to Lady Jean Hume." Mr. Chambers,
who quotes the entire ballad, finds in it many passages
parallel to others in "Gil Morrice," a parallelism in
its rhymes to those of Sir Patrick Spens, and a
marked similarity between the tone and words of
the last lines to those of a verse in "Hardyknute."
Percy had it suggested to him that the ballad
covertly alluded to the indiscreet partiality shown by
Anne of Denmark, Queen of James VI., for the
bonny Earl of Murray. Aytoun admits that it may
have been founded on some real event in Scottish
history, but does not consider that any conjecture
that has been hazarded as to its origin is sufficiently
plausible to warrant its adoption. It is, however, a
tale of royal jealousy—

> " About Yule, when the wind blew cool,
>   And the round tables began ;
> Ah ! there is come to our King's court
>   Mony a weel-favoured man."

The Queen, looking over the castle wall, sees
young Waters riding to the town, splendidly
equipped. A wily lord asks her whose is the fairest
face in the company, when she replies that it is that
of young Waters. The King, who overhears her,
filled with jealousy, says she might have excepted
him. She replies with much ingenuity—

> " ' You're neither lord nor laird,' she says,
>   ' But the King that wears the crown ;
> There's not a knight in fair Scotland
>   But to thee maun bow down.' "

The King would not be appeased, and, in spite of the entreaties of the Queen, the handsome knight was executed on the heading-hill at Stirling.

"The Bonny Earl of Murray" is called by Percy a Scottish song, but he gives us no information as to the source from which he obtained it. The Earl, who was the son-in-law of the Regent Murray, having married his eldest daughter and heiress, was a nobleman of great accomplishments, and very popular. He was, besides, extremely handsome, and it was commonly supposed that he was regarded with favour by the Queen. This is openly expressed in the ballad—

> "He was a braw gallant,
>   And he rade at the glove,
> And the bonnie Earl o' Murray,
>   Oh! he was the Queen's love!"

It is probable that the assumption is one of those libels which the commonalty have in all ages been too apt to file against the illustrious by birth and station. Murray was slain at his seat of Duniebristle, in Fife, by the Earl of Huntly, and his kinsman, Gordon of Buckie, in the prosecution of a feudal quarrel. As the King, James VI., did not call Huntly to account, and was even supposed to have privately countenanced him, he was thought to have been actuated by jealousy.

The authorship, or at least a revival almost equivalent to authorship, of "Young Waters," having been assigned to Lady Wardlaw, because of its resem-

blance in several respects to "Gil Morrice," to "Sir
Patrick Spens," and to "Hardyknute," Mr. Chambers
assigns the authorship of "The Bonny Earl of
Murray" to the same quarter, from the resemblance
of the last stanza to the second of "Young Waters."
The respective stanzas are—

> "O lang will his lady
>   Look owre the Castle Downe,
> Ere she see the Earl of Murray
>   Come sounding through the town."

And—

> "The Queen looked owre the castle wa',
>   Beheld baith dale and down,
> And then she saw Young Waters
>   Come riding to the town."

That there is a similarity is undeniable; but is it
such and so great as to prove identity of authorship?
Many will not readily concede this. However, any
opinion on ballad literature advanced by Mr.
Chambers deserves respectful consideration, for he
was not only specially well informed in this department, but he was eminently fair; though a man who
has adopted a theory, especially if it has been ela-
borated by himself, is ingenious in finding arguments
and proofs to support it.

Beyond the bounds of Percy's "Reliques," Mr.
Chambers finds five ballads passing as old which seem
to him peculiarly liable to suspicion, either from their
general beauty, or from special strains of thought and
expression. These are—"Johnie o' Bradislee," "Mary

Hamilton," the "Gay Goshawk," "Fause Foodrage,"
and "The Lass of Lochryan." Johnie o' Bradislee
seems to have been an outlaw and deer-stealer, and is
supposed to have possessed the Castle of Morton, Dum-
friesshire—a tradition which is favoured by its being
said, in the concluding stanza, that he lies buried at
Durisdeer, a parish in the neighbourhood. Formerly
this district was a celebrated deer-forest, and Johnie
is represented as going to the hunting with his dogs
against the advice of his mother. Having shot a
deer, and sated himself with venison, he fell asleep
between his two greyhounds, when he was seen by
a silly auld carle, who informed the seven foresters
of his helpless condition. These, having attacked
the outlaw, were all slain by him but one, and of that
one he broke three ribs and the collar-bone. He then
laid him "twa-fald" over his horse, and bade him
carry the tidings home. Johnie himself, however,
had received a mortal wound, and he commissions a
starling to let his mother know of her son's fate.
This is done, and Johnie is conveyed to his mother's
home on a bier composed of hazel and sloe-thorn.
There are several different copies extant of this ballad, which Aytoun says is very ancient. The version
in the "Border Minstrelsy" was obtained by selecting the stanzas of greatest merit from each copy,
while Aytoun framed his by collating Scott's version
with various others. But Mr. Chambers holds that
the ballad is by the author of "Gil Morrice" and
"Gilderoy" because of the following parallelisms—

> "The starling flew to his mother's bower stane,
>   It whistled and it sang,
> And aye the overword o' its tune
>   Was 'Johnie tarries lang.'"

This, from "Johnie o' Bradislee," is compared with the following stanza from "Gil Morrice"—

> "Gil Morrice sat in gude green-wood,
>   He whistled and he sang ;
> 'O, what means a' the folk coming ?
>   My mother tarries lang.'"

In all ballad literature there are commonplaces which are no one's property, and can be appropriated at will without the charge of plagiarism. "Tarries lang" seems to be one of these ; it occurs in "Brown Adam" in the "Border Minstrelsy." Therefore its presence in a ballad can of itself in no way indicate the authorship. Another suspicious circumstance, according to Mr. Chambers, is the minute description of the person and apparel of Johnie. The auld carle says—

> "His cheeks were like the roses red,
>   His neck was like the snaw ;
> He was the bonniest gentleman
>   My eyes they ever saw.

> "His coat was o' the scarlet red,
>   His vest was o' the same ;
> His stockings were o' the worset lace,
>   And buckles tied to the same.

> "The shirt that was upon his back
>   Was o' the Holland fine ;
> The doublet that was over that
>   Was o' the Lincoln twine.

> "The buttons that were upon his sleeve
> Were o' the gowd sae guid," &c.

"This," he adds, "is mercery of the eighteenth and no earlier century. Both Gilderoy and Gil Morrice are decked out in a similar fashion; and we may fairly surmise that it was no man's mind which revelled so luxuriously in the description of these three specimens of masculine beauty, or which invested them in such elegant attire." To this it is replied that in the ballad of "Childe Owlet," in Buchan's collection, which, from the revolting nature of the story, was neither conceived by a female mind nor written by a female hand, a "silken seam," "a chain of gold," and "green stays' cord" are introduced, after the manner of the mercery of the deer-stealing Johnie. The ballad, of which various versions are extant, has been pronounced by competent critics to be very ancient. Were we to make any independent criticism, it would be to the effect either that the author knew nothing practically about hunting of the deer, or that hunters in old times arrayed themselves differently from the deerstalkers of our day, who clothe themselves purposely in the roughest attire, and whose necks, however white naturally, soon become completely tanned. It may be noted that Robin Hood and his merry men never need to stalk their deer. They shoot them down, when they are needed, with as little trouble as if they were cooped up in a pinfold.

Mary Hamilton was an attendant on Queen Mary,

and was brought to the gallows-tree for the murder of her illegitimate child. Some suppose that she may have had an intrigue with Darnley, but no such circumstance is on record. Knox, however, in his "History of the Reformation," states that a French-woman who served in the Queen's chamber had given birth to and destroyed an illegitimate child, and was executed for her crime. Mr. Chambers, from passages in it resembling others in "Johnie o' Bradislee" and "Young Waters," makes all three the production of one mind—"a mind having a great command of rich and simple pathos." One stanza of this ballad was a prime favourite with Burns, and he more than once quotes it—

> " O little did my mother think,
>   That day she cradled me,
> What lands I was to travel ower,
>   What death I was to dee ! "

The ballad bears indubitable internal evidence of an earlier era than that of Lady Wardlaw, but the concluding stanza of Aytoun's version is certainly modern—

> " O little did my father think,
>   That day he held up me,
> That I, his last and dearest hope,
>   Should hang upon a tree."

The "Gay Goshawk" is attempted to be proved the production of the same feminine mind by an elaborately minute comparison with "Johnie o' Bradislee," "Hardyknute," "Sir Patrick Spens," " Gil Morrice," " Clerk Saunders," and the " Douglas

Tragedy." It was first published in the "Border Minstrelsy," partly from a ballad with the same title in Mrs. Brown's collection, and partly from a MS. of some antiquity in Scott's possession. Motherwell published a version, which Aytoun prefers to Scott's. Aytoun furnished, by collation and excision, a version shorter than any previous one. The story told in the ballad is this :—The Scottish lover of an English maiden, who is kept secluded from him by her relations, commissions the Gay Goshawk to carry a letter from him to his mistress, in which she is informed that he is dying by long waiting for her. She returns an answer by the same messenger, commencing thus—

> " Gae bid him bake his bridal bread,
>   And brew his bridal ale ;
> And I shall meet him at Mary's Kirk,
>   Lang, lang ere it be stale."

She asks this boon from her father—namely, that if she die in England he will bury her in Scotland, and in the third kirk (Aytoun's version makes it the fourth) which they come to. After the manner of Juliet, the lady simulates death by drinking a sleep-ing-draught. To test the reality of her decease her cruel stepdame drops a drop of burning lead on her bosom, and her father is overwhelmed with grief because his daughter has died without the priest. Uprose her *seven* brethren and hewed to her a bier, while her *seven* sisters sewed a shroud for her. The funeral procession starts, and visits the several kirks

indicated by the lady before her death. At St.
Mary's Kirk there stood spearmen all in a row, Lord
William being their chief. He ordered the mourners
to set down the bier that he might look upon the
corpse. Touching the lady's hand her colour
returned, and, smiling on her lover, she asked him
for a morsel of bread and a glass of wine, as she had
fasted three long days, or, according to Aytoun's
version, nine, for his sake. She orders her brothers
home, commends herself to her aged father, and
imprecates woe on her cruel stepdame. Mr.
Chambers's criticism is very ingenious, but scarcely
conclusive for his theory. He notes the style of
luxurious description, so different from the bald style
of the genuine ballads of the people, and the circumstance that it is *seven* brothers who hew her bier
and *seven* sisters that sew her shroud, *seven* being
the number of the brothers of the heroine in " Clerk
Saunders," who discover the sleeping lovers, and
seven being the number of the brothers of Lord
William's mistress in the " Douglas Tragedy."
Seven is a conventional number in ballad literature,
and cannot be taken as evidence that compositions
in which it occurs have a common origin.

The ballad of " Fause Foodrage," first published
by Scott in the " Border Minstrelsy," chiefly from
the MSS. of Mrs. Brown of Falkland, was at first
suspected by the editor to be a modern fabrication
from the line—

" The boy stared wild like a grey goshawk,"

which is nearly identical with a line of "Hardy-knute." He made the strictest inquiry into its authenticity; but every doubt was removed by the evidence of a lady of high rank (Lady Douglas of Douglas), who had not only been amused by the ballad in her infancy, but could repeat many of the verses. Scott's inference, therefore, was that the author of "Hardyknute" had quoted from the old ballad, which is, at the least, as reasonable as that of Mr. Chambers, that Lady Wardlaw had copied from herself. In fact, Mr. Chambers has so much faith in his critical faculty that he not only saddles Lady Wardlaw with the authorship, but fixes the era of its composition. "It may be observed," he says, "that much of the narration is in a stiff and somewhat hard style, recalling 'Hardyknute.' It was probably one of the earlier compositions of its author." The "probably" is quite superfluous; his mind is made up.

The story of the ballad may be given briefly thus : —The nobles of the land conspire against King Honour and his Queen, who had been barely four months married. Fause Foodrage undertakes to kill the King. He slays the porter in his lodge, possesses himself of his keys, and, penetrating to the royal bed-chamber, pierces the King to the heart with a knife long and sharp. The Queen entreats him to spare her life till it be seen whether the child which she carries be lad or lass. The assassin consents to this, at the same time assuring her that if it be a female it shall be well nursed, but that if it be a male, it shall be hanged as soon as born. Her bower is carefully guarded, but as the time of her travail approaches, she contrives to render her custodiers helplessly drunk, and " big, big " though she is grown, effects her escape by the window, " thro' the might of Our Ladye." She brings forth a son in the " swine's stythe," and Wise William's wife having gone to her, the Queen prevails on her to exchange her female for the royal male child. A secret mode of giving each other intelligence of the welfare of their respective children is agreed on in language, according to Mr. Chambers, " violently figurative." When King Honour's son reached manhood, Wise William took him a-hunting. As they passed a fair castle, Wise William informed his companion that of that castle he was the rightful heir, and that his mother was kept a prisoner by Fause Foodrage, who had, before his birth, killed his father. The youth swears that he will slay the traitor and free his mother that same night.

> " He has set his bent bow to his breast,
>   And leaped the castell wa' ;
> And soon he has seized on Fause Foodrage,
>   Wha loud for help 'gan ca'."

Wise William, of course, is rewarded with the best half of his land, and the "turtle-dow" is made his wife.

The last ballad we shall review in the light of Mr.

T

Chambers's criticism is "The Lass o' Lochryan." It
was first published in a perfect state in the "Border
Minstrelsy," the text consisting of verses selected
from three MS. copies and two taken from recitation.
In this version, which, according to Aytoun, contains
"a deal of extraneous and superfluous matter, which
interferes with, and to a certain extent detracts from,
the simplicity of the story," the lover, Lord Gregory,
is represented as confined by fairy charms in a stately
tower built on a high rock in the sea. A much finer
version was given by Mr. Jamieson in his "Popular
Ballads and Songs," and a completer one by Buchan
and by Motherwell with the title of "The Drowned
Lovers." Burns's song of "Lord Gregory" was suggested by the ballad we are dealing with. Mr.
Chambers assigns it to the Wardlaw group, from its
containing coincidences of treatment and expression
with "Sir Patrick Spens," "The Gay Goshawk," and
"Mary Hamilton." The story is well known. Annie,
who had loved Lord Gregory in usual ballad fashion,
sets out in a ship to find her lover. After a protracted
voyage, she arrives at his castle with her young son
in her arms on a dark and stormy night. He is
asleep, and his mother answers hapless Annie's call,
personating Lord Gregory, and bidding her go home, as
he had got another love. Annie re-embarks. But meanwhile, Lord Gregory, who had dreamed that Annie
had stood at his door, and been refused entrance,
is told by his mother that the case was actually so.
He hastens quickly to the strand, and sees Annie's

ship bearing away. A fierce storm arose; the ship was rent in twain, and the corpse of Annie came floating through the foam, with his young son in her arms. Plunging into the sea, he drew her ashore by her yellow hair—

> "O first he kissed her cherry cheek,
>   And syne he kissed her chin,
> And sair he kissed her bonny lips,
>   But there was nae breath within."

In "Sweet William's Ghost" occurs the following stanza :—

> "Thy faith and troth thou's never get,
>   Nor yet will I thee lend,
> Till that thou come within my bower,
>   And kiss my cheek and chin."

Comparing these two stanzas from different ballads, Mr. Chambers observes, "To kiss cheek and chin in succession is very peculiar; and it is by such peculiar ideas that identity of authorship is indicated." But such kissing is not peculiar to the group of ballads challenged by him; in proof of which it is only necessary to observe that it is noted in "The Bent sae Brown," "Sweet Willie and Fair Maisry," "James Herries," and "The Water o' Wearie's Well," all in Buchan's collection.

The romantic ballad-poetry of Scotland is extensive and of singularly high excellence. But there are degrees of excellence. There are ballads, as "Young Huntin'," and "The Douglas Tragedy," pos-

sessing wonderful power, elevation, pathos, and
beauty; and there are others equally pathetic, as
"The Trumpeter of Fyvie," which are rude in structure and homely in expression. But this is what
might be expected. The poetic faculty is granted in
different degrees: it may be improved by cultivating
it, and deteriorated by neglecting it. In the last-
mentioned ballad the daughter of the Miller of Tifty
describes her passion with perfect naturalness and
feeling, but with no approach to the high-strung romance of many, nay of most, of the romantic ballads
dealing with a thwarted affection—

> " I wish the rose were in my breast,
>   For the love I bear the daisy ;
> So blyth and merrie as I wad be,
>   And kiss my Andrew Lammie.
>
> " The first time I and my love met,
>   Was in the Wood o' Fyvie ;
> He kissed and he dawted me,
>   Ca'd me his bonny Annie.
>
> " He kissed my lips a thousand times,
>   And aye he ca'd me bonny :
> And aye sinsyne himsel' was kind,
>   My bonny Andrew Lammie."

Her father and mother and brother beat her
cruelly for cherishing a passion displeasing to them,
and Annie died ere morn. Her lover, hastening to
the churchyard on his return from Edinburgh, watered
Annie's grave with his tears, and died for her sake.
That there should be such differences of treatment

and expression, the chivalrous in one ballad and the homely in another, means nothing more than that there is a Spenser and a Bloomfield, a Shakespeare and an Allan Ramsay, a Lovelace and a love-struck peasant (not a Burns), inspired for the moment by passion.

CHAPTER VII.

§ 1. THE FAIRY MYTHOLOGY.

ELVES or fairies were spirits of a lower order, not of the diabolical class, but generally harmless, though sometimes freakish, in many respects resembling the sylvan deities of classical mythology. They were not associated in the popular imagination with what was terrible or repulsive, and the belief in their existence and sprightly character was unchecked and but little modified by the introduction of Christianity and the anathemas of the Church. The word *elf* is said to be of Gothic origin, and to signify a spirit, or that which blows or moves, and to be from the same root as the river *Elbe.* Grimm connects it with the Latin *albus* (white), thus indicating their essentially harmless, if not benign disposition. The etymology of *fairy* is by no means settled. To connect it with the French *fée* and the Italian *fata* advances us no step in our inquiries. The term occurs frequently in the Romance language, from which it was introduced into the lays of the old English poets. It has been conjectured that the word has an Eastern origin, being

identical with the Persian *peri*, which, passing into
Europe through the medium of the Arabic, in the
alphabet of which language there is no *p*, would
naturally become *feri*. The graceful and comparatively harmless character of the European elf favours
this etymology. The non-demoniacal character of
the peri, or rather its approximation to the angelic,
has been finely conceived and expressed by Moore—

> "One morn a Peri at the gate
>   Of Eden stood, disconsolate ;
> And as she listened to the springs
>   Of life within, like music flowing,
> And caught the light upon her wings
>   Through the half-open portal glowing,
> She wept to think her recreant race
> Should e'er have lost that glorious place !"

The prototype of the English fairy is said to be the
duergar of the Scandinavians, a dwarfish spirit dwelling in the mountains, with more of the human than
of the angelic nature, malignant rather than beneficent, and vindicating its preternatural origin only
by superior wisdom, by foreknowledge, and by extraordinary skill in the manufacture of arms. The
duergar must have undergone much transformation
before it could assume the airy, graceful, and semi-
beneficent character of the English elf; and Scott
accounts for the modifications which the elfin superstition underwent by, amongst other causes, the traditions of the East. This refers to the intercourse
of France and Italy with the Moors of Spain, who
were familiar with the peris of the Persian mythology,

females beautiful as angels, with nothing malignant about them, and because of their exclusion from heaven evoking in the human breast the liveliest sympathy.

Chaucer, in "The Wife of Bath's Tale," says—

> "In old time of the King Artour,
> Of which that Breton's speken great honour,
> All was this land fulfilled of faerie;
> The Elf Queen, with her jolly company,
> Danced full oft in many a grene mead."

The Fairy Queen, when addressed by "True Thomas" on Huntly Bank as the mighty Queen of Heaven, replies—

> "'O no, O no, Thomas,' she said,
> 'That name does not belong to me;
> I'm but the Queen of fair Elfland
> That hither have come to visit thee.'"

In the ballad of "Alison Gross," the Queen of the 'Seely Court"—that is, of the Happy Court, or of the fairies—restores to his proper shape a wretched wight who, by the charms "of the ugliest witch in the North Countrie," had been transformed into an ugly worm or reptile, and made to "toddle about the tree." Shakespeare's Titania is amiable to everybody but Oberon, her husband, with whom she had a very pretty quarrel, so they had separated and kept rival courts. Puck says to Titania's messenger, who had been sent

> "To dew her orbs upon the green"—

that is, the rings of richer and taller grass sometimes

found in fields, and which were formerly supposed to
have denoted the footsteps of fairies—

> " The King doth keep his vigils here to-night ;
> Take heed the Queen come not within his sight,
> For Oberon is passing fell and wrath."

The quarrel of Oberon and Titania, and their
reconciliation, are the subjects of two well-known
paintings by Sir Noel Paton.

The cause of the quarrel between their majesties
of Elfland was because Titania—

> " As her attendant hath
> A lovely boy, stol'n from an Indian king ;
> She never had so sweet a changeling :
> And jealous Oberon would have the child
> Knight of his train, to trace the forests wild.
> But she, perforce, withholds the loved boy,
> Crowns him with flowers, and makes him all her joy."

It seems, therefore, that human intercourse was
not impossible to the female elf. Thomas the
Rhymer's intrigue with the Fairy Queen is the subject of a well-known ballad. She warned Thomas
as they approached her lord's castle to be discreet :
" I would rather be drawn with wild horses than he
should know what hath passed between you and
me." Guy de Lusignan, Count of Poicton, married
the fairy Melusina, who brought him a large family.
The armorial bearing of persons so born is a leopard,
because that animal was supposed to be the offspring
of the pard and the lioness—that is, an unnatural
birth. Hence a leopard was the cognisance both of

Merlin the prophet and of the first Duke of Guyenne, because they were born of faëry in adultery.

The fairies of Scotland were a less amiable race than those of more southern climes—even than those of England, whose characters were modified in the popular mind by the airy and graceful fancy portraits of Shakespeare, Drayton, and Mennis. The Scottish fairy retained much of the repulsive character of her Scandinavian prototype. This has been accounted for by the more austere character of the people, by the influence of Presbyterianism, and by the stern and sterile aspect of the country. While the English fairies were merely freakish and sportive in their amusements, galloping night by night through lovers' brains, on courtiers' knees, o'er ladies' lips or o'er a courtier's nose, tickling a parson's nose with a tithe-pig's tail, or driving o'er a soldier's neck, each of whom is thus made to dream appropriate dreams, their northern sisters were believed to be vassals of the Prince of Tophet, or at least in close alliance with him; and while some from their dealings with mankind appeared to be beneficent and others malignant, the race being thus divided into good and bad, both classes were the agents of the same foul fiend, the one seeking to be feared and the other to be loved. Hence it was the custom to propitiate them in some way; sometimes by making them an offering, as at the Cheese Well on the top of Minchmuir, sacred to the fairies, and into which passers-by were wont to throw a piece of cheese as an oblation; but more commonly by studiously speaking well of them, as, though invisible, they were always present, and were supposed to be prompt in resenting and punishing any disrespect. Thus the Highlanders called them "Men of peace;" the Irish, "The good people or friends;" and the Lowland Scotch "The good neighbours."

Though their usual dress was green, the fairies of the moors were sometimes clad in heath-brown or lichen-dyed garments, whence the epithet of "elfin grey." Their abodes varied in different localities, but their favourite residence was in the interior of conical green hills, on the slopes of which they danced by the light of the moon, imprinting on them by their tread those circular grassy tufts, sometimes withered, but sometimes of a deep green, within which it was reputed dangerous to sleep. The Irish fairies occasionally inhabited those ancient burial-places known as tumuli or barrows, while some of the Scottish fairies took up their abode under the "doorstane" or threshold of some particular house, to the inmates of which they administered good offices. A favourite occupation was the chase, and the belated traveller often heard them sweeping past in invisible procession, their presence being known by the ringing of the bells attached to their bridles, or to the manes of their horses. Of the Queen of Faëry who revealed herself to "True Thomas" it is said—

" At ilka tett of her horse's mane
Hung fifty siller bells and nine."

They sometimes borrowed mortal steeds, and appear to have been choice in the matter of horse-flesh; for the Isle of Man fairies, contemning the diminutive Manx ponies, selected the English and Irish horses, which they rode desperately, as might have been expected from such agile and light-weight jockeys, and left them panting in their stalls in the morning, with dishevelled manes and tails. In the jocular but richly-imaginative description of Queen Mab, given by Mercutio in "Romeo and Juliet," it is said—

" This is that very Mab
That plats the manes of horses in the night;
And bakes the elf-locks in foul sluttish hairs,
Which, once untangled, much misfortune bodes."

Cattle were favourite objects of elf attention, and cattle seized with cramp, or any sudden and violent affection, were said to be elf-shot. The flint arrow-heads found in Northern countries, and now copiously treasured in museums, were long known as elf-arrows.

Of nothing could the inhabitants of Elfland be less readily suspected than of religious or theological partialities. But Dr. Corbett, Bishop of Oxford and Norwich in the beginning of the seventeenth century, makes them good Catholics, and represents them as deserting England when Protestantism gained the ascendant. His poem is styled "A Proper New Ballad, entitled the Fairies' Farewell; to be sung or whistled to the tune of the 'Meadow Brow,' by the learned; by the unlearned, to the tune of 'Fortune.'"

In the speech of Puck, quoted above, that jovial spirit says of Titania's lovely boy, the cause of quarrel or bone of contention between the King and Queen of Elfland—

"She never had *so sweet a changeling.*"

This is in reference to the most reprehensible of the practices attributed to the elves—that of carrying off and exchanging children. The special agent in transactions of this sort was Queen Mab. Mercutio says—

"O then, I see, Queen Mab hath been with you.
She is the fairies' midwife ; "

which would be better read, "She is the fairy midwife." "She is so called," says Mr. Halliwell, "because it was her supposed custom to steal new-born babes in the night, and to leave others in their place." Unchristened infants were most obnoxious to this calamity—a peculiar power over them, from the corruption of human nature, being from an early period supposed to be vested in demons. Hence, among other reasons, the custom of introducing them into the bosom of the Church when only a few days old. The interval between birth and baptism was an anxious one to the mother. Adults were carried off only when they had in some flagrant manner violated fairy law, such as sleeping on a fairy mount, where the fairy court was for the time being held, or when they had unwittingly or unwarily taken part in their nocturnal revelry. Various charms were resorted to to procure the restoration of a child that had been thus kidnapped, the most efficacious of which was the roasting of the monster of fairy brood that had been substituted for it on the live embers. It was supposed that this would vanish, and the genuine child be found in the spot whence it had been taken.

This practice of stealing children was not a mere caprice, perpetrated for the purpose of inflicting pain on mortals, or for mischief pure and simple. They had to sacrifice a victim to the devil every seventh year, otherwise expressed as paying the "kane" or "teind"—that is, tithe or tenth—to hell, just as in the myth of Theseus and Ariadne the Athenians had to send every ninth year seven youths and seven maidens to Crete to be devoured by the Minotaur. In the indictment of Alison Pearson (28th May 1586), who suffered death for witchcraft, and for consulting with evil spirits, it is written:—"That he (her cousin, Mr. William Sympsoune) told her he was taken away by them, and he bid her sign herself that she be not taken away, for the teind of them are tane to hell everie year." It was natural, if we may use such an epithet in connection with beings that were non-natural, that they should prefer to pay the tribute in the form of a mortal, or, as it is somewhere expressed in connection with this subject, "a human mortal," than in that of one of their own race.

The mode of recovering a person thus provided as tribute to the infernals is minutely described in " The Young Tamlane."

Persons carried off to Elfland were not permitted to revisit their old haunts till the expiry of seven years. Seven years more having expired, they again disappear, and are no more seen among men. This period of seven years is evidently connected with and suggested by the septennial tribute to the infernal potentate. The Fairy Queen dismisses "True Thomas" at the end of seven years, that he may escape this horrible doom, stipulating, however, that he should return when summoned. In the English ballad on the subject she thus addresses her paramour—

> " To morne of helle the foulle fende
>   Among these folke shall chese his fee ;
>   Thou art a fayre man and a hende,
>   Fful wele I wot he wil chese the.

> " Ffore all the golde that ever myght be
>   Ffro heven unto the worldys ende,
>   Thou bese never betrayede for me ;
>   Therefore with me I rede the wende.

> " She broght hym agayn to the Eldyntre,
>   Underneth the grene wode spray,
>   In Huntley Banks ther for to be ;
>   Ther foulys syng bothe nyght and daye."

We fail to discover whether Hogg's " Bonnye Kilmeny " had been in Elfland or in Heaven. She is said to have been in " the land of thochte." The following lines point to Elfland—

> " Quhair gat ye that joup of the lilye scheine,
>   That bonny snoode of the byrk se greine,
>   Ane these rosis, the fayrist that ever war seine ? "

But as it was her stainless purity that commended her to the spirits of the country, who had brought her away from the snares of men,

> " That synn or dethe scho nevir may ken,"—

this does not comport with Fairyland, whose Queen we have just discovered in an intrigue. At all events, the poem was evidently suggested by "Thomas the Rhymer," and, like the second part of that ballad in the "Border Minstrelsy," contains numerous prophecies or visions of incidents in the history of Scotland. The typical seven years are thus introduced—

> " Quhan sevin lang yeiris had cumit and fledde,
>   Quhan greif was caulm and hope was deade,
>   Quhan scairse was rememberit Kilmeny's neme,
>   Lete, lete in the gloamyn, Kilmeny cam heme."

At page 4, vol. iv. of the "Noctes Ambrosianæ," republished in the collected edition of Professor Wilson's works, there is a poem of exquisite melody entitled the "Fairy's Burial." It invests the fairy sisters with the most simple and affecting human feeling. The first stanza is as follows—

> " Where shall our sister rest ?
>   Where shall we bury her ?
>   To the grave's silent breast
>   Soon we must hurry her !
>   Gone is the beauty now
>   From her cold bosom !
>   Down drops her livid brow,
>   Like a wan blossom ! "

Among the best known of the fairy ballads is that of "Thomas the Rhymer," who disappeared from the haunts of men and spent seven years in the elfin world, where the Queen of the Fairies furnished him with that prophetic lore which made him the favourite prophet of his countrymen. He was also a poet—whence his appellative or sobriquet of "Rhymer," being the reputed author of the romance of "Sir Tristrem," the earliest existing specimen of English verse. He flourished in the reign of Alexander III. of Scotland, and resided at Ercildoune, a village on the Leader in Lauderdale, where the ruins of his ancient tower are still to be seen. His patronymic is supposed to have been Lermont or Learmont, though he is designated "Rymour" in a charter in the Chartulary of the Trinity House of Soltra, preserved in the Advocates' Library, by which his son and heir conveys to the convent of the Trinity of Soltra "his whole land, with all its pertinents, which he possessed by inheritance in the tenement of Ercildoune." But we are told that it was not unusual to designate men in that age and in that district, not merely colloquially, but even in legal documents, by the sobriquet which they had acquired from some personal or other peculiarity, or from some marked gift or accomplishment. Thomas was long one of the most important personages in the legendary history of his country, and, in addition to his prophetic gifts, was credited with being a skilled magician.

As Thomas lay on Huntly Bank, on the slope of

the Eildon Hills, near Melrose, he saw a ladye bright, with a skirt of "grass-green silk," and a "mantle of the velvet fyne,"—

"Come riding down by the Eildon tree."

So bright and beautiful was the apparition, that he imagined it to be the Queen of Heaven, when he was informed that it was "but the Queen of fair Elfland." Uncontrollable passion seized him, but he was warned that if he dared to kiss her lips she should be sure of his body, and become arbiter of his fate—

    " 'Betide me weal, betide me woe,
       That weird shall never daunton me !'
    Syne he has kissed her rosy lips,
       All underneath the Eildon tree.

    " ' Now, ye maun go wi' me,' she said—
       'True Thomas, ye maun go wi' me ;
    And ye maun serve me seven years,
       Through weal or woe, as may chance to be.'

    " She's mounted on her milk-white steed,
       She's ta'en True Thomas up behind ;
    And aye, whene'er her bridle rang,
       The steed gaed swifter than the wind."

In an ancient manuscript quoted by Scott, a more elaborate and detailed account is given of the lady and her accompaniments. Her palfrey was dapple grey, and all about her shone like the sun on a summer's morn. Her saddle was of ivory, bright with many a precious stone. The rest of her horse furniture was equally magnificent. Like another Amazon, she bore a hunting-horn about her neck, on which she sometimes blew, while sometimes she sang; and she had besides a bow in her hand, and arrows under her girdle. She led three greyhounds in a leash, and raches, or hounds of scent, ran by her in couples. In the ballad no transformation takes place in her after the consummation of their amour, but in the MS. referred to she then becomes a most hideous hag, with the one side of her head black and the other grey; her eyes seemed to drop from her head; her gay clothing is all away; and her body is "as blue as any lead." It was not till she came in sight of her lord's castle that her beauty of person and accessories returned. The manuscript quoted by Scott is in the British Museum. There are other two manuscript romances on the subject of Thomas and his prophecies; the Cambridge copy has been printed by Mr. Jamieson, and that in the Cathedral Library of Lincoln by Mr. David Laing.

The Queen, accompanied by Thomas, rode on with lightning speed until they reached a desert wide, and left all living land behind them.

> "'Light doun, light doun now, Thomas,' she said,
>   'And lay your head upon my knee ;
> Light doun, and rest a little space,
>   And I will show you ferlies three.'"

These are the "braid, braid road," or path of wickedness, stretching over a lawn of lilies, and by some called the road to heaven; the narrow road thick beset with thorns and briars, the path of right-eousness, after which but few inquire; and lastly, a narrow road, winding about the ferny brae, which conducts to Elfland, to which they must go that night. She further cautions Thomas to hold his tongue whatever he might hear or see, for if he uttered a word in Elfland he should never revisit his own countrie—

"O they rade on, and farther on,
   And they waded through rivers abune the knee,
And they saw neither the sun nor the moon,
   But they heard the roaring of a sea.

"It was mirk, mirk night, there was nae stern-light,
   And they waded through red blude to the knee;
For a' the blude that's shed on the earth
   Rins through the springs o' that countrie.

"Syne they came to a garden green,
   And she pu'd an apple frae a tree—
'Take this for thy wages, True Thomas;
   It will give thee the tongue that will never lie.'"

This implies that he had received the gift of prophecy, of foretelling with certainty future events in the history of Scotland, and is the reason why the Rhymer is distinguished by the epithet "True." Thomas, however, like a man of the world, especially a Border man, given to chaffering over the price of horses and nolt, and like a courtier and gallant looking for favour from prince and peer and grace from lady fair, was not particularly satisfied with the gift of the tongue that would never lie. It was an inconvenient boon, and so far a loss that he could never afterwards avail himself of his tongue as a weapon of fence and offence—as an instrument with

which to obtain advantage over the weaker and less
wise of his fellows. Thomas was henceforth a prophet in spite of himself. Scott remarks—"It is
plain that had Thomas been a legislator instead of a
poet, we have here the story of Numa and Egeria."
Thomas's unavailing rejection of this dubious gift is
thoroughly ingenuous :—

> " ' My tongue is my ain !' True Thomas he said,
>   ' A gudely gift ye wad gie to me !
>   I neither docht to buy nor sell,
>   At fair or tryste where I might be.
>
> " ' I docht neither speak to prince nor peer,
>   Nor ask for grace from fair ladye !'
>   ' Now hauld thy tongue, Thomas !' she said,
>   ' For as I say so must it be.'
>
> " He has gotten a coat of the even cloth,
>   And a pair o' shoon of the velvet green ;
>   And till seven years were come and gane
>   True Thomas on earth was never seen."

In the MS. already referred to, a very rich description is given of the garden through which they passed,
of the fruits which it contained, and of the birds
which sang among the boughs. The festivities and
festal preparations of the royal castle were on a
gorgeous scale. There was all manner of minstrelsy,
harp and fiddle, ghittern and sawtry, lute and "rybid,"
or rebeck, while the dance of knights, and ladies clad
in rich array, moved gaily on. In the kitchen lay
the carcases of forty harts, hounds were lapping the
blood, and cooks were standing with their dressing-
knives brittling the deer. One day the lady told

Thomas he could remain no longer, which grieved the Rhymer sorely. He thought he had not been more than three days, though seven (three in MS.) years had passed away, and to save him from becoming tribute to hell, the Fairy Queen brought him once more to the Eildon tree. For several years Thomas remained in his tower of Ercildoune, disseminating his prophecies, many of which are still preserved. He was under an obligation to return to Elfland whenever his mistress should wish it. At length, while enjoying himself in his own dwelling with the Earl of March and other friends, it was suddenly reported to him that a hart and hind from the forest were quietly traversing the street of the village in the direction of the tower. He recognised these as the messengers of his fate, and rising from the board, followed them into the forest, whence he has not yet returned, though it was long believed that he should once more revisit the earth. His prophecies, with historical comments, will be found in Chambers's " Popular Rhymes of Scotland." They are alluded to by Barbour, Winton, and Blind Harry, though merely historically, as predictions of events that had happened, and of which they were speaking, and not in *ipsissimis verbis.* In the " Border Minstrelsy " there is a second part of " Thomas the Rhymer" given, a sort of cento composed of predictions partly ancient and partly modern, popularly attributed to True Thomas.

Of the King of Elfland we have no distinct por-

traiture either as to person or character. He seems
to have been a good, easy, indolent, placable, luxurious man, leaving the conduct of affairs to his more
active and enterprising Queen, who did not scruple to
hoodwink him and play him false. In the confession
of Isobel Gowdie, Aulderne, Nairnshire, who was in-
dicted for witchcraft in 1662, the following sketches
of their elfin majesties are to be found. The confession is edited by Robert Pitcairn, W.S., author of
the interesting volume, "Criminal Trials in Scotland
from 1428 to 1624." She said—"I was in the
Downie hills, and got meat there from the Queen of
Faërie, more than I could eat. The Queen of Faërie
is brawly clothed in white linens and in white and
brown clothes; and the King of Faërie is a braw man,
weel-favoured, and broad-faced." Aytoun, with a
good deal of humour, says that Thomas yet remains
in Elfland, "an honoured, and possibly an unsus-
pected, guest."

Because True Thomas was "a fayre man and a
hende," or, as another version has it, "a large man
and a hende," he ran the strongest risk of being
appropriated as the devil's "teind." In like manner
the Young Tamlane, because he was "sae fat and fair
of flesh," was in a condition equally perilous. In the
first case, the Queen of Elfland herself effects the
rescue; in the second it is Tamlane's lover, following
instructions which he gave her, and which proved
efficacious, to the grief and mortification of the Fairy
Queen—

" Up then spake the Queen o' Fairies,
    Out of a bush o' broom :
' She that has borrowed young Tamlane
    Has gotten a stately groom !'

" Up then spake the Queen o' Fairies,
    Out of a bush of rye :
' She's ta'en away the bonniest knight
    In a' my companie !

" ' But had I kenned, Tamlane,' she says,
    ' A lady would borrow thee,
I wad hae ta'en out thy twa grey een,
    Put in twa een o' tree !

" ' Had I but kenned, Tamlane,' she says,
    ' Before ye cam frae hame,
I wad hae ta'en out your heart of flesh,
    Put in a heart o' stane !

" ' Had I but had the wit yestreen
    That I hae coft this day,
I'd hae paid my kane seven times to hell,
    Ere you'd been won away !'"

The Young Tamlane, who describes himself as a
son of Randolph, Earl Murray, having been sent for,
when just turned of nine, to keep his uncle company
in hunting, hawking, and riding, was while on his
journey thrown by a sharp north wind into a dead
sleep, and fell from his horse, when the Queen of
Fairies carried him off for herself. Had it not been
for the teind to hell at the end of every seven years,
the term of which was just at hand, and for which
his good condition pointed him out as the probable
victim, he would never have tired to dwell in fairyland. When a child he had loved Janet, daughter of
Dunbar, Earl March ; and on the night preceding

Hallowe'en, when the fairy court sweeps in procession through England and through Scotland and
"the warld sae wide," he suddenly appears to Janet,
who, with feminine caprice, had gone to Carterhaugh
by the light of the moon. With the freedom characteristic of the heroes of ballad poetry, he uses the
privilege of a husband without the blessing of Holy
Kirk. Janet asks him if he had ever been "sained
in Christentie," or been received into the Church by
baptism. He then reveals himself to her as her boy-
lover, and explains the reason of his appearance. He
can only be saved from becoming the tribute of hell
by her "borrowing" him on the following night.
Burns refers to this fairy pageant in his Hallow-
e'en "—

> " Upon that night, when fairies light,
>   On Cassilis Downans dance,
>   Or owre the lays, in splendid blaze,
>   On sprightly coursers prance," &c.

And an older poet, Alexander Montgomery, in his
" Flyting against Polwarth," has a similar reference—

> " In the hinder end of harvest, on All-Hallowe'en,
>   When our good neighbours dois ride, if I read right,
> Some buckled on a bunewand, and some on a bean,
>   Ay trottand in troups from the twilight ;
> The King of Pharie and his court, with the Elf Queen,
>   With many elfish incubus was ridand that night."

Tamlane tells Janet in what manner he is to be
borrowed. She was to abide at Miles Cross, and go
to Miles Moss between twelve and one with holy
water in her hand, "and cast a compass round." In

reply to the question as to how she was to know him among the fairy throng, he answers that three courts or companies would pass by—the first of which she was to allow to pass, the second she was to salute reverently, and in the third, or head court, all clad in robes of green, in which the Queen herself rode, he would be found upon a milk-white steed, with a gold star in his crown—an honour awarded to him because he was a christened man—

> " 'Ye'll seize upon me with a spring,
>   And to the ground I'll fa',
> And then you'll hear an elrish cry
>   That Tamlane is awa'.
>
> " 'They'll turn me in your arms, Janet,
>   An adder and a snake ;
> But haud me fast, let me not pass,
>   Gin ye would be my maik.
>
> " 'They'll turn me in your arms, Janet,
>   An adder and an aske ;
> They'll turn me in your arms, Janet,
>   A bale that burns fast.
>
> " 'They'll shape me in your arms, Janet,
>   A dove, but and a swan ;
> At last they'll shape me in your arms
>   A mother-naked man :
> Cast your green mantle over me—
>   And sae shall I be wan !' "

Though gloomy was the night and eerie the way, Janet, in her green mantle, repaired to the spot that had been indicated to her, and executing her instructions to the letter, was rewarded with the rescue of "her ain true lover" from Elfland, and from the

fate that awaited him there. It is to be observed
that, contrary to the law as laid down in Tamlane,
namely, that a rescue can be effected within seven
years, the popular opinion was, that to be valid
according to fairy law, it must be effected within a
year and a day.

The hero of this ballad is known by different
names, all implying an original identity, such as
Tamlane, Tamlene, Tam-a-line, Tam o' the Linn, Tom
Linn, Thom of Lynn, Thomalin, and Thomlin. He
is supposed to be the same with Tom Thumb, and in
Scott's version of the ballad Tamlane is called "a
wee, wee man." In one or other of his names he
appears frequently in Scottish verse, generally, however, in some ludicrous aspect, as might be expected
of a man no bigger than one's thumb. For
example :—

> " Tam o' the Linn he had three bairns,
> They fell in the fire in each other's arms ;
> 'Oh !' quo' the boonmost, ' I've got a het skin ;'
> ' It's hetter below,' quo' Tam o' the Linn."

An analogous idea is expressed in the old English
song in a comedy entitled " The longer thou livest,
the more fool thou art," quoted by Ritson in the
dissertation prefixed to his " Ancient Songs and
Ballads "—

> " Tom a Lin and his wife and his wife's mother,
> They went over a bridge all three together ;
> The bridge was broken, and they fell in—
> ' The devil go with all,' quoth Tom a Lin."

"Young Tamlane" has been claimed as the finest of the legendary ballads of Scotland. Mr. Chambers, however, classes it among the spurious ballads—at least, among those which have passed through the improving hands of Lady Wardlaw. He notices a slight affinity between it and "Sweet William's Ghost," and tricks of expression and construction common to it with "Sir Patrick Spens," "Gil Morrice," "The Gay Goshawk," and "Sweet Willie and Fair Annie." It must be conceded to Mr. Chambers that in Scott's version of the ballad there are some stanzas of so modern a cast as to prove that this poem has been at least tampered with. For example, the account of fairy life—

> "And all our wants are well supplied
> From every rich man's store,
> Who thankless sins the gifts he gets,
> And vainly grasps for more."

Scott says that his edition is the most perfect that has yet appeared. He collated the printed copies with Glenriddel's MSS., and with several recitals from tradition. He also obtained a copy from a gentleman residing near Langholm, said to be very ancient, though the diction is somewhat of a modern cast. Undoubtedly many of the stanzas are of a most suspiciously modern cast.

At the same time, there can be no doubt of the substantial antiquity of the ballad, as it is mentioned in the "Complaynt of Scotland." Aytoun's version differs materially from Scott's. He rejected the verses which were avowedly modern, and others which were evident interpolations of an earlier period, as well as all doubtful stanzas, and by so doing he has much improved the ballad. For any additions that he made he had warrant in other versions, and he acknowledges his obligations to a fragment given by Mr. Maidment in "A New Book of Old Ballads," printed at Edinburgh in 1843 for private circulation.

§ 2. WITCHES AND WITCHCRAFT.

A less pleasing superstition than the Fairy Mythology is that connected with witches and witchcraft. In Exodus xxii. 18, it is written, "Thou shalt not suffer a witch to live." Hence at one time a confirmed belief among all classes in the existence of such beings, and hence also the barbarously-cruel judicial enactments against them, nowhere more barbarous and cruel than in Scotland. The Reformation in this country, instead of modifying, intensified the severity of the procedure against sorcerers and witches: "as if," says Scott, "human credulity, no longer amused by the miracles of Rome, had sought for food in the traditionary records of popular superstition." As we found that the Scottish elf was a much less amiable being than her English sister, so also, and from the same cause—namely, the sterner aspect of the country—the Scottish witch was a much more dangerous and formidable entity than the

English. In his "History of Civilisation," Mr. Buckle remarks—"Even the belief in witchcraft has been affected by these peculiarities; and it has been well observed, that while, according to the old English creed, the witch was a miserable and decrepit hag, the slave rather than the mistress of the demons which haunted her, she, in Scotland, rose to the dignity of a potent sorcerer, who mastered the evil spirit, and, forcing it to do her will, spread among the people a far deeper and more lasting terror." Hogg has embodied this idea in his "Witch of Fife," who is no "miserable and decrepit hag," but a potent ruler of the elements—

> " The second nycht, quhan the new moon set,
>   O'er the roaring sea we flew ;
> The cockle-shell our trusty bark,
>   Our sailis of the green sea-rue.
>
> " And the bauld windis blew, and the fire-flauchtis flew,
>   And the sea ran to the skye ;
> And the thunner it growlit, and the sea-dogs howlit,
>   As we gaed scouryng by.
>
> " And aye we mountit the sea-green hillis,
>   Quhill we brushit thro' the cludis of the hevin ;
> Than sousit dounright, like the stern-shot light,
>   Fra the liftis blue casement driven," &c.

There are but few Scottish ballads into which witchcraft is introduced as an element. Before proceeding to give a rapid notice of these, we will glance at the difference between the Scottish witch and the witch of Scripture—at least, of the Authorised Version.

The Scottish witch was supposed to have made a compact with the devil, whose vassal she henceforth was, whom she revered and adored, and on whose patronage and assistance she could calculate in her diabolical proceedings. There was supposed to be affixed somehow to the infernal bond, written in her own blood, the stamp or seal of the demon, and there were revellings of Satan and his hags, who, assisted by a familiar lent by Satan, entered into combinations and took active measures against the health, happiness, and prosperity of mankind. The witch was an impersonation of pure malignity. Not so, to anything like an equal extent, was the Jewish or Pagan sorcerer, though Pagan magic was sometimes employed for malicious purposes, as may be learned from the Canidia of Horace. The malignant character of modern witchcraft is attributed to its having "found a point of attachment in a certain cycle of Christian dogma—the doctrine of a devil, and a world of demons over which he rules" (Dr. J. Clark Murray's "Ballads and Songs of Scotland," p. 4).

It has been disputed whether the magicians of Pharaoh, who aided him in his contention with Moses, were sorcerers or sleight-of-hand men. The former view has obtained favour with divines of all ages and sects, who believed that men in ancient times could obtain the assistance of fallen spirits. The inquiry is vain and profitless. The *witch* of Exodus xxii. 18, would have been better translated *sorceress*. Elsewhere in Scripture occurs the sentence, "he used

witchcraft," in which is involved the idea of prayer;
but the word in which this is implied was, like many
other sacred terms of the Syrians, restricted by the
Hebrews to idolatrous services. It means literally to
pronounce or mutter spells, which is just equivalent
to practising magic. The witches of Scripture proceeded by charms or spells, and applied medicines
as remedies or poisons. They gathered herbs, which
were supposed to owe their efficacy to magic spells,
and were most potent when culled by moonlight.
In the moonlight scene (act v. scene i.) of the
"Merchant of Venice," Jessica says to Lorenzo—

> " In such a night
> Medea gathered the enchanted herbs
> That did renew old Æson."

When the magic herbs failed to produce the desired effect, if that were injurious, poison was resorted
to, as in the modern instance of Sir Thomas Over-
bury, who was actually poisoned when the arts of
Forman and other sorcerers failed. The Hebrew
sorceress pretended to rule the elements, and to
direct the effects ascribed to their operation, to regulate the conjunctions of the stars, to tell what were
lucky and what unlucky days, to avail herself of the
power of invisible spirits, and of demons or inferior
deities. Somewhat after the manner of Prospero in
the "Tempest," she might say "by the aid of
spirits and other supernatural powers—

> I have bedimmed
> The noontide sun, called forth the mutinous winds,

And 'twixt the green sea and the azured vault
Set roaring war: to the dread rattling thunder
Have I given fire, and rifted Jove's stout oak
With his own bolt: the strong-based promontory
Have I made shake, and by the spurs plucked up
The pine and cedar. Graves at my command
Have waked their sleepers—oped, and let them forth,
By my so potent art."

The references to witchcraft in Scripture do not involve its reality. Those who dealt in magic were more or less pretenders. Scott, in his " Letters on Demonology and Witchcraft," observes, that " The sorcery or witchcraft of the Old Testament resolves itself into a trafficking with idols and asking counsel of false deities; or, in other words, into idolatry." Hence the justification of the statute which, in a monotheistic theocracy, denounced it with death. Satan was not permitted to assist the sorcerer, according to the modern idea, for he was himself powerless against Job till he received a very circumscribed commission. A good deal of rubbish has been written about the Witch of Endor. She was rather a necromancer—one of those who pretended to call up the spirits of the dead to converse with the living. Saul, in consulting her, rendered himself obnoxious to the same punishment as that denounced by the statute against sorcerers—a punishment which had often been inflicted at his own instance. Many are of opinion that the whole transaction resolves itself into imposture and collusion. Saul was nervous and excitable, and, as Patrick observes, through a long series of vexations and anxieties absolutely delirious. Nor did he himself see the apparition; it was only described to him, and the whole proceedings were conducted under the cloud of night. Others think that the deception was managed by means of ventriloquism. Others, again, accept the narrative as literally true. Who shall decide when the most learned doctors disagree?

The witches in "Macbeth" are, of course, Scottish hags, but they may with greater propriety be termed creatures of Shakespeare's brain. They are hellish monsters, brewing hell-broth, having cats and toads for familiars, loving midnight, riding on the passing storm, and devising evil against such as offend them. They crouch beneath the gibbet of the murderer, meet in gloomy caverns amid earthquake convulsions, or in thunder, lightning, and rain. Shakespeare seems to have taken some hints from Middleton's play of "The Witch," but he has improved on Middleton, for *Nihil tetigit quod non ornavit.*

The conception of the Scottish witch, as we know it, was formed in the Middle Ages, and was derived from the gloomy Scandinavian mythology, in which the Fatal Sisters and other female destructive agencies were leading articles of belief. Witches were supposed to be capable of practising metamorphoses on their victims, and of transforming themselves into animal shapes, generally cats, crows, and hares. The following is the charm which they repeated when they wished to become hares—

> " I sall go intill a hare,
> With sorrow, sigh, and meikle care,
> And I sall go in the devil's name ;
> Ay while I come back again."

While traversing the country in the guise of hares, they were often sorely bestead from the pursuit of hounds, who had no respect for the devil's vassals, and the bites and scratches which they received while in the leporine form were visible on their bodies when they resumed the human shape, the charm for effecting which was—

> " Hare, hare, God send thee care !
> I am in a hare's likeness now,
> But I sall be a woman e'en now ;
> Hare, hare, God send thee care ! "

When travelling in the shape of cats, if they met with any of their neighbours, they addressed them thus—

> " Devil speed thee ;
> Go thou with me ! "

when they were immediately transformed into the feline shape, and accompanied them. When metamorphosed as crows, they were larger than the ordinary bird, and perched on trees. These particulars we learn from the confession of Isabel Gowdie (1662), as given in the Appendix to Pitcairn's "Criminal Trials." A magician who changed himself into a wolf, that he might ravage and devastate, was called a wehrwolf.

No instance of a witch practising actual meta-

morphosis on a victim is to be found in our judicial
records.   Two such instances, however, occur in
ballad literature—the one in " Alison Gross," and the
other in the ballad entitled by Scott " Kempion,"
given from Mrs. Brown's MS., with corrections from
a recited fragment, but designated by Buchan,
Motherwell, and Aytoun, " Kemp Owain," and in
their version excelling " Kempion " in poetical merit.
Both these ballads invest the superstition under
review with a sublimer aspect than that worn by the
witchcraft of the " Criminal Trials."   The former is a
monologue, in which a male describes how he was
wooed by Alison Gross—

> "The ugliest witch in the North Countrie,"

who trysted him one day to her bower and gave him
many fair speeches and caresses—

> "She straiked my head, and she kaimed my hair,
>   And she set me down saftly on her knee ;
> Says, ' Gin ye will be my leman sae true,
>   Sae mony braw things as I wad you gie.' "

The last two lines are nearly identical with two in
Goethe's " Erl-King."   The unfortunate object of her
desire rudely repels her solicitations, though enforced
by the production of—

> " A mantle o' red scarlet,
> Wi' gowden flowers and fringes fine ; "

followed by that of—

> " A sark o' the saftest silk,
> Weel wrought wi' pearls about the band ; "

and then by—

> "A cup o' the gude red gowd,
>   Weel set wi' jewels sae fair to see."

> "'Awa! awa! ye ugly witch!
>   Stand far awa, and lat me be ;
> For I wadna ance kiss your ugly mouth
>   For a' the gifts that you could gie.'"

Naturally her resentment knew no bounds, and producing a silver wand, she turned herself three times round and round, muttering a spell, on which her victim fell senseless to the ground, and was transformed into an ugly worm, doomed to "toddle about the tree." Each Saturday night she resumed her caresses, but in vain, till at last on Hallowe'en, as the "Seely Court" was riding by, the queen had compassion on him, and restored him to his own proper shape. In this instance her elfin majesty was rather the "gude neighbour" of the Lowland mythology than one in any way in league with Satan.

In "Kemp Owain," as given by Aytoun, "dove Isabel" is thrown by her witch stepmother into Craigy's Sea, where she was to remain till she was "borrowed" with three kisses. Meanwhile she was horribly transformed—

> "Her breath grew strang, her hair grew lang,
>   And twisted twice about the tree ;
> And all the people, far and near,
>   Thought that a savage beast was she :
> That news did come to Kemp Owain,
>   Where he lived far beyond the sea."

Hastening to Craigy's Sea, he looked on the savage beast, who came about with a swing and begged him to kiss her, bribing him for the first kiss with a royal belt, the wearing of which would prevent blood ever being drawn from his body; for the second with a royal ring; and for the third with a royal brand—ring and brand possessing each the same virtue as the belt.   He found his reward, for—

> " Her breath was sweet, her hair grew short,
>   And twisted nane about the tree ;
> And smilingly she cam' about,
>   As fair a woman as fair could be."

In " Kempion," as given by Scott, the lady was metamorphosed into a " fiery beast " or dragon, condemned to swim over the salt seas, and climb Estmere crags—probably the rocky cliffs of Northumberland, as opposed to Westmoreland—till she should be relieved by Kempion, the king's son, which is effected precisely as in "Kemp Owain." The tale of "Kempion" bears a strong resemblance to that of the " Laidley Worm of Spindelston Heugh," attributed to Duncan Fraser of Cheviot, a bard of the fourteenth century, but in reality composed, or at least rewritten, by the Rev. Robert Lambe, vicar of Norham.   A similar transformation is recorded in Boiardo's " Orlando Inamorato."

In the ballad of " Willie's Ladye," Willie is represented as having wooed and married a lady contrary to the wishes of his witch-mother, who, by way of revenge, prevents her from being lighter of her young bairn. Consequently she sits in her bower with pain, and to the great grief of her husband, who in vain

attempts to bribe his mother with many precious
gifts to remove her enchantments. His mother, however, is inexorable. Her desire is that Willie's wife
should die, and that he should wed another May.
The difficulty is solved by Billy Blind, a familiar
genius resembling the Brownie, who counsels Willie
to shape an image, "bairn and bairnly like," out of
"a loaf o' wace" or wax, and to invite his mother
to the christening. His mother, taken by surprise,
discloses the means by which the charm could be
removed—

> "O wha has loosed the nine witch-knots,
> That were amang that ladye's locks?
> And wha's ta'en out the kames o' care,
> That were amang that ladye's hair?
> And wha's ta'en down that bush o' woodbine,
> That hung between her bour and mine?
> And wha has killed the master-kid
> That ran beneath that ladye's bed?
> And wha has loosed her left foot-shee,
> And let that ladye lighter be?"

Willie, acting on the knowledge thus obtained, is
soon blessed with a bonny son. A similar spell,
wrought by Hera on Alcmena when she was pregnant
to Zeus, was dissolved by a stratagem of her maid
Galanthis. In the "Golden Ass" of Apuleius a similar legend occurs, in which the wretched woman,
having carried her burden eight years, *velut elephan-
tum paritura, distenditur.* We may pass over the
more vulgar attribute of the Scottish witch by which
she could draw the milk from her neighbours' cattle

by means of tugging at a hair-rope, and chanting the following charm :—

"Cow's milk and mare's milk,
And every beast that bears milk,
Between Saint Johnstoun's and Dundee,
Come a' to me, come a' to me."

In Ben Jonson's "Masque of Queens," presented at Whitehall, February 2, 1609, there is a song of the witches, which, however, as might have been expected from "Rare Ben," is drawn rather from classical antiquity than from the legendary lore of his own country. We give one verse as a sample. There are eleven witches, the tenth of whom sings—

" I from the jaws of a gardener's bitch
Did snatch these bones, and then leaped the ditch ;
Yet went I back to the house againe,
Killed the black cat, and here is the braine."

The judicial persecutions of supposed witches both in England and in Scotland form one of the saddest chapters in history. Statutes against sorcery and witchcraft were passed in England in 1541 and again in 1562, but the number of trials—at least of convictions—was not increased. The leading English clergy regarded all claims to supernatural power by witches as impostures, which were best encountered by treating them with contempt. It was not till the accession of the Scottish James to the English throne that the war against witchcraft broke out in its full fury. James had distinguished himself by publishing a book on "Dæmonologie" at Edinburgh in 1597, which was reprinted at London in 1603. In the preface to the London edition he speaks of "the fearefull abounding at this time in this countrey of these detestable slaves of the Divel, the Witches or Enchanters." We are not, therefore, surprised at the language of the statute against witches enacted the same year. His new subjects were disposed to gratify him by deferring to his wishes in a matter in which he took so deep an interest, and with which, from his special studies, he was supposed to have the most profound acquaintance. One clause of the statute may be quoted as highly curious:—"Any one that shall use, practise, or exercise any invocation or conjuration of any evill or wicked spirit, or consult, covenant with, entertaine or employ, feede or reward, an evill or wicked spirit, to or for any intent or purpose; or take up any dead man, woman, or child, out of his, her, or their grave, or any other place where the dead body resteth, or the skin, bone, or other part of any dead person, to be employed or used in any manner of witchcraft, sorcery, charme, or enchantment, or shall use, practise, or exercise any witchcraft, enchantment, charme, or sorcery, whereby any person shall be killed, destroyed, wasted, consumed, pined, or lamed in his or her body, or any part thereof, such offenders, duly and lawfully convicted and attainted, shall suffer death." James was the more inveterate against witchcraft that he thought his life was constantly aimed at by the emissaries of Satan, and for supposed attempts to poison him by magical arts several persons had been executed. Hence in the statute above referred to witchcraft, in all the modes in which it could be practised, was declared to be felony, without benefit of clergy. Satan and his vassals were supposed to be exceptionally wroth with James for his marriage with Anne of Denmark, he, a Protestant Prince, having married a Protestant Princess.

The prosecutions in Scotland were very numerous, and conducted with remorseless cruelty. Sir George Mackenzie says:—"The persons ordinarily accused of this crime are poor, ignorant men, or else women, who understand not the nature of what they are accused of; and many mistake their own fears and apprehensions for witchcraft." In Scotland, however, persons of the highest rank were put to death for their supposed complicity with witchcraft, such as the Earl of Mar, brother of James III., and Lady Glammis. The British Solomon attended examinations for supposed witchcraft himself. The poor wretches were tortured till they confessed their guilt. Sometimes the nails were torn from the fingers by pincers, and pins driven into the raw flesh, a procedure purely diabolical. Fortunately we live in happier times. The last sentence of death for witchcraft in Scotland was pronounced in 1722.

§ 3. BROWNIES, KELPIES, AND GHOSTS.

Burns chose as an epigraph for his "Tam o' Shanter" a line from Gawain Douglas—

"Of brownyis and of bogilis full is this buke."

We will dismiss "bogilis" in a few words. The bogle, or goblin, was an inferior demon, generally of a freakish disposition, who delighted in terrifying and perplexing timid mortals rather than in serving them, or even doing them harm. Hence the word was applied generally, and without any infernal reference, to mischievous pranks, and even to light-hearted, freakish roystering, especially of harmless romping between the sexes, as in Miss Jean Elliot's song of "The Flowers of the Forest," already quoted—

"At e'en, at the gloaming, nae swankies are roaming,"
'Bout stacks wi' the lasses at bogle to play."

Before proceeding to the consideration of brownies, we may remark that we should have noticed the witches of Burns's "Tam o' Shanter" in the last section. Burns's presentment of the witch bears out our remark that the Scottish witch was a much more formidable and terrible character than her English sister. The accessories of the witch-dance in Kirk-Alloway' were, in the bard's own words, "horrible and awfu'." From the infernal piper in the "winnock-bunker i' the east "—

> " A towzie tyke, black, grim, and large,
>   To gie them music was his charge "—

to the dead in their open coffins, each with a light in its cold hand, and the murderer's bones in gibbet irons, on to the knife which had mangled a father's throat, and to the haft of which the grey hairs still adhered, there is a perfect climax of horrors. The witches themselves are anything but lovely, with the exception of Nannie—

> " A souple jade she was, and strang "—

who, that night enlisted in the corps, afterwards wrought much damage to beast and boat, to corn and bere, in the district of Carrick.

The brownie was a useful household drudge somewhat resembling the English Robin Goodfellow, called *Goblin* by Milton, who in " L'Allegro " thus describes his habits and avocations—

> " Tells how the drudging *Goblin* swet
>   To earn his creame-bowle duly set ;
>   When in one night, ere glimpse of morn,
>   His shadowy flail hath threshed the corn
>   That ten day-labourers could not end :
>   Then lies him down, the lubber fiend,
>   And stretched out all the chimney's length,
>   Basks at the fire his hairy strength,
>   And crop-full out of door he flings,
>   Ere the first cock his matin rings."

The brownie, lurking in the daytime in some obscure recess of the house to which he had attached himself, came forth at night to perform any laborious

office which might be beneficial to the master and
other inmates of the household. In this he resembles
Robin Goodfellow. Not so, however, in his expectation of reward in the shape of cream-bowl or otherwise; though there is some inconsistency in the
legends on this point, as we shall see by-and-by.
He was meagre, shaggy, taciturn, and had a genuine
love of his midnight labours. When the inmates of
the kitchen sat too late round the fire, he appeared at
the door and warned then off—"Gang a' to your
beds, sirs, and dinna put out the wee grieschoch"
(embers); for, like Milton's lubber fiend, he loved to
stretch himself before the fire. If offered reward,
especially in the shape of food, he withdrew from the
house in displeasure, and never appeared again. The
offer of clothes also seems to have been offensive to
him. Consequently it may be surmised that those
who knew his habits and likings would not readily
offend so useful a domestic drudge, who gave his services on such easy and disinterested terms. Brownie
showed his Pagan origin (he is doubless the *Lar
Familiaris* of the Romans) by his ineradicable aver-
sion to the Bible. Brand informs us that a young
man in the Orkneys used to brew and read in his
Bible, which last was brownie's eyesore. He refused
the usual sacrifice to brownie, who spoiled his first
and second brewings, but of the third he had very
good ale, though he had not sacrificed to brownie,
who thereupon took his departure and troubled him
no more. A similar story is told of a lady in Uist,

who refused the usual perquisite and lost two brewings, though the third succeeded, upon which the drudge abandoned the house.   It seems, therefore, that though brownie might be offended with the offer of food or clothes, he rather loved a drink.   According to Olaus Magnus, the Swedish mines were haunted by a class of spirits similar to brownies, and as useful in forwarding mining as brownies were in forwarding agricultural operations.   The last brownie known to have laboured in Scotland had his residence at Bodsbeck," in Moffatdale.   He was borrowed or hired away by the officious and indiscreet kindness of an old lady, who, to reward his services, placed in his retreat a porringer of milk and a piece of money. He was heard crying and howling the whole night, " Farewell to bonny Bodsbeck," and was never seen more.   This incident forms the subject of a tale by the Ettrick Shepherd.

William Nicholson, the " Galloway Poet," is the author of a poem of great merit, entitled " The Brownie of Blednoch."   The brownie's name is Aiken-drum.   We suspect the name was suggested to Nicholson by a popular rhyme which will be found in the " Jacobite Reliques "—

> " There was a man cam' frae the moon,
>   Cam' frae the moon, cam' frae the moon,
>   There was a man cam' frae the moon,
>   An' they ca'd him Aiken-drum."

Nicholson, who was eccentric to the verge of insanity, led a wild, dissipated life, and died a pauper in 1849. We have often conversed with a lady who remembered him travelling through Kirkcudbright-shire with a small pack; and, according to the custom of the time and district, he used, when his rounds brought him that way, to join in the family supper in her father's house, and sleep in the barn. He does not homologate the legend of the brownies' being offended with the offer of meat, for Aiken stipulates for "a cogfu' o' brose," but is ultimately huffed off the premises by a pair of mouldy breeks being placed beside his supper.

> " There cam a strange wight to our toun en',
>   An' the feint a body did him ken ;
>   He tirled na lang, but he glided ben
>   Wi' a dreary, dreary hum.

> " His face did glow like the glow o' the west,
>   When the drumly cloud has it half o'ercast,
>   Or the struggling moon when she's sair distrest.
>   'Oh, sirs ! 'twas Aiken-drum.' "

After describing his matted head, his long blue beard, his glaring eyes, his hairy form, clad with nothing but a philabeg of green rushes, his knotted knees, and his "wauchie arms" tipped with three claws, which were so long that they trailed on the ground by his toeless feet, the poet tells us that the "auld gudeman did sweat;" that he drew a score and sained himself; that the auld wife clutched her Bible as a strong fortress against the Evil One; and that the young wife clasped her wean more closely to her breast. Being conjured to tell what he wants and whence he comes, he answers the last question

first, and then asks if they have work for him. He
describes his qualifications thus—

> " ' I'll shiel a' your sheep i' the mornin' sune,
> I'll berry your crap by the light o' the moon,
> An' ba' the bairns wi' an unkenned tune,
>   If ye'll keep puir Aiken-drum.

> " ' I'll loup the linn when ye canna wade,
> I'll kirn the kirn, an I'll turn the bread ;
> An' the wildest filly that ever ran rede
>   I'se tame't,' quoth Aiken-drum.

> " ' To wear the tod frae the flock on the fell,
> To gather the dew frae the heather bell,
> An' to look at my face in your clear crystal well,
>   Might gie pleasure to Aiken-drum.

> " ' I'se seek nae guids, gear, bond, nor mark ;
> I use nae beddin', shoon, nor sark ;
> But a cogfu' o' brose 'tween the light an' dark
>   Is the wage o' Aiken-drum.' "

The auld wife had sufficient worldly wisdom to
realise the advantages offered by the brownie, and
in spite of the skirling of the wenches, whom she
silenced with a stamp of her foot, she invited Aiken
to "sit his wa's doun." The brownie did not belie
his promises ; he performed prodigies of work by
moonlight or by the streamers' glance, and was an
especial favourite with the children.

> " But a new-made wife, fu' o' frippish freaks,
> Fond o' a' things feat for the first five weeks,
> Laid a mouldy pair o' her ain man's breeks
>   By the brose o' Aiken-drum.

> " Let the learned decide when they convene,
> What spell was him an' the breeks between—
> For frae that day forth he was nae mair seen,
>   An' sair missed was Aiken-drum."

Robin Goodfellow, already alluded to, called also by Shakespeare, in the "Midsummer Night's Dream," Hobgoblin and Puck, was a mischievous, merry spirit of the earth, fond of mixing with mortals, and given to rough practical joking. He was the clown and jester of the Fairy Court—

> "I jest to Oberon and make him smile."

In reply to the fairy who asks him whether he be not that shrewd and knavish sprite called Robin Goodfellow, who frightens village maidens, skims milk, makes the breathless housewife churn in vain, the drink to bear no barm, and misleads night-wanderers, he replies—

> "I am that merry wanderer of the night,"

and he laughingly proceeds to enumerate some of his knavish pranks—

> "And sometime lurk I in a gossip's bowl,
> In very likeness of a roasted crab;
> And, when she drinks, against her lips I bob,
> And on her wither'd dew-lap pour the ale.
> The wisest aunt, telling the saddest tale,
> Sometime for three-foot stool mistaketh me,"

and in consequence comes to grief. However, Reginald Scot, in his "Discoverie of Witchcraft," 1584, has left it on record, nine years before the era of the "Midsummer Night's Dream," that the "Robin Good-fellowe ceaseth now to be much feared."

The water-kelpie was a much more potent and malignant being than the brownie. He haunted the fords of rivers in flood, and laughed wildly when

Y

horse and rider were swept away. Dr. Jamieson, the learned compiler of the Scottish Dictionary, published in 1810, contributed to the "Minstrelsy of the Border" a ballad, entitled "The Water-Kelpie," "descriptive of the superstitions of the vulgar in the county of Angus, the scene of which is laid on the banks of the South Esk, near the Castle of Inverquharity, about five miles north from Forfar." From this we shall give an abstract of the qualities of the sprite, without quoting, as the phraseology is studiously archaic. The poet, reclining on the river bank beneath the dreary shade of the castle, falls into a slumber. An eerie "whush" along the river made his members quake, when suddenly the deep pool was cleft in twain, and the kelpie upreared himself. What seemed his hair consisted of rushes and sedges, entwined with ramper-eels; his eyebrows were of filthy mud, lined with newts and horse-leeches; for eyes glared two huge horse-mussels; while a torrent flew from his mouth and drenched his reedy beard. Two slimy stones formed his shoulder-blades; his broad breast was a whinstone; his ribs were of laminated rock, and each arm was a monstrous fin. From his belly downwards he became a fish covered with shells, and his tail surpassed in power that of the grisly whale. This may be the popular conception of the kelpie, but it is given with the detailed minuteness of an inventory, and is as dull as a sale catalogue. It wants the graphic power, the broad and vigorous touches of the old

ballad, which, few and unpretending, are yet so eloquent and tell so much ; and it shows what a wide
and impassable gulf separates the antiquary, however
learned, from the poet, however unlettered—the mere
man of books from the man with

> " The vision and the faculty divine."

The poet, though mortally afraid, gathers strength
enough to interrogate this fearful apparition, who
shook himself thrice, thrice snorted loud, while
" fire-flauchts " flew from his eyes and flashed along
the floods. When he found words, their hideous
sound, like the northern blast, affrighted bird, fish,
and quadruped. Upbraiding the poet for his temerity
in desiring to speak to him, he promises to spare his
life and give him the information desired—

> " That worms like thee mae ken."

The gist of the information may be thus embodied :
—The rivers from their spring-heads to the sea obey
his laws ; he scampers on the waves like a wild
horse, and becomes the servant of him who succeeds
in bridling him—as proof of which he points to a
bridge for which he had quarried and carried the
stones ; he frightens the lads and lasses watching the
clothes on the river banks, and engaged in amorous
dalliance ; none can be smothered in pool or ford if
he be not there ; and he knows the predestined spot
where each is to meet his fate. For weeks before
such a catastrophe his lights, dancing down the stream,
warn the peasant of approaching disaster, and all run

from the danger save those whose fate is thus pre-
dicted, whose destruction is to him a source of joy.
Like a crocodile on the banks of the Nile, he seems
to mourn the fate of which he is the cause. The
doomed, inspired by him, are deaf to all counsel, and
the night before this interview, though the water was
in flood, a man, "nae stranger to the gate," and
warned that it would not ride, and also that the
kelpie had been heard, took the ford, for the water-
sprite had prepared his shroud. Sometimes he
assumes the human shape, and delights to frighten
mortals—on a starless night leaping on behind a
horseman, grasping him in his arms, and not letting
go his hold till the terrified rider's threshold is
reached. His very name acts as a spell, and is used
by the nurse to still the crying child, who forthwith
sinks into a sleep. This said, he raised a horrid
howl—

> "Thrice with his tail, as with a flail,
>   He struck the flying pool ;
> A thunder-clap seem't ilka wap
>   Resoundin' through the wude.
> The fire thrice flash't ; syne in he plash't,
>   And sunk beneath the flude."

All this is very minute; probably the legend is correctly given; but it is immensely dull, and, instead
of inspiring horror, induces yawning.

In the "Flyting of Polwart and Montgomery,"
"bogles, brownies, gyre-carlingis, and ghaists" are
associated in a single line. The belief in the three
first-mentioned classes of beings has all but evapo-

rated, but the belief in ghosts still maintains its
ground more or less in all climes and in all conditions
of society. Crabbe calls this belief "the last linger-
ing fiction of the brain." Ghosts are seldom seen
but by those who were interested in the party while
alive, as by the son, the husband, the lover, or the
murderer. The apparition is doubtless due to memory
acting on an excited imagination, or to some functional
derangement, such as a disordered stomach, or to a
diseased nervous system. Even the sceptic Lucretius,
while denying the existence of the human soul, admits that the fact of ghostly apparitions was too well
established to be impugned. Of course, the general
belief in ghosts gave room for much imposture. When
the Commissioners of the Long Parliament came
down to dispark the ancient palace of Woodstock—
13th October 1649—they were frightened out of
their wits by the appearance of spectres and the
operation of forces apparently from the infernal
world—all which was but a trick of a clerk of their
own, Joseph Collins, of Oxford, *alias* Funny Joe, a
concealed Loyalist, who, having been brought up in
the neighbourhood, was intimately acquainted with
all the intricacies of the palace. For an interesting
account of the tricks, and an explanation as to how
they were performed, see Scott's "Woodstock." The
Cock Lane Ghost (1762) created a great stir in London. Dr. Johnson, who was constitutionally super-
stitious, was supposed to believe in it, and Churchill,
in a poem entitled "The Ghost," caricatured him, under

the name of Pomposo, as having credited the fraud.
The fact is, that he and Dr. Douglas, afterwards
Bishop of Salisbury, detected the imposture. The
story of the apparition that is said to have appeared
to Thomas, the second Lord Lyttelton, hovers in the
doubtful borderland between truth and fiction. It is
still believed by many that his Lordship, a worn-out
man of pleasure and an invalid, was convinced of its
reality. It is said, on the other hand, that he had
determined to take poison, and hence it was easy for
him to predict the time of his decease. Lord Fortes-
cue, who was in the house with him at the time,
denied that there was any truth in the supposed
visitation. Ghost stories are so numerous, and have
such a striking likeness to each other, that it is unnecessary to multiply them here.

"Mary's Dream," "a song which few have equalled
and none excelled"—such is the dictum of Allan
Cunningham—is the production of John Lowe (Mr.
Chambers calls him Alexander, but this is surely a
mistake), tutor in the family of Mr. M'Ghie of Airds,
in Galloway. The lover of one of the daughters of
the family having been lost at sea, his ghost appears
to Mary in a dream. It is moonlight, which is exquisitely described—

> "Mary laid her down to sleep,
>   Her thoughts on Sandy, far at sea ;
> When soft and low a voice was heard
>   Say, ' Mary, weep no more for me.'

> "She from her pillow gently raised
>   Her head, to ask who there might be :

> She saw young Sandy shiv'ring stand,
>   With visage pale and hollow e'e.
> 'O Mary, dear, cold is my clay,
>   It lies beneath a stormy sea ;
> Far, far from thee, I sleep in death ;
>   So, Mary, weep no more for me.' "

After describing the shipwreck, and bidding her prepare to meet him on the shore where doubt and care had no existence, the shadow fled at the crowing of the cock. "Mary's Dream" was an especial favourite with Allan Cunningham. He says of it, " I scarcely know a song that contains so many popular qualities —a moving tale, with all its natural and supernatural accompaniments, steeped in a stream of melody." Glover, the author of " Leonidas," wrote an admirable party song entitled "Admiral Hosier's Ghost."

§ 4. RETURN FROM THE DEAD—CONCLUSION.

There is a class of Scottish ballads of exquisite beauty and pathos, the subject-matter of which is a return from the dead. In one of them the apparition is called by the poet a ghost, but the persons to whom the apparitions appear evidently regard them as personalities, and really rescued from the realm of Death. These are "Sweet William's Ghost," first published in Ramsay's "Tea-table Miscellany;" "Clerk Saunders," published in the "Border Minstrelsy" from Mr. Herd's MSS., its conclusion much resembling the ballad first mentioned. Professor Aytoun gives a version compacted from those of

Messrs. Kinloch and Buchan, which is more coherent than that given by Scott. "The Wife of Usher's Well," a fragment, first published in the "Border Minstrelsy," Mr. Chambers considers as merely a continuation of the "Clerk's Twa Sons of Owsenford," which in his edition of the ballads he incorporated with the foregoing. Hence some editors would reduce these four ballads to two, while others are of opinion that each is the composition of a different author. Mr. Chambers has, however, put himself out of court: in the development of his hypothesis he assigns all of them to Lady Wardlaw.

The version of "William's Ghost" given by Aytoun was obtained by following in the main that of Motherwell, and collating it with that given by Mr. Kinloch. It differs so much from the ballad as printed by Ramsay, especially towards the close, that the collater was inclined to regard it as a composition distinct from "Clerk Saunders." We shall adhere to Aytoun's version. "The ballad," says Mr. Chambers, "is important as the earliest printed of all the Scottish ballads after the admittedly modern 'Hardyknute.'" And he observes further on, that it "appears as composed in the style of those already noticed—a style at once simple and poetical—neither showing the rudeness of the common peasant's ballad nor the formal refinement of the modern English poet." The last two stanzas, however, were evidently patched on by some contemporary of Ramsay, and they are as stiff, prosaic, and pretentious as

the productions of the minor poets of the beginning
of the eighteenth century usually are.

Both in "William's Ghost" and "Clerk Saunders,"
the apparition requests a restoration of the faith and
troth that he had formerly given to the lady of his
love. We give a short analysis of each ballad.

> "There came a ghost to Marjorie's door,
> Wi' mony a grievous maen ;
> And aye he tirled at the pin,
> But answer made she nane."

Ultimately she asks if it is her father Philip, her
brother John, or her true love Willie, new come
home from England. Being informed that it is her
love Willie, she interrogates him as to whether he
has brought her certain articles of female ornament,
which she particularises, when the ghost replies—

> " 'I've brought you but my winding-sheet,
> And that you wouldna wear !

> " 'Oh, sweet Marjorie, oh, dear Marjorie !
> For faith and charitie,
> Give me again the faith and troth
> That I gave once to thee.'

> " 'Thy faith and troth I will not give
> Nor yet shall our true-love twin',
> Till that you come within my bower,
> And kiss me, cheek and chin.'

> " 'How should I come within your bower,
> That am nae earthly man ;
> If I should kiss your red, red lips,
> Your days would not be lang.'

> " 'The cocks are crawing, Marjorie,' he says,
> 'The cocks are crawing again ;

> It's time the deid suld part frae the quick—
> Marjorie, I must be gane.'"

He again pleads for restitution of his troth, which she refuses to accord till he take her to his "ain ha'-house," and wed her with a ring. His reply is that his house is a lonesome grave, and that it is but his spirit that is speaking to her. She then kilted her robes of green, and followed the corpse of her lover the live-long winter night, till she came to the green kirkyard, where William lay down in the open grave. She inquires at him what are the three things standing at his head, to which the answer is that they are three maidens whom he once promised to marry. Next, she asks what are the three things that stand at his side, when she finds that they are three babies born to him by the three maidens. Lastly, in reply to the question, what are the three things that lie close at his feet, she is told that they are three hell-hounds waiting to keep his soul—

> "Then she's ta'en up her white, white hand,
>   And struck him on the briest ;
> Saying—'Have there again your faith and troth,
>   And I wish your soul good rest.'"

In 1724 there appeared in Hill's periodical, "The Plain Dealer," an exquisitely simple ballad, entitled "William and Margaret," composed by David Mallet (his proper name was Malloch) at about the age of twenty-two. In a note to the ballad Mallet says that the plan was suggested to him by the following stanza of an old song, quoted in Fletcher's "Knight of the Burning Pestle"—

> " When it was grown to dark midnight,
> And all were fast asleep,
> In came Margaret's grimly ghost,
> And stood at William's feet."

"These lines," says Dr. Percy, " have acquired an importance by giving birth to one of the most beautiful ballads in our own or any language." But we agree with Scott that, however the ballad was suggested, Mallet had "Sweet William's Ghost" in his eye, the resemblance between it and his own ballad being too striking to be accidental. Margaret, who had been deceived by William, asks back her maiden vow and her troth, and blames his cruelty and infidelity as the cause of her death. At cock-crow she bids him a long and last adieu, and charges him to come and see the grave of her who had died for his love. Thither he repairs, and stretching himself on the grass-green turf, yielded up his soul in tears. In a publication entitled "The Friends" (1773), an unsuccessful attempt was made to deprive Mallet of the credit of the authorship of this, one of the finest compositions of the kind in our language.

The tale of "Clerk Saunders," of which some suppose " William's Ghost" to be a mere variation, is, according to Scott, " uncommonly wild and beautiful, and apparently very ancient." Alexander Smith, in an essay in his " Dreamthrope," entitled " A Shelf in my Bookcase," speaks of it with boundless enthusiasm.

"If you should happen to lift the first volume of Professor Aytoun's 'Ballads of Scotland,' the book opens of its own accord at 'Clerk Saunders,' and by that token you will guess that the ballad has been read and re-read a thousand times.   And what a ballad it is! The story in parts is somewhat perilous to deal with, but with what instinctive delicacy the whole matter is managed!   Then what tragic pictures, what pathos, what manly and womanly love!   Just fancy how the sleeping lovers, the raised torches, and the faces of the seven brothers looking on, would gleam on the canvas of Mr. Millais!"   But this is presupposing more knowledge of the tale than we have yet supplied—

> " Clerk Saunders was an Earlie's son,
>   Weel learned at the schule ;
> May Margaret was a King's daughter :
>   Baith lo'ed the other weel."

As they walked together over "yon garden green," Clerk Saunders makes a proposition that would now be reckoned indecorous, to which Margaret demurs on the score that they are unmarried, and that if she yielded to his wishes her seven bold brothers might come in, with torches burning bright, and discover them.   As a clerk, and consequently skilled in casuistry, he proceeds to reconcile Margaret's conscience to what she apparently only half disapproved of, her own inclination proving a traitor to her—

> " ' Then take the sword from my scabbard,
>   And slowly lift the pin ;
> And you may swear and save your aith,
>   You never let me in.

> " ' And take a napkin in your hand,
>   And tie up baith your e'en ;
>   And you may swear, and save your aith,
>   Ye saw me na since yestreen.' "

What Margaret had dreaded soon came to pass. At
the midnight hour, when the lovers were fast asleep,
the seven brothers entered Margaret's bower and
stood at her bed-feet. The first, touched with compassion, counselled that they should depart and let
them alone. Other five, equally compassionate,
framed excuses, and bespoke mercy for them, on the
several pleas that Clerk Saunders was the only child
of his father ; that he and Margaret were lovers dear ;
that for many years they had loved each other ; that
it were a sin to twain true love, and that it would be
a shame to slay a sleeping man—

> " Then up and gat the seventh o' them,
>   And never a word spake he ;
>   But he has striped his bright brown brand
>   Through Saunders' fair bodie.
>
> " Clerk Saunders he started, and Margaret she turned
>   Into his arms, as asleep she lay ;
>   And sad and silent was the night
>   That was atween thir twae."

We are now in a position to give Mr. Chambers's
reasons for assigning "Clerk Saunders" to the list of
suspicious ballads. Having, as he conceived, detected
Lady Wardlaw's touch in the "Gay Goshawk" and
"Gil Morrice," he reasons thus :—In the former
ballad, the lady having feigned death after the
device of Juliet, her *seven* brethren rose up and hewed

to her a bier; and he remarks, "It is further very remarkable, that in 'Clerk Saunders' it is *seven* brothers of the heroine who come in and detect her lover." The mode, also, of the doing to death of Saunders is suspiciously like that by which Gil Morrice is carried off, and the resemblance is more complete in Scott's version—

> "Now he has ta'en his trusty brand,
>   And slait it on the strae,
> And through Gil Morrice's fair bodie
>   He garred cauld iron gae."

These are but slender foundations on which to base an hypothesis.

At the dawn, Margaret, who knew not of her lover's murder, warns him to be gone, but receives no answer. When she discovers that he is dead, she invokes woes on her brothers, who had slain the true lover who would have married her. Her father, coming softly into her bower, attempts to comfort her by the prospect of a higher match, but Margaret declares that she shall never be wedded. When she had mourned within her bower for a twelve-month and a day, a knock and cry came to her window, which she at first thought proceeded from a robber, but Clerk Saunders announces that it is he come to speak with her. He cannot rest in his grave till she has restored him his plighted faith and troth. She answers in almost the identical terms employed by Margaret to William, and to these Clerk Saunders replies almost precisely as William does. She

proceeds to say that she will not restore him his troth
till he tell her what becomes of women who die in
travail—

> " ' Their beds are made in the heavens high,
>   Down at the foot of our good Lord's knee,
> Weel set about wi' gillyflowers ;
>   I wot sweet company for to see.' "

Gillyflowers formed part of the popular conception
of heaven—

> " The fields about this city faire
>   Were all with roses set—
> Gillyflowers and carnations faire,
>   Which canker could not fret."

This is from the " Dead Men's Song," as published by
Ritson in his " Ancient Songs." Margaret restores
his troth, and he tells her that if ever the dead come
for the quick he will come for her—

> " Sae painfully she clam the wa',
>   She clam the wa' up after him ;
> Hosen nor shoon upon her feet,
>   She hadna' time to put them on.

> " ' Is there ony room at your head, Saunders ?
>   Is there ony room at your feet ?
> Or ony room at your side, Saunders,
>   Where fain, fain, I wad sleep ? ' "

Mr. Smith observes—" In that last line the very
heart-strings crack. She is to be pitied far more
than Clerk Saunders, lying stark with the cruel
wound beneath his side, the love-kisses hardly cold
yet on his lips." They must have been cold after a
twelvemonth and a day of the grave. Indeed Clerk
Saunders says himself—

" ' My mouth it is full cold, Margaret.' "

Over the companion ballads of "The Wife of Usher's Well" and "The Clerk's Twa Sons of Owsenford" we shall not tarry long. The former was first published in the "Border Minstrelsy." It is a fragment, and is by some, but we think erroneously, considered to be in some measure identical with the latter portion of the second-mentioned ballad. The wealthy wife of Usher's Well sent three stalwart sons over the sea, who perished within a few days. When told this, she wished that the wind might never cease "nor freshes in the flood"—

> " 'Till my three sons come hame to me,
>   In earthly flesh and blood ! '
>
> " It fell about the Martinmas,
>   When nights are lang and mirk,
> The carline wife's three sons cam' hame,
>   And their hats were o' the birk.
>
> " It neither grow in syke nor ditch,
>   Nor yet in ony sheugh ;
> But at the gates o' Paradise
>   That birk grew fair eneugh."

The carline, rejoiced at the return of her sons, feasts all her household, and prepares for her fond ones a bed large and wide, beside which she seated herself wrapped in a mantle. At cock-crow the eldest said to the youngest that it was time they were away, because if they were missed out of their place they would abide a sore punishment. The youngest, touched with compassion for his mother, who had fallen asleep, pleads for some delay, on the

plea that their mother would immediately go mad
when she awoke and discovered their absence. They
hung their mother's mantle on a pin, saying it would
be long ere it happed them again, and with a farewell
to their mother, to barn and byre, and to the bonny
lass, the household servant, they returned to their
dread abode.

The "Clerk's Twa Sons of Owsenford" is thought
by Aytoun to be very ancient, and to be referred to
a period anterior to the Reformation. Owsenford is
probably Oxenford, now a seat of the Earl of Stair in
Mid-Lothian, though some identify it with Oxford.
The two sons went off to Paris to study, which
renders it improbable that they belonged to the
University town of Oxford. They had an amour
with the two daughters of the mayor, who, having
discovered it, swore that he would hang them. Their
mother having ascertained that they were bound in
prison, urged the father to hasten to effect their
pardon. But the haughty mayor was inexorable.
He would free the prisoners neither for gold nor fee,
nor for Christ's sake, but would hang them to-morrow
at noon. The two daughters begged their father to
set their lovers free, even on condition of taking *their*
lives. But he scourged them with a whip, and with
an opprobrious epithet ordered them to their bowers.
Before their father's face each kissed her lover twenty
times, giving him his faith and troth as he had given
her. Aytoun's version ends here; but there is a
second part in which the mother is represented as

sitting on her castle wall awaiting the return of her
husband and her sons.   She sees her good lord returning alone, and having welcomed him, she inquires
after her sons.   He informs her that they are put to
a deeper learning and to a higher school, and that till
the hallow days of Yule they will not be home.

> " The hallow days o' Yule were come,
>   And the nights were lang and mirk,
> When in and cam her ain twa sons,
>   And their hats made o' the birk."

The rest of the ballad corresponds closely with the
conclusion of " The Wife of Usher's Well."   A feast
is prepared because her two sons were well—

> " ' O eat and drink my merry men a',
>   The better shall ye fare,
> For my ain twa sons they are come hame
>   To me for evermair.'

> " And she has gane and made their bed,
>   She's made it saft and fine ;
> And she's happit them wi' her grey mantel,
>   Because they were her ain."

At cock-crowing they disappear for ever.   Mr.
Chambers doubted the genuineness of this ballad as
an antique.   He did not always do so, for in a note to
it in his " Scottish Ballads " (1829) he says—" This
singularly wild and beautiful old ballad is chiefly
taken from the recitation of the editor's grandmother,
who learned it when a girl, nearly seventy years ago,
from a Miss Anne Gray, resident at Neidpath Castle,
Peeblesshire."

Other superstitions might be noticed, such as when

a water-sprite woos a woman to her destruction, or when female elves try to lure men to their abodes.

The " Mermaid " was a formidable being, beautiful above as Aphrodite, with blue eyes, ruddy lips, a smile sweeter than the bee, and a voice surpassing the songs of birds. Doomed was the luckless knight whom her fascinations induced to seize her hand. Soon his drowning scream was heard from the whirling eddy.

Here end our chapters on the " Songs and Ballads of Scotland." The literature which we have attempted to illustrate is of a high order; not, it may be, polished like the literature of scholars, but fresh and healthy, breathing of wood and hill, of stream and sea, of strong passion, of love stronger than death, of horrid cruelty, openly confessed and exulted in, as resulting from a spirit of vengeance supposed to be legitimate, either from private or tribal wrongs, and of an absolutely tumultuous delight in adventure. We have given a list of the titles of old songs and ballads from that beautiful pastoral, " The Complaynt of Scotland." There also will be found the names of the instruments played on by the eight shepherds, and the names of the dances in which the happy Arcadians engaged, as well as the titles of numerous romantic tales which are now irretrievably lost.

INDEX.

PRINTED BY BALLANTYNE, HANSON AND CO.
EDINBURGH AND LONDON

www.ingramcontent.com/pod-product-compliance
Lightning Source LLC
Chambersburg PA
CBHW030912270326
41929CB00008B/664